Cases on Educational Technology Integration in Urban Schools

Irene L. Chen
University of Houston Downtown, USA

Dallas McPheeters
Sr. Learning Consultant, Cerner Corporation, USA

T0338703

Information Science
REFERENCE

Managing Director:	Lindsay Johnston
Senior Editorial Director:	Heather Probst
Book Production Manager:	Sean Woznicki
Development Manager:	Joel Gamon
Development Editor:	Michael Killian
Acquisitions Editor:	Erika Gallagher
Typesetters:	Mackenzie Snader
Print Coordinator:	Jamie Snavely
Cover Design:	Nick Newcomer, Greg Snader

Published in the United States of America by
Information Science Reference (an imprint of IGI Global)
701 E. Chocolate Avenue
Hershey PA 17033
Tel: 717-533-8845
Fax: 717-533-8661
E-mail: cust@igi-global.com
Web site: http://www.igi-global.com

Library of Congress Cataloging-in-Publication Data

Cases on educational technology integration in urban schools / Irene L. Chen and Dallas McPheeters, editors.
    p. cm.
  Includes bibliographical references and index.
  ISBN 978-1-61350-492-5 (hardcover) -- ISBN 978-1-61350-493-2 (ebook) -- ISBN 978-1-61350-494-9 (print & perpetual access) 1. Educational technology--United States--Case studies. 2. Education, Urban--United States--Case studies. 3. Motivation in education--United States--Case studies. I. Chen, Irene. II. McPheeters, Dallas, 1959-
  LB1028.3.C325 2012
  371.33--dc23
                           2011038332

British Cataloguing in Publication Data
A Cataloguing in Publication record for this book is available from the British Library.

All work contributed to this book is new, previously-unpublished material. The views expressed in this book are those of the authors, but not necessarily of the publisher.

List of Reviewers

Jane Thielemann-Downs, *University of Houston Downtown, USA*
Sue Mahoney, *University of Houston Downtown, USA*
Robert Johnson, *University of Houston Downtown, USA*
Laura Mitchell, *University of Houston Downtown, USA*

Table of Contents

Section 2

Detailed Table of Contents

Section 1

Chapter 1

    Deepak Verma, Classroom Teacher, USA

A middle school teacher proposed that since students these days are more at ease with technology due to the excessive use of technology gadgets in their lives, why not make the best use of technology by way of electronic whiteboards to engage students? This brought about some changes in this inner city school which had failed the state Annual Yearly Progress (AYP) report more than once. However, was the sudden surge in student motivation the result of the novelty effect or the Hawthorn effect? And might that surge in student motivation soon fade away?

Chapter 2

    Alicia Martinez, School Teacher, USA

In an effort to control paper supplies and budget, an elementary school initiated a "No/Low Paper Policy." Under this policy, teachers are encouraged to use the technology available in classrooms instead of worksheets, and teachers were assigned quotas and pin numbers to discourage excessive paper usage. Despite the forward thinking attitude of the school, the campus technology specialist continues to struggle with being heard by campus and district administration on issues dealing with the purchase and upkeep of technology.

A school was able to receive the "Technology for All" grant to issue a large number of laptop computers for students to check out and use at home. A policy for checking out the laptops was developed that included a software utility to keep track of the amount of time students may keep the laptop, the implantation of antitheft tracking software to minimize loss, the maintenance plan of the laptops, how they were to be insured, and other information. Later on, the school principal had to devise a new plan so that the laptop checkout policy would not escalate into damages and possible lawsuits.

The story describes how three school institutes are grappling with the loss of private information, each through a unique set of circumstances. Pasadena City Public Schools discovered that it had sold as surplus, several computers containing the names and Social Security numbers of employees. Stephens Public Schools learned that personal information about students at one of its middle schools was lost when a bag containing a thumb drive was stolen. And Woodlands Public Schools accidentally exposed employee personal data on a public Web site for a short period of time. How should each of the institutes react?

A small group of technology application teachers and campus IT specialists exchanged ideas about how the latest round of budget cuts might impact their jobs and technology on campus in general. Issues brought up included how schools "can do it all cheaper" if more online courses are added, how dual credit courses – that count both for high school graduation requirements and college credits – are becoming popular among families with much smaller tuition budgets, how teachers have to wait for 6-8 years for new computers instead of 4-5, how campus Web sites are outdated due to lack of maintenance fees, and how campus instructional technologists are too busy fixing obsolete computers and equipment.

Chapter 6

Tamika Washington, Future School Teacher, USA

Many times in the urban schools, computers and learning software are either at a shortage or simply do not exist. In schools like that, the ratio of students to computers can be as high as 20 to one. This case study compares the learning technology resources and opportunities accessible to William and Terrance, two cousins who attended 4th grade in two different school districts.

Chapter 7

Dallas McPheeters, Sr. Learning Consultant, Cerner Corporation

E-Rate is a funding source established by the Federal Communications Commission (FCC) on May 7, 1997. The purpose of the funding is to ensure Universal Telecommunications Service is available to public schools and libraries. Telecommunication services include voice, data, internet, and classroom learning solutions. Schools and libraries apply for E-Rate assistance when adding telecommunications infrastructure upgrades. If approved, applicants are required to follow and maintain strict accounting procedures and any red flags raised during the continual compliance assurance process can immediately stop funding until a resolution is found. The potential for a good deal of tension among education stakeholders exists when E-Rate funding is put on hold due to such audit questions. Such experiences are common as detailed in this case study.

Chapter 8

Blanca Rodriguez, School Teacher, USA

Prairie School District believes in integrating technology into classroom learning for all students. However, for some schools "all students" does not include the special education population. Rolando was a 7 year old autistic boy additionally labeled with mental retardation. Pretend you were Rolando's teacher. Would you have done differently?

Chapter 9

Martina Ramos-Rey, School Teacher, USA

Paul was a 12 year old 6th grader diagnosed as Bipolar, ADHD, and having difficulty controlling impulses. He attended a public school and remained all day in the general education classroom. After trying multiple research-based interventions over a period of weeks, Paul's teacher and the behavior specialist decided to try computer software designed to help him reflect on his behaviors and how his behaviors made others feel.

Chapter 10

Leanne Spinale, Future School Teacher, USA

It is now commonplace for students to bring PDA's and smart phones into the classroom which gives them swift access to the internet. While this technology is a benefit for students conducting research for a project, it can also be detrimental for educators conducting assessments. "Pop Quiz Debacle" describes a particular quandary for educators who work with advanced placement or Gifted/Talented students. For students with a very high GPA and other academic performance, what distinguishes them is how perfect they are. So there's no room for any kind of error. And if there's no room for error, students tend to cheat – even though these students would have done just fine on the test. They say they cheat because, "this is my safety net."

Chapter 11

Irene Chen, University of Houston Downtown, USA

In recent years Facebook, MySpace, and other social-networking sites have been blamed for the suicides of teenagers in Missouri, Massachusetts, and New York. Parents complained their children were traumatized by nasty comments posted by cyberbullies on social-networking sites. Schools and districts are taking action in response. According to a T H E Journal survey conducted in 2009, 68 percent of respondents replied that their districts banned social networking sites for students and teachers, 19 respondents replied that they banned social networking sites only for students, and another 12 percent said there was no ban in their districts. In the following case study, a middle school principal calls for parents to yank their children from all social-networking sites after a so-called "Naughty List" was posted on Facebook. Is his extreme measure justifiable?

Chapter 12

Rarshunda Hudson-Phillips, School Teacher, USA

Ms. Turner, an eighth grade History teacher, assigns students a research paper on Cuba and communism. She asks the students to use only paper media for their research materials. Her students argue, "Why should we waste time using books to find information, when we can just look it up on the Web quickly?" Angry parents also question why the students should have to use only books for research when they have been given laptops by the school.

Students in classrooms face challenges of which teachers and adults are either unaware or simply do not notice. Neither Jonathan's parents nor his teachers knew about the difficult situation Jonathan was experiencing with his classmates. Like so many parents and teachers, they did not have any reason to suspect that ten-year-old Jonathan was a victim of a cyber gang's activities occurring right in his own living room and inside his classroom.

If homework assignments that require the use of a computer are given to students, should they be penalized for what their family cannot afford? In this case study, Mrs. Lincoln, who developed her course using a web-based course management system named Moodle, spent time working on her Moodle pages and posting assignments. She then explained to students how the site worked. She also spent a week in the computer lab training her students to become proficient using the Moodle application. After a couple of weeks, Mrs. Lincoln noticed that a quarter of her students were not completing their Moodle based assignments.

Among Mrs. Grant's 22 first graders, ten are English language learners, while another two are autistic and have special needs. One of the autistic students is physically and verbally aggressive. Mrs. Grant realized that the classroom had many obstacles to overcome before becoming an emotionally and physically safe place for all the students. Mrs. Grant played a video explaining the importance of classroom rules. She showed another YouTube video showing students following their classroom rules.

A great deal goes into ensuring a smooth-running classroom when a teacher is absent. Mrs. Truman, a substitute teacher, highly recommends pre-regulated set-up and training in technology for substitute teachers.

Mrs. Long's integration of video games in the classroom is a work in progress. She has observed how video games are a great way to motivate and engage students. On the other hand, she has observed how video games can lead to behavior and academic problems.

Roosevelt School District, a small urban elementary school district, is trying to find a way to purchase new digital technology for campuses. The bases of this case study are to develop a plan for how the district can pay for new technology.

Despite recent online learning inroads in schools, many professional educators and administrators remain hesitant, reluctant, and even resistant to teaching with technology. The cause of resistance to technology is often misinterpreted. Teachers do not resist the technology itself. Teachers resist what the technology may represent - change, confusion, loss of control, and impersonalization. As long as these concerns remain unaddressed, technology adoption in any organization will be an uphill battle.

Ms. Gonzalez, librarian/media specialist of an urban high school, is asked to prepare a presentation to explain to a panel of campus stakeholders, the results of her study of the current status of technology use. The goal of the presentation is to inform the panel of stakeholders so they can develop a plan to further implement the use of technology as a teaching and learning tool on campus.

The ability to navigate the Web and to use technology effectively and efficiently is no longer an option but a requirement in schools and in the workplace. Information literacy is widely accepted as embracing rapid advances in technologies and recognizing the multiple literacies required of students living and learning in this century. Information literacy has grown to include traditional literacy, computer literacy, media literacy, and network literacy. School library media specialists in the twenty-first century face both challenges and opportunities in the recent high expectations of information literacy. Among the challenges is keeping up with changing technologies and taking the necessary steps to ensure students and teachers have appropriate access to resources and instruction. Opportunities include the chance to transform today's library into a resource center of the future where information literacy can be easily obtained. Welcome to the world of Ms. West, a middle school teacher turned high school librarian, and see how she ponders upon her new role as being the instructor/specialist of information literacy skills on the campus, a reading advocate and provider of reading materials, as the manager of the resources both information and library resources, and lastly being a collaborator with teachers concerning information literacy issues.

Mr. Taylor, a new and techno savvy teacher, stays connected by maintaining his own social network pages. However, after seeing that other students were using his social network page as a medium for negativity, gossip, inappropriate conversations, and unsuitable remarks, he questioned its continued use as a helpful teaching tool for those utilizing it appropriately.

Section 2

Digital participatory media offer urban social studies teachers a unique opportunity to foster students' civic skills and public voice while enhancing their understanding of social justice within a democratic society. This case study addresses how an 8th grade U.S. history teacher in a New York urban school, when using wikis and online discussion with his students, came to realize that "what [technology] users need in order to take charge of their own online decision making is at best an art and, more often than not, a series of trial-and-error solutions" (Lankes, 2008, p. 103), while operating within two constraints identified by Bull et al (2008): "Teachers have limited models for effective integration of media in their teaching; and, only limited research is available to guide best practice" (p. 2). While using digital collaborative tools enabled students to develop collaborative and communication skills and begin to learn social justice oriented content, the teacher faced challenges related to technology integration, curricular alignment, selection of appropriate digital tools, and fostering online academic norms among students. This chapter focuses on a teacher's three-year journey from his first day of teaching to his connecting the use of technology to relevant curricular content to promote his students' use of online public voices for social justice.

Chapter 24

Sheri Vasinda, Texas A&M University-Commerce, USA
Julie McLeod, University of North Texas, USA

The continuing improvements and access to digital technology provide opportunities for capturing student thinking never considered or available in the past. Knowing the importance of thinking processes and understanding children's resistance to writing them down, mathcasts were used as a way of supporting students during their problem solving. Mathcasts are screencaptures of students' work and thinking as they write and talk about their thinking during mathematical problem solving. Viewers of the mathcast gain unique insight into the students' problem solving process, thinking process, and mathematical conceptions or misconceptions. The authors found screencasts to be a good technological match with mathematical problem solving that provided a more powerful opportunity for both self-assessment and teacher assessment that was not available with traditional paper and pencil reflection. When students can revisit their verbal thinking several times throughout the year, they are equipped to self-assess in new, powerful, and more reflective ways.

Chapter 25

Selcen Guzey, University of Minnesota, USA
Gillian Roehrig, University of Minnesota, USA

Why do some science teachers successfully integrate technology into their teaching while others fail? To address this question, educational researchers have conducted a growing body of research focused on technology integration into classrooms. Researchers are studying everything from teachers' philosophical approaches to teaching that influence efforts at technology integration to classroom-level barriers that impact technology integration. Findings indicate that while some teachers fail in utilizing technology due to the personal and classroom barriers they experience, others eagerly work to overcome the barriers and achieve technology integration. In this case, Mr. Bransford, a novice science teacher who has incorporated technology into his classroom practices within his first five years of teaching, is discussed. Mr. Bransford teaches 8th grade Earth Science using a range of educational technology tools. The barriers he has faced, his strategies to overcome those barriers, and his technology enriched classroom practices are presented.

Chapter 26

This case focuses on a case study that involves the incorporation of ICT in particular gaming technology into the subject area of Citizenship Education (CE), a non-traditional ICT focused subject. The case study is within the context of a K-12 classroom, and it explores the processes in which a classroom teacher may have to navigate to be able to use innovative ICT within their classroom. The case highlights the main issues as relating to pedagogical and institutional considerations.

Chapter 27

These two cases address issues related to using technology as a tool to develop pre-service teachers' Technological Pedagogical and Content Knowledge (TPACK) in mathematics and science methods courses. The chapter assumes the following scenario and overarching case study question: You and your colleagues are the course instructors of a mathematics and a science methods course. Your pre-service teachers typically lack content knowledge in mathematics and science. Further, you must also address pedagogies and how to use technology as a tool to support student learning of mathematics and science concepts. What activities can you create to simultaneously develop knowledge of content, pedagogies and how to teach with technology?

Chapter 28

Preservice teachers need to acquire both technological skill and understanding about how technology rich environments can develop subject-specific knowledge as a part of their teacher education programs. The purpose of the research project, as described in this case study, was to examine the impact that immersion in technology-infused social studies pedagogy courses had on preservice teachers' willingness to use computer and online tools as well as how they used them during their student teaching. Teacher education students enrolled in two pedagogy courses were surveyed at the beginning and end of the courses and interviewed over the duration of the courses regarding the nature and extent of their technological knowledge and skill. Following the completion of the pedagogy courses, six volunteered to have their technology use tracked during their nine-week practice teaching experience. Findings showed that while the preservice pedagogy courses did increase the student teachers' knowledge of and skill with a variety of computer and online tools as well as their desire to use them during their student teaching, the elementary schools in which they were placed for their practicum were poorly equipped, and the mentor teachers were not using the tools that were modeled on campus. If preservice teachers are to truly understand the benefits of learning and teaching with technology, teacher education institutions and school districts need to work together to present a consistent vision of technology integration and schools need to provide environments that encourage and support technology use.

Chapter 29

Cheng-Yao Lin, Southern Illinois University Carbondale, USA
Fenqjen Luo, Montana State University Bozeman, USA
Jane-Jane Lo, Western Michigan University, USA

This case study explored the efficacy of web-based instruction on preservice elementary teachers' mathematics learning. Web-based instruction is appealing to many schools in urban settings because it helps them to face the two big challenges most akin to their schools: to motivate students' interests and to meet the diverse students needs with its interactive feature and adaptive capability. Ten preservice elementary teachers were interviewed regarding their ability to model and reason with fractions after receiving web-based instruction on these topics in their regular mathematics method course. The interview transcripts were used to provide information about the strength and weakness of participants' conceptual and procedural understanding of fractions. The findings of this case study identify promises and challenges in supporting the recommendations of many national reports, such as the NCTM Professional Standards for School Mathematics (2000) and the National Mathematics Advisory Panel (2008), in incorporating technology into the compulsory mathematics classrooms.

This case reports the preliminary findings associated with the planning, development, and implementation of Module 1 of the Pathway to Nevada's Future project. Baseline data, participant characteristics, findings, and results from participation are reported. Data sources include online surveys, online discussions, and informal interviews of project personnel.

The current reform agenda in mathematics education promotes the view that mathematics should be taught and assessed in a variety of meaningful and authentic ways, including incorporating technology in the mathematics classroom. However, the incorporation and sustained use of technology into mathematics classrooms presents technological, content, and pedagogical challenges to teachers and students. As the necessity and availability of technology in mathematics classrooms increases, so must supporting technology usage in teachers' content delivery and assessment practices and their professional development (Roblyer & Edwards, 2000; Newby, Stepich, Lehman, & Russell, 2000). This empirical case study reports on the advancement of 8th grade Algebra I teachers' mathematical assessment practices of technology-based activities and classroom artifacts during a two year professional development program. As a part of the professional development program, participating teachers documented their use of examining and assessing algebraic work on a handheld Computer Algebra System (CAS).

Effective professional development holds the power to transform teaching practices that invigorate teachers and increase student engagement. Arizona Classrooms of Tomorrow Today (AZCOTT) was one such experience. Eighteen elementary teachers completed a yearlong, rigorous, sixty-hour workshop experience that focused on integrating technology in content area instruction. Participants integrated technology effectively, began to develop leadership skills, and experienced changes in attitude, beliefs, knowledge, and skills as technology influenced existing curricula.

Chapter 33

This case will focus on the following situation: As the technology coordinator for a school district you receive a state grant to provide technology resources and professional development for every teacher in the intermediate (Grades 5-6), middle (Grades 7-8) and high school (Grades 9-12) classrooms in your district. Your superintendent and school board have asked you to: design differentiated professional development to meet all teachers' needs; include some outside consultants but quickly build teacher capacity so future professional development can be facilitated by district employees; provide educational materials for teachers and parents about internet safety and legal issues; determine that the use of technology has positively impacted student learning outcomes. This case study describes the story of how one school district responded to this challenge.

Foreword

When I was asked to write this foreword for a book on technology use, my mind went back to the days when I was doing the literature review for my dissertation study. I remembered how a report published in 1995, by the now defunct Office of Technology Assessment, discussed how important it was for teachers to make "the technology connection." In fact, rereading that resource I found a citation to a report published in 1986 with the title *A Nation Prepared: Teachers for the 21st Century*; obviously, we were already trying to get ready for "the 21st century" and the kind of teacher, learner, and school that it would require. After almost two decades, and now *in* the 21st century, we wonder if most teachers have been able to make that technology connection to educate the new workforce. But, to be fair, we should wonder not only if teachers have been able to make that connection but if faculty in teacher preparation programs at higher education institutions have also made that connection. Unfortunately, it seems that we still have a long way to go to finally and truly establish the so much sought after link to technology.

Just to mention a few facts, we know that many K-12 schools, especially those situated in inner cities, ban the use of cell phones, music players, video games, even an open Internet connection. At least in the last fifty years, the school curriculum has not changed much even when technology and science have advanced by leaps and bounds; in fact, our students are learning outdated facts from textbooks even if the books are brand new.

In terms of teacher preparation programs, there is a nagging obstinacy on training educators to become the experts and center of the classroom; the complement of this equation is clearly to hold the view of students as the expert-less. In schools across the nation, and in the name of accountability, schools maintain an inflexible, one-size-fits-all curriculum that emphasizes memorization, outdated knowledge, and standardized testing that are irrelevant to most of the students and their future. Finally, in many classrooms, teachers still resist letting their students use new (and sometimes old) technology because they themselves lack the ability to do it – as if this would stop students from making full use of the devices.

Marc Prensky, in an article published in 2008, summarized the feelings about schooling that our students hold. In that article, he quoted a student saying, "Whenever I go to school I have to power down." Then the author added, "He's not just talking about his devices—he's talking about his brain." It is no wonder that most high school and middle school students report to be bored 50% to 70% of the school day (Prensky, 2008).

Given the wide availability and low cost of cell phones, its ownership is now widespread even among student populations with low socioeconomic means. As it is well advertised by the phone networks and phone manufacturers, many of those telephones are actually mini-computers with capabilities only dreamt about 20 years ago. Different from older generations, the cell phone is not used to talk but mostly to connect to others via text messaging and Internet postings on networking sites. The young generation leads a connected, up-to-the-moment life with multi-modal identities and abilities. As a corollary, we cannot expect today's students to learn the same way we did when they are experiencing virtual worlds, individually designed multiple identities and looks represented by avatars, and keeping open communications and collaborations with people halfway around the world–people whom they have never met in person–as part of everyday life. If we stop and think of all these experiences that happen *outside* our classrooms, by necessity we need to ask ourselves: Is our education system still relevant to our students? Even more important: is our teaching style still relevant and effective to our students?

So, how do we teach the 21st century student? How do we prepare future teachers and provide professional development to existing ones to educate for this century? The answers to those questions are many and varied. However, we know that the only way to keep this country's world leadership is through a well prepared workforce, a workforce that is conversant with technology to develop innovation and creativity; to accomplish it, we need to challenge the structure of PK-12 education to allow those values to sieve through the curriculum. A good start to this challenge is to recognize that teachers need to be the facilitators of deep inquiries in their students' minds–not the holders of all knowledge. Teachers need to make the pedagogical connections among the students, knowledge, and technology; they need to teach their students how to retrieve, organize, evaluate, assess, and categorize information. In order to create these inquiries, curriculum cannot continue to be the "one size fits all" of the past but it will require being as personalized as our students' interactions with technology; it will require that students are the co-designers of their learning experiences. In the end, the full integration of technology in education will happen regardless of the teacher–or should we say, in spite of the teacher, when our students cannot finally "power themselves down" to go to school. A clear issue that we need to question *now* is whether teachers are able to take full advantage of the technology and their technology-savvy students to maintain the global-edge of the US.

A good tool to continue to sharpen our pre-service and in-service teachers' technology skills is the use of vicarious experiences as the ones presented in this book. The varied repertoire of case studies with situations faced by teachers, and for which there is little or no training in teacher preparation programs, is invaluable; the questions presented before the case studies focus the reader's attention on the details of the case and then place him or her at the center stage of the situation, while the questions presented *after* the case study facilitate troubleshooting to come up with the best possible response. This vicarious experience will allow future and present teachers to anticipate similar situations and how they can make the most out of each one. An excellent characteristic of the book is that it does not stop with the "how-to" of using technology in the classroom but also engages the reader in ethical and cultural issues, assessment, classroom management when using technology, and teacher professional development.

Finally I came to this conclusion: I am not writing a foreword for a book on technology use; I am writing a foreword for a book on how to be a teacher that happens to use technology to engage students who otherwise are mostly disengaged–the inner-city students.

Laura Sujo-Montes
Northern Arizona University, USA

Laura E Sujo-Montes, PhD, earned a Master's of Arts degree in TESOL and a Doctor of Philosophy degree in Curriculum and Instruction with emphasis on Learning Technologies at New Mexico State University, Las Cruces, NM. She is currently teaching undergraduate and graduate Educational Technology courses and Bilingual Multicultural Education courses at Northern Arizona University in Flagstaff, AZ. Her research interests include online learning environments and the use of technology to teach English Second Language Learners.

Preface

The Industrial Revolution of the 19th century encouraged vast migration to American cities. By the 1990s, three out of four Americans lived in an urban setting. The complexity of modern urban life has heavily impacted the public school system. These changes, coupled with technological advances, have created a unique urban environment for learning. Many writers make notes of the distinguishing features of urban schools and delineate urban schools as places that operate with large ineffective bureaucracies, have high levels of diversity, high population density, profound income disparity, and high levels of student, teacher, and administrator mobility. At the dawn of the Internet era, the priority was figuring out how to let more students and teachers access the world's information. Now the challenge is managing all that information and users' behaviors. Because these distinctively urban traits impact student learning, many researchers argue that education must address these matters.

This book contains a spectrum of case studies aimed at understanding technology integration in urban schools. Section 1 is a collection of cases based on original stories composed by current teachers on issues relevant to the students, staff, faculty, and administrators in K-12 urban school settings. Topics in these cases include: student motivation, equipment upkeep, data security, lack of technology, budget shortfalls, technology funding and fraud, and assistive technology for students with behavioral and emotional problems.

An ongoing challenge for most urban teachers is finding ways to involve students in learning activities that promote retention and engagement, what is usually described as "effective learning." This challenge has become even more pronounced as students have adapted to the essential egocentrism of the mobile communications device.

As most parents of adolescents know all too well, text messaging, video games, and mobile phones in general play an indispensable role in the lives of today's K-12 students. Tech savvy youths know what they can do with technology but may not know the proper limitations of technology. The speed of technological advances available to American youth has caught uninformed parents and teachers by surprise.

Section 1 is a collection of cases based on original stories composed by current and future teachers. Teaching requires preparation that can respond to the rigorous demands of the contemporary classrooms. The overall aim of these case studies is to provide a series of easy to read stories about issues that are considered important in the integration of technology in urban schools. The cases discuss topics relevant to technology abuses, funding, student motivation, professional development, video game addiction, resource allocation, and cyber bullying.

Section 2 contains a number of cases written by teacher educators in relevant to K-12 urban school settings, training of preservice teachers, and professional development of inservice teachers. This section presents a collection of case studies that illustrate preparing teachers to integrate technology in urban schools from many angles.

Depending upon interest, the readers may decide to focus attention on Section 1 of the book: a section that explores issues and themes as they relate to integrating technology, from future and current teachers' perspectives. Readers who would like an insight into preparing future teachers will find Section 2 relevant.

An ongoing challenge for most urban teachers is finding ways to involve students in learning activities that promote retention and engagement, what is usually described as "active learning". The first case in Section 1, "Use of Technology to Motivate Students," describes how a middle-school teacher transformed students from being mere visitors "who only come to the classroom to chat with friends rather than learn any subject or skills," into active learners. The introduction of electronic whiteboards in the mathematics classroom increased student engagement. However, was the sudden surge in student motivation the result of the novelty effect? Would the effect soon fade and the school return to the status quo? These questions and more are addressed in this case study.

In an effort to control paper supplies and budget, the next case describes how an elementary school initiated a "No/Low Paper Policy and Equipment Upkeep." Under this policy, teachers were encouraged to use the technology available in classrooms instead of worksheets. Teachers were assigned quotas and pin numbers to discourage excessive paper usage. Despite the forward thinking attitude of the school, the campus technology specialist continues to struggle with being heard by campus and district administration on issues dealing with the purchase and upkeep of technology.

Two additional case studies address concerns over campus data security. Schools are allowed to collect public information including names, e-mail addresses, phone numbers, addresses, types of business, genders, dates of birth, behavior and assessment records, customer preference information, and other related personal information. Schools collect, store, and use the personal information of students and parents, for defined purposes. Discover how data security is being handled by reading these case studies.

"The Laptop Tracking Plan" case describes how a school was able to receive the "Technology for All" grant and issue a large number of laptop computers to students for use at home. A policy for checking out the laptops was developed that included a software utility to keep track of the amount of time students may keep the laptop, the implantation of antitheft tracking software to minimize loss, the maintenance plan of the laptops, how they were to be insured, and other information. Later, the school principal had to devise a new plan so that the laptop checkout policy would not escalate into damages and possible lawsuits.

Some data security incidents occur at the most unexpected moments and places. The case of "School Districts Stumble on Data Privacy" depicts how three school institutes are grappling with the loss of private information, each through a unique set of circumstances. Pasadena City Public Schools discovered that it had sold as surplus, several computers containing the names and Social Security numbers of employees. Stephens Public Schools learned that personal information about students at one of its middle schools was lost when a bag containing a thumb drive was stolen. Woodlands Public Schools accidentally exposed employee personal data on a public Web site for a short period of time. How should each of these institutions react?

Lately, the headlines clamor about budget cuts to public education. Reductions in school funding will only guarantee further declines in the technology applications of public education in America. In the case, "Budget Woes," a small group of technology teachers and campus IT specialists exchanged ideas about the impacts of the latest round of budget cuts to their jobs and technology on campus. Issues brought up include how schools "can do it all cheaper" if more online courses are added, how dual credits courses that count both for high school graduation requirements and college credits are becoming popular among families with reduced tuition budgets, how teachers have to wait for 6-8 years for new computers instead of 4-5, how campus Web sites are out-dated due to lack of maintenance fees, and how campus instructional technologists are increasingly spending valuable time and dwindling resources fixing obsolete computers and equipment.

Many times in the urban schools, computers and learning software are found in either short supply or simply nonexistent. The case study, "Lack of Technology in Urban Schools," compares the learning technology resources and opportunities accessible to William and Terrance, cousins who are both in the 4th grade. While William attended a school located in the middle-class suburb, Terrance attended an inner-city public school in the same metropolitan area.

The case, "Large School District Struggles to Obtain E-Rate Funds After Bid-Rigging Probe," discusses E-Rate as a funding source for school districts as well as some pitfalls associated with this federal program. The purpose of the funding is to ensure Universal Telecommunications Service is available to public schools and libraries. If approved, applicants are required to follow and maintain strict accounting procedures, and any red flags raised during the continual compliance assurance process can immediately stop funding until a resolution is found. The potential for a good deal of tension among education stakeholders exists when E-Rate funding is put on hold due to such audit questions. Such experiences are common as detailed in this case study.

In "Technology in the Special Education Classroom," Prairie School District believes in integrating technology into classroom learning for all students. However, for some schools, "all students," does not include the special education population. Rolando was a 7 year old autistic boy labeled with Autism and mental retardation. Read the case story, and decide if you were Rolando's teacher, would you have reacted differently?

In the case study, "Emotional and Behavioral Disorders Students Using Computer-Assisted Devices", Paul, a 12 year old 6th grader diagnosed as Bipolar, ADHD, and having difficulty controlling impulses, attended a public school and stayed in the general education classroom all day. After multiple research-based interventions had been tried over a period of weeks, Paul's teacher and the behavior specialist decided to try computer software to help him reflect on his behaviors and how his behaviors made others feel.

It is now commonplace for students to bring PDAs and smart phones into the classroom which gives them swift access to the internet. While this technology is a benefit for students conducting research for a project, it can also be detrimental for educators conducting assessments. "Pop Quiz Debacle" describes a particular quandary for educators who work with advanced placement or gifted/talented students. For students with a very high GPA and other academic performance, what distinguishes them is how perfect they are, so there's no room for any kind of error. If there's no room for error, students tend to cheat – even though these students would have done just fine on the test. They say they cheat because, "this is [our] safety net."

In recent years Facebook, MySpace, and other social-networking sites have been blamed for the suicides of teenagers in Missouri, Massachusetts, and New York. Parents complained their children were traumatized by nasty comments posted by cyberbullies on social-networking sites. Schools and districts are taking action in response. According to a *T H E Journal* survey conducted in 2009, 68 percent of respondents replied that their districts banned social networking sites for students and teachers, 19 respondents replied that they banned social networking sites only for students, and another 12 percent said there was no ban in their districts. In the case study titled "Principal's Letter to Parents: Take Kids off Social Networking," a middle school principal calls for parents to yank their children from all social-networking sites after a so-called "Naughty List" was posted on Facebook. Is his extreme measure justifiable?

The case, "Students' Reliance on the use of Technology for Classroom Assignment," describes how Ms. Turner, an eighth grade History teacher, assigns students a research paper on Cuba and communism. She asks the students to use only paper media for their research materials. Her students argue, "Why should we waste time using books to find information, when we can just look it up on the Web quickly?" Angry parents also question why the students should have to use only books for research when they have been given laptops by the school.

Cyber bullying has increased with the use of the Internet. Increasingly, youths are using their tech gadgets and social media to abuse others in romantic relationships. According to new results from the Cyberbullying Research Center, a research group dedicated to tracking bullying behaviors among online youth, about 10 percent of interviewed teens reported receiving a threatening cell phone message from their romantic partner. Abusive teens may also exert their control by preventing their partners from using technology, experts say. About 10 percent of teens interviewed said a romantic partner forbade them from using a computer or cell phone. Many students are at a disadvantage because they do not know how to identify cyber bullying, neither do they know what to do once they have identified that they or someone they know is being bullied. The case "Cyber Gangs inside the Classroom" describes how neither Jonathan's parents nor his teachers knew about the difficult situation Jonathan was experiencing with his classmates. Like so many parents and teachers, they did not have any reason to suspect that ten-year-old Jonathan was a victim of a cyber gang's activities occurring right in his own living room and inside his classroom.

In the case study titled "Technology Integration in the Home?" Mrs. Lincoln, who developed her course using a Web-based course management system named Moodle, spent time working on her Moodle pages and posting assignments. She then explained to students how the site worked. She also spent a week in the computer lab training her students to become proficient using the Moodle application. After a couple of weeks, Mrs. Lincoln noticed that a quarter of her students were not completing their Moodle-based assignments. If homework assignments that require the use of a computer are given to students, should they be penalized for what their family cannot afford?

Cell phones in the classroom have become as common as pencil and paper. Teachers are faced with the challenge of making sure that students are not using the phone during class time. One of the features that the cell phone offers is the ability to take pictures and create videos. Not only can these features contribute to cheating, but it can also be used to capture unflattering photos or live moments of teachers and students. Students can take pictures of their unsuspecting classmates in the locker rooms or restrooms, violating privacy. In an act of harassment, they can distribute pictures of classmates to others. They can promote violence by recording fights at school. They can also use their video capability to provoke teachers and then post their video on sites such as YouTube. Teachers also try to integrate YouTube videos for teaching purposes.

"YouTube in the Classroom" tells the story that among Mrs. Grant's 22 first graders, ten are English language learners, while another two are autistic and have special needs. One of the autistic students is physically and verbally aggressive. Mrs. Grant played a video explaining the importance of classroom rules. She showed another YouTube video showing students following their classroom rules. Mrs. Grant realized that the classroom had many obstacles to overcome before becoming an emotionally and physically safe place for all the students.

A great deal goes into ensuring a smooth-running classroom when a teacher is absent. The case, "Technology and the Substitute Teacher," describes why Mrs. Truman highly recommends pre-regulated set-up and training in technology for substitute teachers.

Mrs. Long's integration of video games in the classroom is a work in progress. In "Video Games in the Classroom: A Success or Game Over," she has observed how video games are a great way to motivate and engage students. On the other hand, she has observed how video games can lead to academic and behavior concerns.

Roosevelt School District, a small urban elementary school district, is trying to find a way to purchase new digital technology for campuses. The basis of the case study titled "How Do We Close the Gap between Technology Innovation and Available Funding?" is to develop a plan for how the district can pay for new technology.

The case "Technology and Traditional Teaching" explains how despite recent online learning inroads in schools, many professional educators and administrators remain hesitant, reluctant, and even resistant to teaching with technology. The cause of resistance to technology is often misinterpreted. Teachers do not resist the technology itself. Teachers resist what the technology may represent - change, confusion, loss of control, and impersonalization. As long as these concerns remain unaddressed, technology adoption in any organization will be an uphill battle.

In "Technology Use on My Campus", Ms. Gonzalez, librarian/media specialist of an urban high school, is asked to prepare a presentation to explain the results of her study of the current status of technology use. The goal of the presentation is to inform the panel of stakeholders so they can develop a plan to further implement the use of technology as a teaching and learning tool on campus.

The author of the case "A High School Librarian's Participation in Supporting Information Literacy on Her Campus" argues that the ability to navigate the web and to use technology effectively and efficiently is no longer an option but a requirement in schools and in the workplace. Information literacy is widely accepted as embracing rapid advances in technologies and recognizing the multiple literacies required of students living and learning in this century. Information literacy has grown to include traditional literacy, computer literacy, media literacy, and network literacy. Opportunities include the chance to transform today's library into a resource center of the future where information literacy can be easily obtained. Welcome to the world of Ms. West, a middle school teacher turned high school librarian, and see how she ponders upon her new role as being the instructor/specialist of information literacy skills on the campus, a reading advocate and provider of reading materials, as the manager of the resources both information and library resources, and lastly being a collaborator with teachers concerning information literacy issues.

The case "Social Networks: Education beyond the Classroom" describes how Mr. Taylor, a new and techno-savvy teacher, stays connected by maintaining his own social network pages. However, after seeing that other students were using his social network page as a medium for negativity, gossip, inappropriate conversations, and unsuitable remarks, he questioned its continued use as a helpful teaching tool for those utilizing it appropriately.

Distress signals seen in today's American urban schools include increasingly overloaded and underfunded schools, a growing population of indifferent students, limited access to technology, aging school facilities, and outdated books and classroom resources. Teaching requires preparation that responds to the rigorous demands of the contemporary urban classroom. Section 2 contains a collection of cases written by teacher educators in higher education institutes on issues relevant to K-12 urban school settings.

The first four cases in Section 2, written by university faculty, focus on enhancing K-12 students' learning with technology. Interestingly, the cases concerning youth cultures, collaborative tools, and gaming align closely with previous cases written by current and future K-12 teachers in Section 1, but through a difference lens.

This first case study in Section 2, "Using Online Collaborative Tools to Foster Middle School Students' Public Voices: Payoffs, Perils and Possibilities," addresses how an 8th grade U.S. history teacher in a New York urban school, using wikis and online discussion with his students, came to realize that what technology users need in order to take charge of their own online decision making is a series of trial-and-error solutions. This case describes a teacher's three-year journey beginning from his first day of teaching until he finally connected the use of technology to relevant curricular content in order to promote his students' use of online public voices for social justice.

The next case discusses how improvements and access to digital technology can provide opportunities for capturing student thinking never previously considered. The case "Digitally Capturing Student Thinking for Self-Assessment: Mathcasts as a Window on Student Thinking during Mathematical Problem Solving" discusses how mathcasts were used as a way of supporting students during their early attempts at problem solving. Mathcasts are screen captures of students' work as they write and talk about their thinking during mathematical problem solving. The authors found screencasts to be a good technological match with mathematical problem solving that provided a more powerful opportunity for both self-assessment and teacher assessment that was not available with traditional paper and pencil reflection.

The next case provides reasons for the successful integration of technology into science classes. The case, "Educational Technology in a Novice Science Teacher's Classroom," describes how Mr. Bransford, a novice science teacher, incorporated technology into his classroom practices within his first five years of teaching. In the study, he describes the barriers he faced, his strategies to overcome those barriers, and the final outcome of his technology enriched classroom practices.

"The Case Study of Game-based Learning in a Citizenship Education K-12 Classroom: Opportunities and Challenges" focuses on technology incorporation, in particular gaming technology, into the subject area of Citizenship Education. The case study takes place within the context of a K-12 classroom and explores the processes in which a classroom teacher may have to navigate to be able to use innovative technology within their classroom. The case highlights the main issues relating to pedagogical and institutional considerations.

"Leveraging Technology to Develop Pre-Service Teachers' TPACK in Mathematics and Science Methods Courses" presents two cases that address issues related to using technology as a tool to develop pre-service teachers' Technological Pedagogical and Content Knowledge (TPACK) in mathematics and science methods courses.

In "Issues and Challenges in Preparing Teachers to Teach in the Twenty-First Century," Gibson examines the impact that immersion in technology-infused social studies pedagogy courses had on preservice teachers. The case describes the teachers' willingness to use computer and online tools as well as how they used them during their student teaching. Teacher education students enrolled in two pedagogy courses were surveyed at the beginning and end of the courses and interviewed over the duration of the courses regarding the nature and extent of their technological knowledge and skill. Following the completion of the pedagogy courses, six volunteered to have their technology use tracked during their nine-week practice teaching experience.

The case study "Web-Based Instruction: A Case Study of Preservice Elementary Teachers' Efficacy in Modeling and Reasoning with Fractions" explores the efficacy of web-based instruction on preservice elementary teachers' mathematics learning. Ten preservice elementary teachers were interviewed regarding their ability to model and reason with fractions after receiving web-based instruction on these topics in their regular mathematics method course. The interview transcripts were used to provide information about the strength and weakness of participants' conceptual and procedural understanding of fractions.

An online, statewide technology professional development project was implemented for middle school teachers in Nevada. The case study, "The Pathway to Nevada's Future: A Case of Statewide Technology Integration and Professional Development," reports the preliminary findings associated with the planning, development, and implementation of the Pathway to Nevada's Future project. Baseline data, participant characteristics, findings, and results from participation are reported.

The empirical case study discussed in "Using Technology to Support Algebra Teaching and Assessment: A Teacher Development Case Study" reports on the advancement of 8th grade Algebra I teachers' mathematical assessment practices of technology-based activities and classroom artifacts during a two-year professional development program. As a part of the professional development program, participating teachers documented their use of examining and assessing algebraic work on a handheld Computer Algebra System.

In "ABCs and PCs: Effective Professional Development in Early Childhood Education," Hansen describes how effective professional development seminars can transform teaching practices, invigorate teachers, and increase student engagement. Eighteen elementary teachers completed a yearlong, rigorous, sixty-hour workshop experience that focused on integrating technology in content area instruction. Participants integrated technology effectively, began to develop leadership skills, and experienced changes in attitude, beliefs, knowledge, and capabilities as technology influenced existing curricula.

The case described in "Designing District-Wide Technology-Rich Professional Development" focuses on the following scenario: As the technology coordinator for a school district you receive a state grant to provide technology resources and professional development for every teacher in the intermediate (Grades 5-6), middle (Grades 7-8) and high school (Grades 9-12) classrooms in your district. This case study describes the story of how one school district responded to this challenge.

The book is designed to fill the gaps left in the technology and teacher education field, as typical textbooks for technology and teacher education usually present skills to be learned such as word processing, database management, multimedia creation, and to provide the background required for insight into more advanced issues for integrating technology in education.

Based on the critical issues found in each case, discussion questions have been generated for classroom engagement. Discussion questions provided discussion starters for further investigation, debate, and discovery. For some cases, sample answers to the discussion questions are offered to encourage further development. The response to these questions is open-ended and although research appears to be moving in one direction, there does not seem to be one "right" answer. The case study approach has been effective to train students to think critically and make reasonable judgments. These discussion questions make it relatively easy to facilitate investigation and class participation.

This is a text for graduate students in instructional technology or curriculum and instruction programs with a serious interest in technology. In-service and prospective teachers may also benefit from the insights and understanding that can be gained from deep thinking and discussions. This collection of case studies contains ideas that we are confident the reader will find worthy of consideration.

This book can be approached from a variety of ways, depending on the reader's interests and needs. It can be read in sequence or can simply be dipped into as needed. We the contributors hope you find it useful, stimulating and at times, a little challenging.

Irene L. Chen
University of Houston Downtown, USA

Dallas McPheeters
Colorado Mountain College, USA

Acknowledgment

The authors would like to acknowledge the support of the students and faculty of Department of Urban Education at University of Houston Downtown. A special thanks to the students at the ETC 3301 Educational Technology and MAT 6318 Advanced Educational Technology at University of Houston Downtown, Spring 2010, who provided initial ideas on the case stories. We also appreciate the following reviewers for their input and suggestions: Drs. Sue Mahoney, Jane Thielemann-Downs, Robert Johnson, and Laura Mitchell, with the University of Houston Downtown.

Irene L. Chen

The compilation of such a work as this requires the help of many people. First and foremost, I am thankful to Dr. Irene Chen for inviting me to participate as a contributor and co-editor of this exciting work. Her encouragement coached me through from beginning to end and for that, I am grateful.

In addition, I thank all those who contributed valuable case studies to serve as examples for the learning of future educators and education stakeholders. So many isolated cases are more than one teacher, school, or even district institution could ever experience. However, these selfless contributions, when added together, become a much needed resource to those preparing to educate the next generation in tomorrow's classrooms. Added thanks must be expressed to so many of our contributing authors for their willingness to provide additional supporting materials when asked, without regard to their own busy lives and schedules.

Last but not least, I thank my dear wife, Pam, for giving up so many weekends so I could take care of editing duties rather than engage in family outings. For her encouraging support I am beholden. Her generous love and devotion make me one of the most fortunate of men.

Dallas McPheeters

Section 1

Chapter 1
Use of Technology to Motivate Students

Deepak Verma
Classroom Teacher, USA

EXECUTIVE SUMMARY

A middle school teacher proposed that since students these days are more at ease with technology due to the excessive use of technology gadgets in their lives, why not make the best use of technology by way of electronic whiteboards to engage students? This brought about some changes in this inner city school which had failed the state Annual Yearly Progress (AYP) report more than once. However, was the sudden surge in student motivation the result of the novelty effect or the Hawthorn effect? And might that surge in student motivation soon fade away?

BACKGROUND INFORMATION

In urban neighborhoods where education is generally not viewed as life-transforming training, but instead as free daycare, teaching can be a daunting task. And if there is a huge pressure place on teachers by administrators to either perform or perish, the challenge becomes even more pronounced.

One such inner city school, which has failed the state Annual Yearly Progress (AYP) report for the last 3 years, is Elm Middle School. Some of the main reasons for failing AYP standards have been low math and reading results combined with other non-evaluative contributing factors such as; lack of parental support, poor student attendance, and low student motivation in classrooms. Although several

DOI: 10.4018/978-1-61350-492-5.ch001

useful teaching strategies have since improved the student results last year, the school has miles to go before it can be counted as a success by the community and school district leaders.

The teachers of Elm Middle School work very hard. They stay late in the afternoons to teach after-school tutorials. They attend on Saturdays to help struggling students. Miss Villarreal, a math teacher, asked the following question in a faculty meeting: "Even though it is true that we all work hard, do we work smart enough?" Miss Villarreal proposed that since students these days are more at ease with technology due to the excessive use of cell phones, IPODs, video games, Internet, and many other electronic devices, why not make the best use of this untapped resource.

It just so happened that teachers at Elm Middle School were lucky to have the school district recently purchase 10 electronic whiteboards for the school along with LCD projectors and laptops. The proposal of Miss Villarreal seemed a perfect solution for the problem.

The main focus for this case study was to observe the change in students' attitudes towards learning as Miss Villarreal implemented activities via electronic whiteboards.

THE CASE

Miss Villarreal had been teaching for five years total, all of it at Elm Middle School. When she joined the school, the average passing rate of math students was just 40%. As a result, a lot of solutions were tried. The teachers were asked to tutor struggling students after school, use peer tutoring in classes, and make classroom lessons more engaging. Although learning results significantly improved, the AYP expectations also increased, and the school is still considered barely "acceptable" by state standards. There was nothing left that teachers had not tried in their attempt to increase the students' engagement in their studies. Of course, despite the teachers' efforts, school administrators acknowledged the students' responsibility to learn and be focused in the classroom.

Teachers in Elm Middle School made up the term "student visitors" to refer to the unmotivated student groups who just came to visit the classroom–rather than to learn any subject or skills–to chat with their friends without bringing their needed classroom supplies. A high percentage of students on campus comprised the unmotivated "student visitor" group.

Miss Villarreal took the initiative of introducing the electronic whiteboard in her math classroom. She understood that it was imperative to involve students in the use of the technology. When these students come to class loaded with electronic gadgets filled with music, videos, games–and no parental control–it becomes difficult for them to listen to a teacher standing in front of a blackboard giving a lecture

2

on the Pythagorean theorem. Miss Villarreal knew these problems and tried to use the "weapons of classroom distractions, aka technology" to her advantage. She was lucky to be given one of the school's 10 new electronic whiteboards to use in her classroom.

To regain the students' attention focus, Miss Villarreal planned to consistently use the electronic whiteboard to build student desire to learn more about math. She understood that in the beginning, there would be occasions when the use of the technology might appear cumbersome, but that with time and effort the technology may bring about the desired effect in student understanding.

The very first day when she got this big white screen to work in the classroom, students thought Miss Villarreal had merely installed a new whiteboard on which to write. But when she connected the board with her laptop and LCD projector, the students anticipated something more. Miss Villarreal asked for student volunteers to come to the board and help her complete the electronic whiteboard configuration. After this, more students demonstrated willingness to come to the board in order to see the computer screen working through the whiteboard screen. It was explained to the class that electronic whiteboards can control the software loaded in the computer. The different colors on the whiteboard appealed to students and they asked if there were some particular colors they would prefer. With bright colors of their choosing on the screen, students felt like it had become "their own" electronic whiteboard.

But the best part was yet to come. When Miss Villarreal searched on the electronic whiteboard for 3 dimensional objects such as cubes, and got them to spin, students became enthusiastic. From that moment on, most students wanted Miss Villarreal to teach using the electronic whiteboard only. Since then, flipping a coin, plotting the graph of a function, probability concepts, measurement, integers and equations have become class favorites.

Miss Villarreal implemented some of the action research techniques she learned from the graduate courses she was taking. The effect of student understanding on several different levels was tallied to see if the effect is similar for all levels of students. In her informal experiment, students were grouped based on their level of understanding and basic needs in four groups: Special education students, ESL students, regular students and Pre-AP/Gifted students. The same desired effect–increased student motivation–was quite noticeable in all classrooms irrespective of student grouping.

The visual models available with electronic whiteboard use transformed the classrooms. The so called "student visitors" are no longer visitors and have now become electronic whiteboard configuration masters; helpers to move objects on the screens; helpers to search for activities on the electronic whiteboard; and drawing artists. These students are now actively making choices about how to generate, obtain, manipulate, or display information. The electronic whiteboard technology has allowed many students to actively think about information, make choices, and execute skills. The benchmark results comparing student growth indicate an increase of 15-20% in scores for all student groups.

The most noticeable effect on students was an increase in motivation. Miss Villarreal and her students were sometimes surprised at the level of technology-based accomplishment displayed by students who had shown much less initiative with traditional chalk and paper classroom settings.

Other teachers at Elm Middle School also frequently cite technology's motivational advantages in providing a venue in which a wider range of students can excel. Compared to conventional classrooms with their stress on verbal knowledge and multiple-choice test performance, the electronic whiteboard technology provided a very different set of challenges and different ways in which students can demonstrate what they understand (e.g., by programming a simulation to demonstrate a concept rather than trying to explain it verbally).

However, Miss Villarreal feared that after a few days of electronic whiteboard use, the students' interest may fade and the same old lack of motivation habits might creep back into her classroom. It was therefore imperative for Miss Villarreal to keep herself updated with other technology skills and Web resources and to stay connected with the groups of teachers who incorporate innovative technology in classrooms. Miss Villarreal would also need to work harder so that her comfort level with the instructional technology remained high.

Was the sudden surge of students' motivation the results of the novelty effect or the Hawthorn effect? Might the increase in motivation fade soon and Elm Middle School return back to its former status quo?

Chapter 2
"No/Low Paper" Policy and Equipment Upkeep

Alicia Martinez
School Teacher, USA

EXECUTIVE SUMMARY

In an effort to control paper supplies and budget, an elementary school initiated a "No/Low Paper Policy." Under this policy, teachers are encouraged to use the technology available in classrooms instead of worksheets, and teachers were assigned quotas and pin numbers to discourage excessive paper usage. Despite the forward thinking attitude of the school, the campus technology specialist continues to struggle with being heard by campus and district administration on issues dealing with the purchase and upkeep of technology.

BACKGROUND INFORMATION

In its second year of service, A.W. Jones Elementary School is as advanced as any public school could be in the metropolitan area. It has the latest projector systems, computers, and many other gadgets. Many visitors to the campus have commented on the abundance of technology and opportunities for students to get more familiar with programs and equipment that they may be expected to use in their future professions.

In its first year of operation, the administration learned a lot of lessons from their mistakes. One of these mistakes was letting teachers have too much control over copies and printing. So, in an effort to control paper supplies and the budget for

DOI: 10.4018/978-1-61350-492-5.ch002

supplies, the school initiated a "No/Low Paper Policy." Under this policy, teachers are encouraged to use the technology available in classrooms instead of worksheets, and teachers were assigned quotas and pin numbers to discourage excessive paper usage. However, there have been many drawbacks to this policy about which the teachers have subsequently expressed their displeasure.

Mr. Lee is the technology specialist on the campus and is in charge of all the technology equipment. He is the "go-to guy" on campus for any questions or concerns about software and hardware. Unfortunately, Mr. Lee is also the person that everyone on campus approaches about complaints concerning technology. Although he tries his best to solve everyone's problems, with over fifty teachers to deal, with this can be a difficult and sometimes impossible job.

Students at Jones Elementary love having new and advanced technology available to them. They usually put their efforts into behaving in order to earn points towards computer time and opportunities to play computer games. Since a large portion of Jones students are from economically disadvantaged homes, teachers hate to deprive students of opportunities to use equipment and other technologies that they do not have the chance to use elsewhere.

THE CASE

Mr. Lee is a ten year veteran employee for the Metropolitan School District. A.W. Jones Elementary School is his current campus location. He has spent the majority of his employment with the District as a technology specialist and computer teacher. As part of his job, he must stay current with the latest technology available in the field of education. Many campus employees approach him with questions and concerns about educational technology. When it comes time for purchasing new software or gadgets for the school, he is often approached about giving his input into the final purchase and to answer questions about the item being purchased and how it could benefit the campus.

In his second year of working at A.W. Jones Elementary, he was asked to join the team of professionals deciding what changes needed to be considered for the new school year. One of the decisions made at this meeting was that the school would initiate a "No/Low Paper" policy. Many other schools were considering similar policies due to recent budget cuts and past abuse of supplies. The administration decided that cutting back on paper use in the classroom—such as worksheets and student handouts—would be a huge step in supporting this new policy. Mr. Lee was approached about whether this would be too much of a problem due to recent additions of new technology and supplies. He expressed that this would be a better question for the teachers to debate but that using the technology involved in the process would not be a problem. However, he also advised that technology like projectors, computers, printers, and screens would require a certain level of upkeep.

At this time, he also shared that among the new interactive whiteboards available for the schools to purchase, the M Brand would be a better purchase than the previously suggested S Brand. The M Brand would cost a third of the price of the S Brand and were much easier to reposition and store.

However, in the end, the school decided to continue on their main course of purchasing twenty S Brand electronic whiteboards. By the middle of the school year, there were still five S Brand electronic whiteboards locked in a closet with no teacher willing to use them since they were so large and inconvenient to use with the type and placement of the projectors already installed in the classrooms. The S Brand electronic whiteboards also were rejected by a lot of teachers because they would have to be placed in front of dry erase boards that the teachers felt were easier to use and not as valuable.

Mr. Lee was also in charge of the set-up and initiation of the new Accelerated Math program that the campus purchased. The program required the purchase of at least twenty printers, scanners, and large amounts of paper supplies for each student. Everything was finally in place a few months after school began and teachers and students were really enjoying the program and all it had to offer. However, shortly after the program began the large number of printouts that each student required daily became too much for the small printers. Ink consumption was also surprisingly high. This worked against the objective of the No/Low Paper Policy.

Even though Mr. Lee had cautioned that this would become a problem, the restriction of supplies had led to replacement ink cartridges not being ordered and the program was stopped. It took months for the replacement supplies to finally come in. By the time the supplies were available to teachers, the majority of the students had to be reintroduced to the routines involved in using them and precious class time was lost.

During all these incidents dealing with technology, the argument of whether teachers should be allowed to bring their own supplies from home was raised quite a few times. In teachers' opinions, if they were willing to spend their money and risk their equipment then they should be allowed to use their products, especially if the District was not willing or able to purchase the items. Mr. Lee had to explain over and over to teachers that if it were up to him then he would be in favor of the teachers bringing their own items but the district was in charge of the policies dealing with technology use.

Mr. Lee continued to struggle with being heard by the campus administration and district on issues dealing with technology. He tried to pick his battles but could not refrain from speaking his mind and sharing what he knew was best for the students and teachers. As long as there was a demand to improve schools with technology and other advancements, there would continue to be people like Mr. Lee who would have to argue on what products should be purchased and what actions should be taken in the field of technology.

Chapter 3
The Laptop Tracking Plan

Jessie Munks
School Teacher, USA

EXECUTIVE SUMMARY

A school was able to receive the "Technology for All" grant to issue a large number of laptop computers for students to check out and use at home. A policy for checking out the laptops was developed that included a software utility to keep track of the amount of time students may keep the laptop, the implantation of antitheft tracking software to minimize loss, the maintenance plan of the laptops, how they were to be insured, and other information. Later on, the school principal had to devise a new plan so that the laptop checkout policy would not escalate into damages and possible lawsuits.

BACKGROUND INFORMATION

Edison Elementary is a school that is located in the suburbs of a major US city. The district itself boasts of being one that is more suburbia than urban but this particular school lies right on the border of the two. The physical building is located in a suburban neighborhood but its' students actually live in urban areas and are bused in to attend class.

The school received unique funding from the state for offering education to students from/in urban areas, which the district enjoyed greatly. Because the students bused in are classified as being from urban and socially disadvantaged areas, the district was able to apply for funds that would not otherwise be available. As

DOI: 10.4018/978-1-61350-492-5.ch003

a result of the school having a large number of students with low socio-economic status the school was able to apply for and receive the "Technology for All" grant.

The school administered a survey to assess student and community needs. After administering the community survey, the school discovered that many students did not have computers to use at home. The school technology committee decided that the best way to use the grant money would be to purchase student laptops. The committee came to a consensus that it would be most beneficial for students to be able to check out these laptops from the school library and use them at home. A policy for checking out the laptops was developed. This policy included the amount of time students may keep the laptop, the implantation of antitheft tracking software to minimize loss, the maintenance plan of the laptops, how they were to be insured, and other information. The response by the students and community was overwhelming. The laptops were continually checked out. The laptop program was proceeding as planned until it was found that student privacy might be in jeopardy due to the antitheft tracking software.

THE CASE

Edison Elementary officials were very proud that, thanks to the Technology for All" grant, they were able to give each of their 900 students, a laptop computer to "ensure that all students have 24/7 access to school-based resources."

One afternoon, Principal Skinner rushed into the library asking for both the librarian, Ms. Trang, and the media specialist, Mr. Larson, at once. He asked them about the laptop tracking software. Both Ms. Trang and Mr. Larson were unsure of what the principal wanted to know about the software. Mr. Skinner asked Mr. Larson to show him how to look up a checked out laptop computer. Mr. Larson then quickly logged into the network and under administrative tools used the "locate" option to find laptop "XM616". The principal was horrified to see this. He instructed Mr. Larson to shut this portion of the tracking software off immediately. He then instructed Ms. Trang to suspend all laptop check out until further notice. Mr. Larson and Ms. Trang began to question the principal when he explained that the recording or viewing of others' information without consent is considered illegal. Since parents and students were not made aware of this and it was not in the signed form students were required to have in order to check out the laptops, that portion of the software must be disabled. Even with prior knowledge, viewing the information was still a sticky situation. He called for an emergency after-school staff meeting to devise a plan to prevent the laptop checkout policy from escalating into damages and possible lawsuits.

The Laptop Tracking Plan

"Good afternoon", Mr. Skinner stated. "One of the nearby schools has informed me that we may have arrived at a small problem. It seems the nearby school has an angry mob of parents on their hands and, if we are not careful, we will be facing a similar situation".

He began giving all the details about how a parent at a nearby school had come to realize that she was being watched by someone while she was using a borrowed laptop from the school. She noticed a red blinking indicator light that would blink sometimes, while other times not. She did some online investigation and discovered that the blinking light signaled that the tracking software was activated and that she was being watched without her consent. Without consulting the principal, she gathered a group of parents and they started boycotting that school. The principal and other personnel got the situation under control but were afraid that the information would spread like wildfire. The principal at the other school tried to save other schools the headache that he was currently experiencing by informing them that they needed to revise their laptop tracking policies immediately.

Another teacher brought up an infamous federal class action lawsuit on behalf of students of two high schools in the Pennsylvania suburbs. The suit alleges that the schools secretly spied on the students while they were in the privacy of their homes by remotely activated webcams embedded in school-issued laptops.

Realizing the potential trouble of the laptop tracking plan, the staff broke into small collaboration groups in order to come up with a new contingency plan for the tracking software. After the collaboration was complete, the following four options were suggested:

1. Do not track the checked out laptop computers with software tools.
2. Find a new tracking software tool to replace the current software.
3. Get rid of the checkout plan altogether and do not allow laptop computers to be checked out.
4. Change the consent forms to indicate that the tracking software is on the laptop and must be checked out at the individual's discretion.

Chapter 4
School Districts Stumbled on Data Privacy

Irene Chen
University of Houston Downtown, USA

EXECUTIVE SUMMARY

The story describes how three school institutes are grappling with the loss of private information, each through a unique set of circumstances. Pasadena City Public Schools discovered that it had sold several computers containing the names and Social Security numbers of employees as surplus. Stephens Public Schools learned that personal information about students at one of its middle schools was lost when a bag containing a thumb drive was stolen. Also, Woodlands Public Schools accidentally exposed employee personal data on a public Web site for a short period of time. How should each of the institutes react?

BACKGROUND INFORMATION

Most parents know that school districts request information when:

- Registering for emergency announcements.
- Providing feedback in an online survey.
- Subscribing to a newsletter or a mailing list.

Parents allow schools to collect information including names, e-mail addresses, phone numbers, addresses, types of business, genders, dates of birth, behavior and

DOI: 10.4018/978-1-61350-492-5.ch004

assessment records, customer preference information, as well as other sensitive personal information. They collect, store and use the personal information of students and parents, for defined purposes. They use the information to provide service and support and share news and information with families and communities. We all assume that they strive to protect the security of personal data by use of appropriate measures and processes. More importantly, we also trust that they do not sell our personal information.

When talking about data security, most of us think of procedures and practices for data encryption, audit logging and incident handling, and secure remote access. However, some data security incidents occur at the most unexpected moments and places.

Keeping data secure, safe, and legal is everyone's responsibility and needs to be embedded into campus culture and ways of working. Therefore, we encourage you to discuss data handling and information security and to give feedback after reading the three incidents below.

THE CASE

Three school institutes in the western United States are grappling with the loss of private information of students, parents, or employees, each through a unique set of circumstances.

Pasadena City Public Schools allowed the leak of personal information on about 650 employees as a result of auctioning surplus computers. The sale of six obsolete computers included hard drives containing names and Social Security numbers of district employees. The district dissemnated a letter to the employed and then posted the letter to the district's homepage outlining that standard procedures had not been followed with the sale of the Division's outdated computers, and that the hard drives from some of the outdated computers were not removed prior to the sale. Luckily, the district has since recovered the drives. The individual who purchased the computers signed a statement verifying that no material had been copied or disseminated. In an effort to further protect employees, the district took the following measures:

1. A letter with more detailed information was sent to affected employees.
2. A hotline was created for employees to call with questions/concerns. The hotline was available within 36 hours of the release of the news and the number included in the letter.
3. Free credit monitoring services were provided to affected employees.
4. The Division would work closely with the City Police Department to provide assistance to employees.

5.   The district was reviewing existing protocols and implementing additional procedures to prevent future incidents.

In the case of Stephens Public Schools (<u>student population 1,600</u>), parents of students at Wake Lake Middle School (<u>student population 1,600</u>), received a letter from its principal in September regarding the theft of confidential school division data. The data was maintained on a thumb drive taken off school property for the sake of emergency backup and was in a bag taken during a burglary off campus. The data included student identification numbers, student names, parent/guardian names, parents' cell, home, and work phone numbers, and student bus numbers or walker status. Additional "identifiable data" might also have been recorded. The school held an informational meeting to answer questions from concerned parents. Two assistant principals of the school were assigned to handle in-coming phone calls and media attention.

The district posted the information in Table 1 on its homepage to inform the community.

Not long after the above incident happened, Woodlands Public School learned that it had posted on a Web site, encrypted personal information about some employees, including names, home and work addresses, and individual employee pay scales. The data was contained in a spreadsheet outlining proposed budget cuts for the next academic year. The spreadsheet was e-mailed to an external consulting company that was hired to assist with budget calculation and was posted on a Web site.

Even though the file had been deleted and is no longer available on the Internet, the school department was urging employees to be alert to the possibility of identity theft.

In a memo sent out to the employees, the Superintendent warned that the information was accessible February 6 through February 11. It also urged employees to

Table 1.

September 21, 2010
SPS Addresses Theft of Student Information
Stephens Public Schools recently learned that certain personal information relating to Wake Lake Middle School was stolen during a burglary off of school property. This information was contained on a USB "thumb drive" and used by school administrators to contact parents/guardians in the event of an emergency occurring outside school hours or in emergency circumstances where the building might be inaccessible.
The exposed student information was limited to students who attend Wake Lake Middle School and the parent/guardian of each student received a letter on Friday, September, 21.
An informational meeting will be held in the Wake Lake Middle School cafeteria at 7 p.m. on Monday, September 24 to address community concerns. In the interim, parent/guardians who would like to confirm the exact data on the stolen "thumb drive" which relates to their child may contact the following school administrator between 9 a.m. and 5 p.m. on Saturday, September 22 and Sunday, September 23 at the following number:
Dr. Sharon Huskin 932-7322

educate themselves about identity theft, monitor credit reports and act immediately if they notice any suspicious activity in their accounts. However, the district indicated that the encrypted data would not be easily accessed by someone who had downloaded the file.

The local newspaper, The Busy Bee Tribune, released a full coverage of the story. "You have to really search the file in a lot of different ways in order to access that information," said Mr. Smith, the district Chief Information Officer (CIO). "It really would take a great deal of sophistication in order to access the encrypted data."

Mr. Smith told the journalists of that the school department received an anonymous phone call Tuesday from someone informing them that personnel information was contained in the file. He said the list of employees was "partial," but he did not want to specify which employee information was exposed. "We're still investigating how it all happened," he said.

Chapter 5
Budget Woes

Irene Chen
University of Houston Downtown, USA

EXECUTIVE SUMMARY

A small group of technology application teachers and campus IT specialists exchanged ideas about how the latest round of budget cuts might impact their jobs and technology on campus in general. Issues brought up included how schools "can do it all cheaper" if more online courses are added, how dual credit courses–that count both for high school graduation requirements and college credits–are becoming popular among families with much smaller tuition budgets, how teachers have to wait for 6-8 years for new computers instead of 4-5, how campus Web sites are out-dated due to lack of maintenance fees, and how campus instructional technologists are too busy fixing obsolete computers and equipment.

BACKGROUND INFORMATION

We have been hearing so much about budget cuts to public education in the news lately. For some states, revenue numbers are showing a steady decline in tax collections. Several governors announced that the state budgets were under water by millions of dollars.

In the United States, K-12 as well as higher education are suffering huge budget cuts from the government. K-12 programs are being affected in many of the following ways: Losing licensed teachers, reduction in programs such as art, music, and sports programs, elimination of special education for children with additional

DOI: 10.4018/978-1-61350-492-5.ch005

needs, increased class sizes, loss of teaching assistant positions, increased teacher workload, elimination of needed programs and activities, reduction in administrative positions such as assistant principal.

Educators and communities are beginning to see how billions of dollars have been invested with little appreciable return in the form of improved instruction and better educated students.

And reductions in school funding will only guarantee further declines in the technology applications of public education in America. Without new technology initiatives and projects, technology administration positions in district central offices are being reduced or eliminated. Distance courses are expanded to avoid hiring more teachers and to save on other costs. Instead of helping teachers with curriculum design, campus technical support personnel have to spend most of their time fixing old computers and defective parts. School Web sites are not updated, software subscription fees not paid, and campus hardware and software are not upgraded. These are just some measures being forced upon schools in the midst of budget woes.

Everyone wants quality public education, but no one seems to be able to afford it.

THE CASE

After attending a trade show, a small group of technology application teachers and campus IT specialists from several school districts gathered and discussed the impacts of the latest round of budget cuts affecting their jobs and technology on campus in general.

Melinda: I have seen districts having to adjust faculty and staff salaries, cut maintenance spending, and implement department and campus cutbacks. When students return to campus this fall, they'll find crowded classrooms, less access to faculty and counselors, fewer campus services, and more difficulty getting classes they need to graduate. The schools have responded by asking parents to pay more fees while at the same time expanding class sizes, eliminating programs, laying off staff, and furloughing teachers and other employees. It is likely that we will continue to see these cascading effects from budget cuts across the board.

Barry: These funding/spending changes have already drastically hindered the ability of schools to make "bonus" additions of technology implementations on all levels.

Mark: What worries me about these budget cuts is that I have heard a few people up in the hierarchy claim that they "can do it all cheaper" if we add more online courses. While I don't yet think this can be considered a trend like the one in online higher education, I worry that online courses may be increasingly viewed by the state and administrators as the equivalent to industrialized farms: do it quicker, cheaper, faster.

Deborah: Campus-based activities and programs with small student numbers will be eliminated and teachers can be let go once online programs are available. I wonder if this may become more widespread, and if so, the incentives for quality online education do not exist. It's all about the money.

Barry: I heard that the state has contacted a number of distance education consortiums and virtual school networks to look for ways to expand current online course offerings with the expectation of enrolling thousands of more students in fall courses.

Melinda: By the way, Mark, you teach a course for the state's virtual school network. What are popular online courses for K-12 students nowadays?

Mark: Routinely offered online courses are Algebra I & II, Geometry, Astronomy, Art, Biology, Biology AP, Business Computer Information System, Calculus AB Advanced Placement, Driver And Safety Education, Economics With Emphasis On The Free Enterprise, English IV, English Language And Composition AP, Languages Other Than English I through IV, Mathematical Models With Applications, Physical Education, United States Government And Politics AP, United States History, World Geography, Psychology AP, and Physics.

Melinda: How about dual credit courses? I heard that courses that count as high school graduation requirement and college credits are becoming popular in financial situations like this because some families with much smaller tuition budgets ask their students to consider dual credit courses instead.

Mark: That is true. Courses that would likely benefit a student in obtaining admission to a postsecondary institution are popular. Dual credit courses also allow a student to earn college credit or other advanced credit. As I remember, courses that are routinely offered as dual credit courses are COSC 1336: Programming Fundamentals I An Introduction to JAVA, ENGL 1301: Composition I & II, ENGL 2322: British Literature, ENGL 2326: American Literature, and HIST 1301: American History History of the US.

Deborah: Online courses are quick and cheap answers to a budget crisis like we are going through. Families and students welcome them also. But I am afraid that they will water down the quality of education. This is the kind of activity that threatens to destroy the education system we've worked to build over the last decade. What the administrators don't realize is that it could also severely damage the reputation of their institution, which has taken decades to establish.

Barry: Yes, look at Enron. A reputation is something that is built over many years but can be destroyed in a heartbeat.

Melinda: The state's response to these economic pressures to change must be holistic, attending to the varying needs of stakeholders. E-learning does not function in isolation. Multiple stakeholders are involved in the credibility and success of e-learning: learners, instructors, higher education institution, parents, communities, standards setting organizations, and so on. The growth and value of e-learning is directly related to the ability of institutions to attend to the needs of each stakeholder. Online education can succeed when the stakeholders are invested in the quality. If budget cuts do indeed lead to more online education, we will have to hope that those bearing the new responsibility will have taken both the right approach and attitude to deliver positive opportunities.

Barry: The state administrators and district central office people are growing by leaps and bounds while classroom-based teachers are shrinking. As a school's technical specialist, I'll make $5,000 less this year than two years ago. I have not had a raise in two years. Next year I am projected to take a $400 a month pay cut; all of this with the ever increasing demands that all of my students perform at grade level or I will lose my job. I heard that some tech support persons like me have to support two campuses instead of one in order to keep their jobs. How much more should I lose?

Deborah: I think we are lucky to work as campus tech support, because I heard administrators in the technology department of some district central offices are laid off because the districts do not plan on any major technology renovations for the next few years.

Mark: That's also what I heard. Some who were let go from the technology department have either returned to classrooms, teach at local colleges, or work as private consultants.

Melinda: These funding changes have changed people's lives. They have already changed the ability of districts to make "bonus" additions of technology implementations on all levels.

Barry: That is exactly right. Our district's Web site page hasn't been updated for 2 years. Some information is more than three years old. Campus faculty directories are seriously outdated. Contact information for new teachers and staff can't be found anywhere. Parents have to call the campuses to find out a teacher's phone number. It is like going back to 5 years ago. Check out our school's Web site for yourself.

Mark: Good thing that my district budget plan was approved 2 years ago before the budget crisis–to build the parent portal my district implemented last semester that allows parents to view grades, school announcements, and other student records online. Otherwise, I do not think it would happen.

Deborah: My school's 5-year desktop computer replacement cycle is now extended to a 7-year replacement cycle or even longer. The Operating System has remained the same for at least 5 years now. Expensive subscriptions to online services such as streaming video archives, e-mail account maintenance, online learning modules, and other perks have been cancelled due to budget shortages. Teachers have to look for free resources as class supplements. No major upgrade of software either.

Melinda: Same here. In the past, I would spend half my day installing new computers and configuring new equipment. I would also spend lots of time attending planning meetings for new Web projects or hardware/software upgrades. And now I am without new computers or equipment to purchase and no new project initiatives. I am running around most of my day fixing old computers, and replacing defective parts.

Barry: I found that I have to explain to teachers and students why the Internet is so slow all the time. That's because our Web servers are growing obsolete and the software is lagging at least 3 years behind the industry. These challenges cause some compatibility issues from server to server.

Deborah: The other day, I even showed teachers how to use the Century Gothic font to replace Times New Roman in order to save on the money for toner cartridges and other stuff.

Barry: I think instead of running teachers around, every district central office administrator needs to take a pay cut or furlough themselves.

Melinda: Furloughs add to the problem. When employees are furloughed, they cut out spending on extras such as dining out, hiring cleaning and lawn services, visits to the mall, movies, weekend trips, athletic and music events, etc. This in turn decreases income for people in the service industry, and the downward spiral continues.

Barry: Enough is enough. Teachers need to show that they are effective in the classroom, agree to have their pay at least partially indexed to student performance on standardized tests, be willing to pay for some of their benefits like the rest of the community, and agree to pension reductions. Many professionals like myself will flee the State if this train wreck is allowed to continue, and with a progressively shrinking tax base.

Melinda: The rich send their children to private schools. The charter school is set up to take the children who have strong parent and/or family support who cannot or will not pay tuition to the private schools. The public schools have all the children leftover who have no other choices. The charter school is funded by the public school but it's the public school that must bear the burden of larger class sizes, the brunt of AYP, the rigid mandates of NCLB and the state standards, and the nonsensical inclusion. What's wrong with this picture?

Mark: So much of our financial woes could be eased by simply raising the sales tax a cent or two.

Melinda: I am not sure. It is a trend but I see it more as a cycle. It has happened before, not quit the same. The farther I look back, the more of the cycle can be seen with the future witnessing a medium term downward trend in financing for K-12 education.

The reduction in budgets forces change. What are the future trends that come from these observations?

Chapter 6
Lack of Technology in Urban Schools

Tamika Washington
Future School Teacher, USA

EXECUTIVE SUMMARY

Many times in urban schools, computers and learning software are either at a short-age or simply do not exist. In schools like that, the ratio of students to computers can be as high as 20 to one. This case study compares the learning technology resources and opportunities accessible to William and Terrance, two cousins who attended 4ᵗʰ grade in two different school districts.

BACKGROUND INFORMATION

For those urban schools that cannot provide simple necessities such as textbooks and heat or air conditioning, educational technology is defiantly at the bottom of the agenda. Such basics as computers and learning software are either at a short-age or simply do not exist. Many times in the urban schools the ratio of students to computers is as high as 20 to one. Without these resources, school graduates are not prepared for the world's demand of information literacy and technical skills. Research shows that although there are dramatic increases in the use of computers in the school system, children in public urban schools have less access to computers than those in the suburban and private school systems. As a result, many of the urban students are not prepared for the level of technology expected in colleges or among the work force.

DOI: 10.4018/978-1-61350-492-5.ch006

Because of the importance of computer access in everyday life, there is little wonder that such a large "digital divide" across school districts exists. While some students have unlimited access to computers and the Internet at any given time between school and home, others have minimal to no access at either location. Another discouraging fact is that this separation is ever growing. One source states that the technology gap between whites and minority groups has increased by five percent since 1997. Middle and upper class students, given access to technology resources are more likely to continue their education after high school and with a greater degree of success.

Research conducted in 1994 by Software Publishers Association showed that "educational technology has a significant positive impact on achievement in all subject areas, has positive effects on student attitudes, and makes instruction more student-centered". Studies also revealed a better success rate on standardized tests when the students were exposed to educational technology. With the results of many studies showing that students with more exposure to educational technology are excelling in present and future educational tasks as well as in future careers, it is critical that students in urban schools get the same opportunities in order to reach their full potential. Students, who are products of schools with limited access to technology, go out into the real world with major disadvantages.

THE CASE

William and Terrance were both in the 4th grade and are cousins. While William attended a school located in the middle-class suburb, Terrance attended Reagan Elementary, an inner-city public school in the same metropolitan area. William's school had a large amount of available computers and students were taken to computer lab four times a week. On the other hand, Terrance's school only had a handful of working computers that were shared between 1st, 2nd, 3rd, and 4th graders and only had computer lab time once a week. During William's lab time the students were exposed to many different computer applications, computer vocabulary, and different computer software programs to enhance their learning experience. During Terrance's computer class, the students were rushed through assignments. Terrance had to take turns with other classmates when doing hands-on assignments and did not get the full effect of putting into action what he had learned. To make matters even more challenging, Terrance did not have a computer at home.

However, his cousin William did have a computer at home. Because William had access to a computer at home, he benefited by being able to become more familiar with computers outside of school. Although Terrance was a bright child, his mother was disappointed to find during visits that William was a lot more comfortable with the computer than Terrance was and realized that this could be a serious problem for Terrance in the future. She was very concerned about the quality of education her son was receiving at the school he attended and knew that the problem needed to be addressed.

Terrance's teacher, Mrs. Bradley, also noticed the difference in her students as it related to technology when compared to her students from previous years. This year, Mrs. Bradley changed schools, moving to Reagan Elementary from an upper class subdivision. Mrs. Bradley knew there would be differences between the schools but looked forward to the opportunity to work towards improving education at her new school. However, she did not expect the resources to be as limited as they were. The school Mrs. Bradley taught at previously had enough computers for each student to have their own during computer lab time. On the other hand, Reagan Elementary had such a limited amount of computers that two to three students shared one computer during their computer class. Also, Reagan Elementary only offered computer lab once a week. Because of the lack of computer resources at Reagan Elementary, Mrs. Bradley feared that her students would not have the necessary skills to succeed; she knew that this environment was setting her students up for failure and could not just stand by and watch as the "digital divide" grew larger between her students and those in suburban and private schools.

Mrs. Bradley decided to work towards improving the school's resources and, as an advocate for educational technology, her first goal was to get more computers and software in the school. She knew the importance of educational technology for the future of her students and was determined to make sure they had the resources required to be successful. She started by writing a letter to the parents of the students in her class to find out if they had any ideas to help raise awareness about the "digital divide" in their school. She also asked for ideas to help raise money for better educational technology in their school.

When Terrance's mother read the letter Mrs. Bradley sent home, she became very excited. She knew that this would be a great opportunity for her son and his classmates to get the resources they needed. Eager to help better the situation for these students, she talked to Mrs. Bradley about her idea to apply for a grant in order to get funds for more computers at Reagan Elementary. She also met with different organizations within the school to get some fundraisers started and went around to local businesses to find sponsors. Faculty and staff at Reagan Elementary, and members of the community were eager to help with this cause. They knew that if these students were given the resources they needed, they would be one step closer to future success.

Chapter 7
Large School District Struggles to Obtain E-Rate Funds After Bid-Rigging Probe

Dallas McPheeters
Sr. Learning Consultant, Cerner Corporation, USA

EXECUTIVE SUMMARY

E-Rate is a funding source established by the Federal Communications Commission (FCC) on May 7, 1997. The purpose of the funding is to ensure Universal Telecommunications Service is available to public schools and libraries. Telecommunication services include voice, data, internet, and classroom learning solutions. Schools and libraries apply for E-Rate assistance when adding tele-communications infrastructure upgrades. If approved, applicants are required to follow and maintain strict accounting procedures and any red flags raised during the continual compliance assurance process can immediately stop funding until a resolution is found. The potential for a good deal of tension among education stakeholders exists when E-Rate funding is put on hold due to such audit questions. Such experiences are common as detailed in this case study.

DOI: 10.4018/978-1-61350-492-5.ch007

BACKGROUND INFORMATION

E-Rate is a funding source established by the Federal Communications Commission (FCC) on May 7, 1997. Money for the fund is generated from phone bill taxes collected by the government. The purpose of the funding is to ensure Universal Telecommunications Service is available to public schools and libraries. Telecommunication services include voice, data, internet, and classroom learning solutions. Schools and libraries apply for E-Rate assistance when adding telecommunications infrastructure upgrades. The fund is applied as a discount off upgraded services required and can range from 20-90% depending on economic and geographic factors of the applicants.

Once approved, applicants are required to follow and maintain strict accounting procedures and any red flags raised during the on-going compliance assurance process can immediately stop funding until a resolution is found. For this reason, applicants often hire E-Rate vendors who are experienced in the detailed record-keeping required by the federal guidelines. These E-Rate vendors generally include in their bids, a promise to handle any compliance challenges as they arise. The potential for a good deal of tension among education stakeholders exists when E-Rate funding is put on hold because of audit questions. Such common experiences bring us to the following case study.

THE CASE

A prominent school district in the southwest (we'll call District 1 for the purposes of this case study) was approved for $9 million in annual E-Rate funding for a period of five years. Local officials were thrilled with the award and looked forward to improving District 1's technology infrastructure to match needed 21st Century learning technologies. Such learning technologies require fast bandwidth in order to stream data-intensive applications to schools and students. The district's 100 school buildings were quite dated and required electrical upgrades to accommodate 21st Century hardware and software demands. The district's Chief Technology Officer (CTO), Mr. Secor, expressed his delight at the prospects the E-Rate funding would provide for modernizing District 1 and a five year technology plan was developed and approved by local governing authorities.

Based on the E-Rate funding award, District 1's new technology budget was approved by the community's education stakeholders and infrastructure upgrades were ordered by district officials to bring high-speed Internet to the schools. Installation of the costly upgrades began as local contractors got to work retrofitting old buildings with new network infrastructure. Yet, just after the first year of upgrades were completed, a bid-rigging probe began and three district officials were put on leave while E-Rate funds were halted pending a thorough investigation. Halting E-Rate funds is standard procedure whenever there is a question concerning compliance with the strict Federal guidelines that govern the E-Rate program. Beyond bid-rigging accusations and investigations, other questionable budget issues arose with each new school year. As one local newspaper account reported:

"In March 2004, two district Technology and Telecommunication Services (TTS) employees independently called the federal whistle-blower hotline, concerned with how district officials planned to use the federal funds they were seeking. Though budget items were approved with certain compliance requirements, it appeared district technology officials were making unusual arrangements to obtain non-budgeted items by ambiguously labeling purchases so as to confuse auditors."

Meanwhile, unfinished infrastructure upgrades crippled District 1's 5 year technology plan which was based on the increased bandwidth provided by the now-halted upgrades. Because of the anticipated funding, new hardware was placed throughout the district's 100 schools. In addition, more demanding software purchases were made to take advantage of the upgraded infrastructure and hardware.

However, the lack of bandwidth left the new technology sitting idle. Community stakeholders were confused and upset that the steep financial commitments toward improving education were suddenly put on hold mid-stream, so-to-speak. District CTO Secor was continually being questioned at board meetings and by local media about how District 1 would maintain its course toward 21st Century technology integration. Heated debate spread among local media outlets and the situation grew from bad to worse. District monies were pulled from other budgets and allocated to technology expenditures with a promise to reimburse once the E-Rate funding resumed. However, years passed and promised resumption of E-Rate funding remained dormant along with new requests being denied during the complex and lengthy investigation process (see Table 1).

Table 1. E-Rate Funding

Regional Districts	Amount Requested 2004	Amount Awarded	Amount Requested 2006	Amount Awarded
Case Study District 1	$16 Million	$0	$19 Million	$0
Nearby District 2	$1 Million	$570,000	$800,000	$490,000
Nearby District 3	$186,000	$183,000	$326,000	$285,000
Nearby District 4	$167,000	$70,000	$138,000	$138,000
Nearby District 5	$163,000	$163,000	$276,000	$75,000
Nearby District 6	$52,000	$46,000	$130,000	$69,000

E-Rate funds requested by District 1 presented in this Case Study along with funds requested by nearby school districts during the same time period.

Despite the fact that monies from E-Rate funding had been withheld since 2002, District 1 continued to approve budget additions based on juggling budgets for items labeled as so-called "E-Rate eligible." District public announcements led stakeholders to believe the items would be paid for once funding was restored, with the implication that it was only a matter of time before the inevitable restoration of E-Rate funds. An example of this arrangement can be seen in the minutes from District 1's Technology Task force meeting held in July of 2009 (Table 2).

This reasoning was echoed on many occasions during the years that E-Rate funding has been on hold pending resolution of the alleged non-compliance issues. To date, no funds have been received. Yet community stakeholders are led to believe an eventual resolution will solve the resulting budget shortfalls. The situation has been further exacerbated by sporadic resignations of key people within District 1's technology department. A recent article in a local paper records Table 3.

Despite the setback of existing E-Rate funding delays, District 1 has continued to apply for new E-Rate funding by hiring E-Rate vendors who specialize in the application process and its related compliance requirements. E-Rate vendors do not work for free but rather can charge large sums for their services with no guarantees of success in securing funding. District 1 recently approved a $150,000 budget expenditure to hire an E-Rate vendor to help with a new application for the upcoming academic year. Justification for such an expense was based on a fear that without communication infrastructure upgrades, school children would not be safe in cases of emergency. The local news source reported it this way: "Last year, District 1's governing board applied for E-Rate money because members were told public safety hinged on it." According to CTO Secor, upgrades were encouraged because of possible problems with schools dialing 911 and not getting through, exposing the community's children to potential danger. After further investigation, however, it was concluded that such speculation was unfounded. In fact, authorities discovered there was never any real danger as reported by district officials to community stakeholders.

Over the course of several years of E-Rate funding requests (see Table 4 Timeline), District 1 has not received any funding since the first year it applied, while five neighboring districts all received significant E-Rate funding without a single denial (Table 1). Mr. Secor resigned in frustration after ten years of E-Rate funding

Table 2.

What was the intent of the Bond funds? The CTO, Mr. Secor, explained that the bulk of the money was loaned to District 1 to purchase infrastructure needs, and upon E-rate reimbursement District 1 would repay the monies to the bond fund.

Table 3.

Since federal funds for technology improvement—E-Rate funds—became available in 1998, District 1 has had problems obtaining them, and hasn't received any since 2002. Despite the investigations, District 1 continues to apply for the federal funds—because there's no other single source with that much money to give. State education officials say the investigations hurt District 1's chances but that it's still possible the district could receive funds, as long as all application rules are followed. The 2007-2008 application from District 1 would get reviewed just like all the other applications submitted this year," wrote the director of educational technology for the State Department of Education."However, final approval will depend upon the results of the pending investigation."

failures and none of the hired E-Rate vendors has been successful yet in recouping the halted funding since the original award. Neither have they been successful in gaining approval for a single new E-Rate funding application. Such challenges within a school district can be devastating to community stakeholders as students suffer from the inadequate infrastructure affording 21st century learning opportunities. Without the needed infrastructure upgrades, bandwidth remains inadequate to take full advantage of new hardware and more demanding software as well as online education services provided to schools.

Table 4. Timeline of the case

Timeline of the Case A history of the trouble in District 1's technology department and its application for federal E-Rate money, which funds technology improvement: **1999** The Technology and Telecommunication Services Department is created. **Oct. 7, 2003** Mr. Secor is appointed district CTO. **February 2004** District 1 applies for nearly $16 million in E-Rate funds, including more than $10 million for contracts with ABC Vending. The request is later denied. **March 2004** Technology department employees call an anonymous federal whistle-blower hotline, concerned by the 2004 E-Rate application. **May 24, 2004** New Superintendent and the District 1 Governing Board are given memos from Technology department employees about concerns with the 2004 E-Rate application and Secor. **December 2004** Attorneys for the U.S. Department of Justice interview Technology department employees. **February 2005** District 1 applies for slightly more than $1 million in E-Rate funds. The request is later denied. **Nov. 4, 2005** An independent audit notes procurement problems resulting in the inability to file for 2004 E-Rate funds. **Feb. 16, 2006** District 1 applies for $19 million in E-Rate funds under the condition the State Attorney General's Office investigate its E-Rate consultant and the procurement policies. **June 2006** With no word from the Attorney General's Office, District 1 withdraws its 2006 E-Rate application. **October 2006** District 1 employees give sworn testimony in depositions. **Jan. 19, 2007** CTO Secor resigns.

Chapter 8
Technology in the Special Education Classroom

Blanca Rodriguez
School Teacher, USA

EXECUTIVE SUMMARY

Prairie School District believes in integrating technology into classroom learning for all students. However, for some schools "all students" does not include the special education population. Rolando was a 7 year old autistic boy additionally labeled with mental retardation. Pretend you were Rolando's teacher. Would you have done differently?

BACKGROUND INFORMATION

Technology usage in the classroom is at an evident high. Many classrooms are fully equipped with electronic white boards, projectors, computers, document cameras, and the like. Teachers also have up-to-date software programs and streaming videos that can accompany any lesson on the state curriculum guidelines. Professionals are constantly sent to trainings to improve the way technology is used in their classroom.

Assistive technology service is any service that directly assists an individual with a disability in the selection, acquisition, or use of an assistive technology device. Among all the technological advances, it is very obvious that there is not much focus on equipping special education classrooms with the latest technology tools.

According to the Technology-Related Assistance for Individuals with Disabilities Act of 1988 (Public Law 100-407), an assistive technology means any item, piece

DOI: 10.4018/978-1-61350-492-5.ch008

of equipment, or product system, whether acquired commercially, off-the-shelf, modified or customized, that is used to increase, maintain, or improve functional capabilities of individuals with disabilities. Adaptive technology is both an essential and critical educational tool that every student should be provided, regardless of disability.

THE CASE

Technology touches almost every aspect of our lives, including schools, communities, and homes. Prairie School District has several schools that are technology-based and teach students not only the fundamentals but even the extras. The school district gives every campus a $1.5 million grant to be used on technological resources or trainings that may be needed. Prairie School District believes adamantly in integrating technology into classroom learning for all students. However, for some schools "all students" does not include the special education population.

Rolando was a 7 year old autistic boy additionally labeled with mental retardation. He was born into a single-parent home with his mother and older sister. He entered into the Lexington Lake Elementary School in Prairie School District at the age of 3 when he was diagnosed with special needs. He was immediately placed into a preschool program for children with disabilities, otherwise known in the State as Preschool Programs for Children with Disabilities (or PPCD). The process of Rolando entering a new school came as a surprise for his mother, who spoke only limited English and required a translator for every Admission, Review and Dismissal (ARD) teacher meeting.

Rolando exhibited a remarkable memorization quality. He was able to memorize numbers and several sight words using sight cards. However he was unable to identify the words in actual story. He also had impaired social skills. He would usually play by himself or cling to an object throughout the day that he would talk to and with which he would engage in dramatic play. He also had a speech delay which correlated with his lack of social interaction. Since Rolando was labeled with mental retardation by the school's diagnostician, his mother was unable to qualify for a trained behavior therapist to come to the home and help with Rolando's disruptive behaviors. Nor did his mother have the funds to send him to an outside behavior specialist. Consequently he could only see a school speech therapist once a week for 30 minutes.

Typically, children with autism process visual information easier than auditory information. Any time teachers use assistive technology devices with autistic children, they are giving them information through their strongest processing area (visual). Therefore various types of technology from "low" tech to "high" tech could be incorporated into daily living in order to improve the functional capabilities of children with autism.

Rolando was a visual child and he functioned throughout his day using PECS picture schedules. Rolando's mom was still waiting for her own PECS (acronym for "Picture Exchange Communication Systems") schedule to use with him at home. She had been waiting for 6 months now. Her financial situation inhibited the resources she needed for her son.

Based on the above information given on Rolando, it was evident the child would benefit from assistive technology relating to his disability of Autism. There were several assistive technological tools that could help Rolando within the classroom. At school, Rolando would benefit from an adaptive keyboard with larger keys and less distractions. A touch screen computer, similar to many of the electronic whiteboards, would also help students with both visual and physical impairments. The average cost of one electronic whiteboard is $2,400, not including the $150 professional training that each teacher is required to attend. The average cost for an adaptive keyboard is $75 and a touch screen monitor is $1,200.

Lexington Lake Elementary has sent all 43 of its teachers to electronic white-board training sessions, with the exception of the special education teachers. All 47 classrooms now have electronic whiteboards, with the computer lab housing 2 electronic whiteboards. When Ms. Washington, Rolando's teacher, brought up at a faculty meeting, the following adaptive tools that would benefit her students, she was declined by her principal, Mr. Hitchcock, based on the reason of insufficient school funds. Mr. Hitchcock did have her fill out a waiting list, which she had done for the previous 2 years. Lexington Lake Elementary had enough funds to distribute a new electronic whiteboard to every teacher on campus, but the school could not fund an essential $1,275 adaptive tool for the special education classroom. Ms. Washington also requested a membership to a special needs website which helped students with their phonetic skills. She was declined the request for the $75 yearly membership fee. The average general education teacher at Lexington Lake Elementary had a minimum of 3 memberships' to websites. Ms. Washington was offered the 3 current membership accesses to use with her students; however the sites were not special-needs friendly. Lexington Lake Elementary was allocating its resources to serve the general education population, but it was not meeting the needs of "all" students.

The average classroom at Lexington Lake Elementary is equipped with 3 computers, 1 electronic whiteboard, interactive centers, an electronic projector, a document camera, and a printer. In contrast, the average special-needs classroom at Lexington Lake Elementary has 1 computer for its students and 1 for the teacher. In the average special needs classroom, there are no interactive centers, no projector, no document camera, and the special education teacher shares a printer with a first grade teacher. The general classrooms are also allowed computer time for 1 hour each week. Priority is given to the general students when it comes to computer lab usage.

Ms. Washington was given computer time on Monday mornings, but due to many of the student's intensive needs she would need the help of at least 2 teacher aids. On Monday mornings Ms. Washington's second aide was sent to help the fifth grade classes. Mr. Hitchcock requested that all available aides report to grade levels 3 through 5 and assist all teachers as much as possible. During the months of January through April, priority was given to all grade levels scheduled to take the state mandated exams. During the months of December through January, priority was given to all grade levels that were scheduled to take another standardized exam. This left Ms. Washington with only 4 months of full access to both her aides as well as computer class-time usage. Since Mr. Washington's students were neither a state mandated exam nor other standardized exam grade level, her aides were the first ones to be pulled. Ms. Washington must also attend ARD'S frequently, which adds up to more time that she is pulled from her students.

According to the US Department of Education, the Individuals with Disabilities Education Act (IDEA) is a law ensuring services to children with disabilities throughout the nation. IDEA governs how states and public agencies provide early intervention, special education and related services to more than 6.5 million eligible infants, toddlers, children and youth with disabilities. Children and youth (ages 3-21) receive special education and related services under IDEA Part B.

Rolando's mother had been to several ARDS. She was given clearly stated IEPs for her son and which were determined by assessments and observations. These goals stated specifically that Rolando was delayed in developmental, behavioral, physical, and pre-vocational skills. It was also determined that Rolando would benefit from modifications made on his instructional content, his setting, methods, and materials which were required to achieve and maintain satisfactory progress. It was identified that assistive technology would be crucial to Rolando's success in school. The goals were created and everyone at the ARD, including the principal, signed off on the IEP.

According to Rolando's IEP, Lexington Lake Elementary was required to have a voice output device in the school to assist him throughout his day. The device must be ordered by Rolando's speech therapist. His therapist had requested an order through the District during the previous November; however, the principal had since denied the funding. The voice output device would help Rolando at reducing his echolalia patterns of speech. Echolalia is when a child orally repeats a word constantly without using it correctly in context. Rolando's language consists of predominantly echolalia which his therapist had listed as non-speech. He was not thinking of the words he was saying, instead he just repeated them. The voice output device would have assisted him in processing the words prior to speaking.

The Prairie School District typically provided employees with a wide variety of trainings and professional development opportunities throughout the school year and summer. However at Lexington Lake Elementary, Mr. Hitchcock, the principal, preferred that the staff took free or low-cost trainings. Even though he did allow teachers to attend several trainings after school, the trainings were preselected. This year, of the trainings that were approved were actually geared more toward the general education teachers as opposed to ancillary or special education teachers. If teachers decided to select a training given during school hours, they were required to submit applications for approval and were almost always denied. The District did provide several professional development opportunities for special education teachers, however, all were offered either during school hours or were costly.

As Ms. Washington's professional development opportunities were decreasing and her annual evaluation was drawing near, she was forced to select trainings that would not improve her effectiveness as a special education teacher. Simply stated, at Lexington Lake Elementary, staff development training was more geared towards the general education population and not toward the individual needs of students or staff.

The new Superintendent was also expected to make a decision for the upcoming school year that would impact the special needs children in the district. He was proposing to remove all special needs classroom appointed funds and hire staff who would visit each classroom and assess the needs of the students. The appointed staff would meet with specialists and therapists and decide what materials, professional development, and adaptive technology were needed. This was an effort to modify and enforce the way schools were allocating and distributing funds for special needs programs. If this plan took effect, it was expected to greatly improve Lexington Lake Elementary and make the schools accountable for their actions.

Do you think the proposed plan would help Ms. Washington's classroom and other campuses like Lexington Lake Elementary, to equally distribute adaptive technological tools to all classrooms so that students like Rolando would be able to build up the ability to communicate and learn despite their physical and neurological challenges?

Chapter 9
Emotional and Behavioral Disorders Students Using Computer–Assisted Devices

Martina Ramos-Rey
School Teacher, USA

EXECUTIVE SUMMARY

Paul was a 12 year old 6th grader diagnosed as Bipolar, ADHD, and having difficulty controlling impulses. He attended a public school and remained all day in the general education classroom. After trying multiple research-based interventions over a period of weeks, Paul's teacher and the behavior specialist decided to try computer software designed to help him reflect on his behaviors and how his behaviors made others feel.

BACKGROUND INFORMATION

The presence of students with behavioral disorders is becoming more common in the general education classroom. These students present a challenge to the school and the teacher. EBD is diagnosed in 1% of school age children. The National Research Council and Institute of Medicine of the National Academies published the numbers in Table 1 in 2009.

DOI: 10.4018/978-1-61350-492-5.ch009

Table 1.

DISORDER	PERCENTAGE OF YOUNG PEOPLE AFFECTED
Learning Disorder:	5.0%
Substance use / addiction disorder:	10.3%
Conduct Disorder:	3.5%
Oppositional Defiant Disorder:	2.8%
Attention Deficit Hyperactivity Disorder:	4.5%
Anxiety Disorders (various):	8.0%
Unipolar Disorder:	5.2%
One or more disorders:	17.0%

With laws such as IDEA focusing on the least restrictive environment for these children, teachers who are not trained in working with EBD students face major obstacles, such as students' behavior and finding instructional strategies that work with EBD children. One of the instructional and behavioral strategies that has been scarcely researched, but has shown good results, is using technology such as hand-held computers and computer software developed specifically for EBD children to help them self monitor their behavior.

Many teachers are not trained on how to work with these students. While there are many research-based behavioral interventions available to implement in the class-room, technology has now afforded educators the ability to incorporate innovative interventions using hand-held devices, computers, and computer software. Using these resources to help EBD students self-monitor their behavior in and out of the general education classroom will allow the teacher to teach and the students to learn.

Implementing hand-held devices and computer-assisted instruction will be very beneficial for EBD students, schools, and teachers. Beginning the process can be challenging, but with a few simple adjustments this behavioral and instruc-tional intervention can be integrated into the regular education classroom quickly and efficiently.

Funding for hand-held devices and computer-assisted instruction can come from the school's technology budget. If needed, schools can apply for grants to acquire funds. If the funds are planned into the budget the year prior, it will be easier to purchase hand-held devices; the costs of which can range between $200 to $700 apiece. Typically, schools do not need more than a few hand-held devices.

The devices and other software would be managed by the Special Education department or campus behavior specialists. Students would be trained on the device and/or software. The Special Education department and classroom teacher could decide what would work best for the student; either a hand held device which prompts self monitoring, or computer software that allows the student to work at his/her own pace.

THE CASE

Paul was a 12 year old 6th grader diagnosed as Bipolar, ADHD, and as having difficulty controlling impulses. He attended a public school and stayed in the general education classroom all day. His teacher, Mrs. Sheldon, had been teaching for 9 years. She had excellent classroom management and good communication skills, but she had never worked with a bipolar student. The class make-up consisted of mainly Gifted and Talented and high achieving students. Paul's classmates noticed that he behaved differently and tried to keep their distance from him. He had no friends and often acted out. He complained to his parents and teachers that no one liked him. Due to lack of opportunities to interact with others, he had poor social skills and felt isolated.

Paul's daily behaviors were a problem. In class, he struggled to pay attention, fell asleep, threw paper, talked to himself, and rarely finished his class work. He also had difficulties outside the classroom. For example, during lunch Paul would throw food at other students. He had been warned and given consequences for his behavior many times, but because of his inability to control his impulsivity, he continued exhibiting the behavior.

After multiple research-based interventions had been tried over a period of weeks, Mrs. Sheldon, together with the behavior specialist, Mr. Griggs, and the principal, Mrs. Wright, decided to try computer software to help Paul reflect on his behavior and how his actions made others feel. Paul had already been doing this orally with the school counselor. The software prompted Paul to answer some simple questions such as, "How do you feel after you have done something you aren't supposed to? What made you choose to do what you did? How do you think your classmates feel when you do that?"

The first day, Paul was uneasy about using the software. He felt silly typing in his answers which took a long time because of his lack of keyboarding skills. Mrs. Sheldon continued to have Paul use the software every time he broke a rule or did something outlandish. Eventually, Paul began to like the software. In the diary, he typed:

"Now I'm into computers a lot; I really am. I enjoy getting my work done on my own."

"If people were nice to me, I'd be a lot happier."

"I walk to school to type a few things in MY COMPUTER before school."

"Kids tell me I get in trouble too much or say I'm dumb and won't hang out with me. My friends are okay with me and we usually talk about computer games."

"Mrs. Sheldon showed me how the computer lets you color things so I can see the differences in my classes, like how much work there is in one class and how much in another. Maybe, I will remember to do my assignments."

"I heard the bell ring for lunch and jumped out of my seat so I could get to MY COMPUTER."

"Mom told another teacher about this diary thing I am doing. I hope I can change. I don't like feeling like a jerk."

"I don't think I'm dumb like some kids tell me; some stuff in school is really fun like when we got to do reports on marine life."

"Mr. Griggs says that my marine life report was good and that I might be able to teach the teachers some things."

"Mr. Griggs told my mom that some teachers just won't give me a chance. What he said made me feel like it isn't always my fault. I don't choose to forget and to be messy."

Paul also began to love having new and advanced technology available to him. He put more efforts into behaving and getting longer computer time and opportunities to play computer games. His behavior slightly improved and even though he still made bad choices at times, his behavior was not as bad as before. Mrs. Sheldon also noticed that his keyboarding skills improved.

Both Mrs. Sheldon and Mr. Griggs agreed that inclusive software such as the one Paul used offered teens who have behavior problems a welcoming, nonthreatening environment in which to practice positive social skills. Teachers were very encouraged by Paul's success with the software. They discovered that early intervention and treatment offers the chance for students with bipolar disorder to gain the best possible level of wellness.

When it comes to technology and the latest tools for helping students, research is Mrs. Sheldon's motto. She put a lot of effort into finding the most affordable and user friendly products to help students like Paul. Mrs. Sheldon and Mr. Griggs talked to other experts and attended conferences and found that popular options for bipolar disorder included auditory therapy software programs and cognitive training games. Good auditory therapy software programs have helped individuals make improvements in many areas, including attention span and focus, speech and motor control, Self-esteem, mood, motivation, social interaction, and Physical balance and coordination - sensory integration. This can result in improvements from academic performance to emotional balance. Besides, good cognitive training software programs consists of a variety of exercises designed to help improve functioning in areas such as sustaining attention, memory, thinking before acting, visual and auditory processing, listening, and reading. The principle behind cognitive training is to help improve the "core" abilities and self-control necessary before an individual can function academically with success. The exercises "drill for skill" and work directly in the areas where specific cognitive difficulties occur.

Some of these software programs required around forty hours to complete each unit. Since Paul might require repetition and one-to-one instruction, the computer was the easiest and most cost effective way to implement this type of program. The computer also provided the option of game-like structure to motivate inattentive students like Paul to complete the training in order to build skills essential for success in school and life.

Mrs. Sheldon and Mr. Griggs decided to discuss these software options with other EBD experts before making recommendations for the school to acquire the software applications during the next purchase cycle.

Chapter 10
Pop Quiz Debacle

Leanne Spinale
Future School Teacher, USA

EXECUTIVE SUMMARY

It is now commonplace for students to bring PDAs and smart phones into the classroom, which gives them swift access to the internet. While this technology is a benefit for students conducting research for a project, it can also be detrimental for educators conducting assessments. "Pop Quiz Debacle" describes a particular quandary for educators who work with advanced placement or Gifted/Talented students. For students with a very high GPA and other academic performance, what distinguishes them is how perfect they are, so there's no room for any kind of error. If there's no room for error, students tend to cheat–even though these students would have done just fine on the test. They say they cheat because, "this is my safety net."

BACKGROUND INFORMATION

The vast advances in computer technology in recent years have changed the way we use computers. Gone are the days where you had to sit at a desk to operate a computer, nowadays you have powerful computer access in the palm of your hand. It is now commonplace for students to bring PDA's and smart phones into the classroom which gives them swift access to the internet. While this technology is a benefit for students conducting research for a project, it can also be detrimental for educators conducting assessments. Additionally, the boundaries defining right and wrong are becoming blurred. Everyday the news reports of public figures involved in criminal activity, immoral activity or deceit. It seems that integrity is no longer revered in

DOI: 10.4018/978-1-61350-492-5.ch010

our society. The combination of the decrease in integrity along with technological advances poses significant concerns for educators. Not only is cheating on the rise nationally, but there has also been a cultural shift in who cheats and why.

Ask a high school or college student about cheating and most will justify it by saying, "Everybody does it." Survey statistics back up the statement.

Researchers found that nationally, 75 percent of all high school students cheat. But the ones who cheat more are the ones who have the most to lose–the honors and advanced placement students. Eighty percent of honors and AP students cheat on a regular basis.

The following case study describes a particular quandary for educators who work with advanced placement or Gifted/Talented students.

THE CASE

Mrs. Washington was a GT Specialist at Jefferson Creek Intermediate School. She enjoyed working with the GT students and strived to not only properly educate them, but to instill in them a desire to achieve higher goals.

Jefferson Creek Intermediate School had both an honor code policy and cell phone policy that was explained to the students at the beginning of each year. However, Mrs. Washington was aware that these policies were violated several times a year. The school administrators recognized that the technology policy in conjunction with the existing code policy and cell phone policy needed to be reviewed and revised, but they were concerned about parents' viewpoints regarding more stringent guidelines and how it would affect emergency communication with their child.

One of Mrs. Washington's favorite groups of students to work with was from Mr. Walters' class. Lindsey, Tracy, Heather, Ian, and Brady were all very motivated learners. She could always count on them to provide lively viewpoints during class discussions. She considered them to be some of the best students in the school.

On Tuesday Mrs. Washington and the students were discussing the movie The Count of Monte Cristo. She wanted to discover how the students perceived the character's actions. She queried first about Villefort's decision to imprison Dantes even though he had done nothing wrong.

The students offered many possible reasons for Dantes' decision however it seemed to Mrs. Washington that the students were dismissing Villefort's behavior and not holding him accountable for his actions. Mrs. Washington prompted. "so you are saying that Villefort's actions were permissible?"

Again, the students offered possible reasons why such a decision may be permissible.

*"Last week we discussed the concept of integrity. Did Villefort act with integrity?"
asked Mrs. Washington.*

*"Well," said Brady, "it's all about honesty and Villefort wasn't being honest, but
I bet if you asked him he could explain why he did it. I bet he felt like he had a
good reason."*

The students agreed, "He sure didn't act with integrity."

*"Well," said Mrs. Washington, "it sounds like you think Dantes didn't show integrity
when he hid his identity, but you're giving Villefort a pass on his actions."*

*"Well, haven't you told us that there are two sides to every story?" asked Ian. "The
movie didn't really explain why Villefort did it, but we know Dantes did it for revenge
and that's wrong," continued Ian.*

*Mrs. Washington pondered this discussion for several days and wondered if the
students would make decisions to forward their own goals or take the harder path
and make decisions with integrity. At their next meeting she discussed the concept
of integrity again and how it might apply to them.*

They brainstormed for a while and then a colleague came in the room and asked
to speak with her. She asked the students to complete a quiz while she spoke with
her colleague. She quickly passed out the quiz which was on the book The Adven-
tures of Huckleberry Finn, a book that they had not yet read nor discussed. She
realized that she had passed out the wrong quiz by mistake and began to interrupt
her colleague to rectify the situation, but noticed something disconcerting. Some
of her students were cheating.

It was at this point Mrs. Washington observed the following: Tracy began to
frantically complete the quiz. She moved from question to question and appeared
to have a grasp on the answers. Brady gradually moved his chair closer to Tracy
and peered frequently at Tracy's paper. At the outset, Lindsey seemed anxious and
she even put her head down on her desk. But after a few minutes she sat back up
and began to write. She repeated this several times and it caught Mrs. Washington's attention. Mrs. Washington ambled to the other side of the room and noticed
that Lindsey's cell phone was in her hand under the table and when she would put
her head on the desk she was accessing information on her phone. Heather, on the
other hand, seemed intent on sharpening her already sharpened pencil which she
did three different times whilst walking slowly by Lindsey and staring intently at
her paper. Mrs. Washington couldn't believe they were cheating, especially after the

discussion about integrity depicted in the movie The Count of Monte Cristo. These were her best GT students and she expected more from them. Why did they cheat?

Back in the teachers' lounge, Mrs. Washington told Mr. Walters about the incident in private, as the latter is the homeroom teacher for Lindsey, Tracy, Heather, Ian, and Brady.

"Back in my old school days, the most high-tech cheating trick consisted of exchanging calculators with the answers in it. But times have changed." Mrs. Washington sighed at the end of the conversation.

"But other teachers have not detected any cheating behaviors among that group of students. Maybe it's because we assume students are naturally honest. I did not think they are capable of doing that," said Mr. Walters.

"I heard that in a nearby high school, teachers have had students who have been caught using photo copies of notes or photo copies of other information during exams," said Mrs. Washington. "I also read from online news that in other state, some students were found with phones in the soles of their shoes and pagers under their clothes, by examiners using metal detectors. "

"But why did these GT students cheat?" asked Mr. Walters.

"I asked Lindsey, Tracy, Heather, Ian, and Brady to come talk to me in private after the incident. For students with a very high GPA and other academic performance, what distinguishes them is how perfect they are. So there's no room for any kind of error. And if there's no room for error, you tend to cheat, even though these students would have done just fine on the test. They say they cheat because "this is my safety net."

The speed of such technological advances has caught teachers by surprise, ill-informed of the varied capabilities of wireless devices. After other similar cell phone cheating incidents, school district attorneys are sounding an alarm; recommending their client school districts consider the potential dangers of text messaging.

Chapter 11
Principal's Letter to Parents:
Take Kids off Social Networking Sites

Irene Chen
University of Houston Downtown, USA

EXECUTIVE SUMMARY

In recent years Facebook, MySpace, and other social-networking sites have been blamed for the suicides of teenagers in Missouri, Massachusetts, and New York. Parents complained their children were traumatized by nasty comments posted by cyberbullies on social-networking sites. Schools and districts are taking action in response. According to a T H E Journal survey conducted in 2009, 68 percent of respondents replied that their districts banned social networking sites for students and teachers, 19 respondents replied that they banned social networking sites only for students, and another 12 percent said there was no ban in their districts. In the following case study, which is a true story based on a news report in the Spring of 2010, a middle school principal calls for parents to yank their children from all social-networking sites after a so-called "Naughty List" was posted on Facebook. Is his extreme measure justifiable?

BACKGROUND INFORMATION

In recent years Facebook, MySpace and other social-networking sites have been blamed for the suicides of teenagers in Missouri, Massachusetts, and New York.

DOI: 10.4018/978-1-61350-492-5.ch011

Parents complained their children were traumatized by nasty comments posted by cyberbullies on social-networking sites.

Retrevo surveyed more than 1,000 adults in the US and found that parents not only want to learn more about their kids through technology, they also have solid opinions on how their kids should use it. According to a new survey by Retrevo, almost half of parents said that they were "friends" with their teenagers on social networks.

Close to 12 percent of surveyed parents ban social networking as a form of punishment, and 18 percent ban all Internet usage. This is creeping very close to the 22 percent who nix TV, showing that parents understand how valuable Internet access is to their teens. Additionally, 29 percent of all parents ban the use of mobile phones and texting while at the dinner table. That number goes up to 36 percent for parents of teenagers. Still, many parents see the value in trying to "friend" their kids on social networks, even though it might be a bit awkward at times.

According to the same survey, most parents who are Facebook friends with their kids have teenagers—only 8 percent of parents said kids under 12 should have Facebook accounts in the first place—and they say that they learn a lot about their teens this way.

Schools and districts are taking action in response. According to a T H E Journal survey conducted in 2009, 68 percent of respondents replied that their districts banned social networking sites for students and teachers, 19 respondents replied that they banned social networking sites only for students, and another 12 percent said there was no ban in their districts.

In the following case study, a middle school principal is calling for parents to yank their children from all social-networking sites after a so-called "Naughty List" was posted on Facebook.

THE CASE

The names of dozens of female students at Reagan Middle School community in Pearson District had their names posted on a so-called "Naughty List" on Facebook, officials said. The page, called "The Whimsical Girls of Pearson ISD" claimed the girls were promiscuous. "I haven't done anything to deserve to be put on that list," said an 8th-grade victim who did not want to be identified. Parents complained to the district.

A spokeswoman said the district persuaded Facebook to remove the page and the case was turned over to the County Sheriff's Office. "We felt it was serious enough to get involved and try and help our kids and get to the bottom of it," said the spoke person of the District. "The ramification of cyber-bulling, in my opinion, is huge because it's like a snowball. It splatters in ways that you don't even imagine that it would," said Mrs. Mallow, a student's mother.

If the author of the list is identified, he or she could face expulsion, school officials said. However, the district attorney's office said it determined that no crime was committed. (see Table 1)

Facebook issued a news release soon afterward about its new, expanded Safety Center. Two days later, Daniel Romero, the school principal, sent an e-mail blast to the Middle School community on April 17, urging parents to take down their children's online profiles on Facebook, MySpace, and elsewhere. Here is the e-mail:

Dear parents,

As you know, the school's guidance counselors for years have been mediating spats that originated online. It is time for every single member of the school community to take a stand! The recent incidents that happened here in Reagan Middle School has reminded me to urge you, as parents, to take down your child's online profiles on Facebook and elsewhere.

Table 1.

Important Information from the Fort Bend Independent School District Regarding Online Harassment/Cyberbullying

This information has been prepared collaboratively by the Pearson District Departments of School Administration, Safe and Secure Schools, Student Support Services, Technology, Auxiliary Services, Police and Community Relations and Partnerships for our students, parents, staff and community.

Because Pearson District has recently been asked to address an incident of cyberbullying on a non-district website, we thought it would be helpful to:

• Raise the awareness regarding the seriousness of cyberbullying.
• Provide insight concerning the District's policy on bullying.
• Provide helpful information on how to support responsible use of the Internet at home.
• Provide a reminder of the District programs, resources and activities provided in support of our students and their families.

Cyberbullying is defined as the use of the Internet or other electronic devices to intentionally engage in repeated or widely disseminated acts of cruelty towards another that results in emotional harm. Sometimes teens engage in hurtful online behavior because they feel more invisible online and yet, they do not understand the harmful consequences of their actions. Sometimes they see others being bullied and join in because they are themselves being bullied at school. Many of the most harmful incidents of cyberbullying occur when students post hurtful material on public sites. What they do not take into consideration when they engage in harmful conversations on public sites is the harmful impact their postings have at school.

The Pearson District Freedom from Bullying policy Board Policy FFI (Local) addresses written or verbal expression or physical conduct that would be considered bullying of its students. The District policy defines bullying, timely reporting, reporting procedures, district action and confidentiality. If this type of activity is a concern at school, please contact your school administrator so they can help resolve these problems. We want all of our students to feel welcome, physically safe, emotionally secure and happy.

The District takes the issue of cyberbullying very seriously and encourages you to monitor your child's internet activity. Please report any acts of online bullying to your child's campus administrator immediately.

The threat to your son or daughter from online adult predators is insignificant compared to the damage that children at this age constantly and repeatedly do to one another through social networking sites. The main problem is that tweens do not have the resilience to withstand Internet name-calling. The casual cruelty of an unsupervised 12-year-old online is a more realistic threat to their children than the oft-raised specter of sexual predators.

There is absolutely no reason for any middle school student to be a part of a social networking site! Let me repeat that - there is absolutely, positively no reason for any middle school student to be a part of a social networking site!

Sincerely,

Mr. Daniel Romero

Principal of Ronald Reagan Middle School

"They are simply not psychologically ready for the damage that one mean person online can cause," he wrote in the e-mail. "The school's guidance counselors for years now have been mediating spats that originated online"

The **last straw** for Mr. Romero was students' growing use of a social-networking upstart where members ask and answer questions about one another.

Mr. Romero singled out the site for blame in his e-mail to Reagan Middle School parents, calling it a "scourge" that exists "simply to post mean things about people anonymously."

"The nicest thing you see on it is, 'Jessica loves Zack,'" he said in a phone interview with a journalist.

A Facebook spokesman pointed out that many middle school-age children are formally barred from the site. "We prohibit children under the age of 13 from using Facebook both for safety reasons and to comply with the Children's Online Privacy Protection Act," the Facebook spokesman said.

Ian Smither, the parent of a student, said he agreed with the principal's point, but her daughter was "completely up in arms" when he raised the possibility of shutting down her Facebook account. He said she remained hopeful they could work out "an amicable solution."

Mr. Romero says that, on the whole, parental response to his e-mail has been overwhelmingly positive, and that parents from as far away as Israel and Korea have e-mailed him to say, "thank you for saying something."

Parents can also friend Mr. Romero on Facebook, of which he is a member. In Table 2 is a log of what parents had to say.

Table 2.

Parent A: I think the point is this...at that age, what is the need to be on a social network? Really...through the eyes of a child, not our adult eyes, what benefit is it really?
Parent H: Finally someone who is willing to stand up and do the right thing. Too many schools do not want to own any responsibility once the kids are back home.
Parent I: The only difference between name calling in real life and on the Internet is that you can lash out in real life, but on the Web you can only leave a comment. Different forms of communication have always brought problems but they also bring good things. I think the good outweighs the bad.
Parent J: Facebook is touted like so many other modern toys as making it easier to network and keep in touch. What it accomplishes most of the time is in fact wasting time. I assure you the economic productivity of those not on Facebook is far greater than those on Facebook.
Parents K: While I like that a school principal has taken up a cry against young kids on social networking sites, it's unfathomable to get every single kid off of sites like Facebook. What this principal is doing, however, is bringing more attention to the subject of cyber bullying.
Parent B: Well, you're not going to get children off of Facebook. We have the freedom of speech and schools and other things are trying their very hardest to take it away in my opinion. It is not the school's choice if people need to get off of Facebook. It is the child's and their parents.
Parent C: I remember when I first joined Facebook in 2004. Many people don't remember this was originally strictly for college students and you could only join through your college's e-mail addresses. I think it's great that they have opened Facebook up to everyone but what concerns me is that these are elementary and middle school students.
Parent D: There is absolutely no reason for a school principal to be a decision maker in this issue. Do your job by teaching and safeguarding kids IN SCHOOL and let parents do their jobs at home.
Parent E: The problem is many parents don't do their jobs. Some parents are completely clueless & naive as to what is said and what is shared on Facebook.
Parent F: Facebook for my kids and myself is strictly family and friends. We have family all over the country. We keep in touch and send each other pictures. We also play the games together. I know everyone's ID and password. No teasing or bullying happening. I would assume parents are not checking. Some parents do not even know how to use computer, but their kids do.
Parent G: There is a bunch of social networking sites for small children, through Disney and other sites. They just are not very popular because Facebook is for older kids.

Chapter 12
Student's Reliance on the Use of Technology for Classroom Assignment

Rarshunda Hudson
School Teacher, USA

EXECUTIVE SUMMARY

Ms. Turner, an eighth grade History teacher, assigns students a research paper on Cuba and communism. She asks the students to use only paper media for their research materials. Her students argue, "Why should we waste time using books to find information, when we can just look it up on the Web quickly?" Angry parents also question why the students should have to use only books for research when they have been given laptops by the school.

BACKGROUND INFORMATION

Today's students cannot conceive of a time that technology was not readily available to them. For them, the use of the Internet plays a major role in their relationships with friends, family, and school. Many young people do not understand arguments that schools should limit their use of personal technology in the classroom. They view education as an extension of their social networking experience. And the parents of teens think the use of technology enhances the social life and academic work of their teenage children. They see technology as the answer to every question, accessible instantly. Therefore, they do not comprehend restricting the use of the limitless

DOI: 10.4018/978-1-61350-492-5.ch012

capabilities of technology. Proponents of the use of technology in the classroom argue that students complete their schoolwork more quickly; they are less likely to get stymied by material they don't understand; their papers and projects are more likely to draw upon up-to-date sources and state-of-the-art knowledge; and, they are better at juggling their school assignments and extracurricular activities when they use technology gadgets.

During the early 1980s, there was little if any use of technology in everyday life. The use of technology in the classroom at that time was typically limited to the use a typewriter and occasionally a television. Teachers did not have computers on their desks, and student computers were unheard of. The only way to have access to information was through books and newspaper articles. Students were expected to find written documentation for information included in their school work. Students were provided the tools to complete research by using the school or public library as their main source of information. High schools in the 1980s still offered courses in typewriter usage. The tasks afforded by technology were limited to typing papers. When students needed to research information, hard-back books were the only medium available to students.

Today's students have grown up with the use of technology readily available to them. Since the 1990s the use of technology has become a necessity few could live without. With the advent of home computers and the Internet, students have had more access to information than ever before. Some researchers believe that readily accessed information from the Internet has diminished the use of books, high-level critical thinking, and learner ability to discern valid information. Other critics have written and spoken extensively of their beliefs that schools should not use technology. These critics offer a variety of reasons ranging from how the use of technology can create social isolation, to technology preventing students from learning critical basic skills. In other words, current students are not developing higher order thinking skills. They lack the cognitive skills of investigation, research, and comprehension of text. Students copy and paste information and do not verify validity through any other media outlet. The subsequent question is the accuracy of websites and blogs. With so few safeguards or policing of web information, how can students ascertain the correctness of information obtained there? If education is the great equalizer and technology is the future instrument of education, are we certain that all students have equal access? While technology is increasingly available, some schools enjoy more opportunities than others. In larger, more affluent school districts, the use of laptops is becoming common place.

THE CASE

At a local area school district, eighth grade middle school students were given laptops that were checked out to them for the duration of the school year. Ms. Turner, a first year History teacher, assigned her students a research paper on Cuba and communism. She asked the students to use only paper media for their research material. The students argued that they should be able to use the laptops and the Internet for their research. The next day, Ms. Turner received two angry emails from parents and was called into the assistant Principal's office to discuss her assignment. The parents questioned why the students should have to use only books for research when they have been given laptops by the school. The parents did not want students to 'waste' time in libraries looking up information. The assistant principal explained to Ms. Turner that the students should be able to use a variety of outlets to do their research. She asked Ms. Turner to explain her stance. Ms. Turner explained that a number of the online sources that the students had used on previous assignments were inaccurate and that the students lacked the skills to complete research without their dependence on the Internet. Ms. Turner further explained that she would like the students to become less dependent on the Internet and spend time using the school and local library. She elaborated that when higher level critical thinking was required, students did not possess the thinking skills as they should have. Furthermore, they were unable to look for books on their topic or use the library to locate books. Ms. Turner also explained that she had viewed several Internet sites about Cuba and found numerous inaccuracies. She did not want the students to receive poor information and unwittingly stop searching any further for the truth.

Ms. Turner was told by the assistant principal that she must allow the students to use the laptops and the Internet as part of the project. The assistant principal explained that students are not comfortable with using only the library and that the *use* of technology outweighed possible inaccuracies. The assistant principal explained that it was Ms. Turner's job to point out the inaccuracies and offer possible solutions. Ms. Turner was not happy with the outcome and wondered if this entire experience was not typical of why students were losing the critical thinking skills they would need in their academic futures.

Chapter 13
Cyber Gangs inside the Classroom

Evelyn Martinez
School Teacher, USA

EXECUTIVE SUMMARY

Students in classrooms face challenges of which teachers and adults are either unaware or simply do not notice. Jonathan's parents nor his teachers knew about the difficult situation Jonathan was experiencing with his classmates. Like so many parents and teachers, they did not have any reason to suspect that ten-year-old Jonathan was a victim of a cyber gang's activities occurring right in his own living room and inside his classroom.

BACKGROUND INFORMATION

There has been a push since the late '90s to make technology accessible to as many people as possible in order to eliminate the gap between those with the resources to access technology, and those lacking the resources; but no true balance or equalizer has been found as yet. And for those who do have access, once students click on that Internet browser icon, a new world opens up before them; a world which might not be the best thing for their life. In fact, today's generation has adopted a new set of standards when it comes to issues surrounding the use of technology. Activities such as illegal downloading, jail breaking mobile phones, and cheating using handheld devices present just some of the challenging technology-related issues we

DOI: 10.4018/978-1-61350-492-5.ch013

face today. While there is a tremendous push to integrate more technology into the educational curriculum, there are many circumstances where such technologies can take a negative turn in classrooms. As teachers look around their classrooms, which typically include many at-risk learners, they see some of these negative influences technology has had on students. For example, while teachers are discussing a topic like literature, students often seem uninterested. But as soon as teachers introduce more trendy topics such as video gaming or mobile access to television shows, these same teachers report a rise in student interest levels. Even at the elementary level, students nowadays act more like mini-teenagers who are trying to grow up too fast; and the Internet may be affording them the opportunity. Children now have access to the Internet even *without* a computer. A Nintendo Wii or Sony PlayStation game console gives children unlimited access to the web as it opens up portals of communication without requiring that the games themselves be played.

Students in our classrooms face many challenges of which teachers and adults are unaware or do not notice; like being bullied into committing forms of cyber crime, or being harassed by groups of students who form cyber gangs. Even if parents and teachers do not always agree on the degree to which technology should be used in the classroom setting or at home, the fact is it is impossible to escape it. Teachers and parents both have to remain vigilant of the kind of access and the amount of involvement children have when it comes to technology. At-risk students are more likely to join real as well as cyber gangs because it offers them a sense of belonging. When students feel a sense of acceptance while doing something that may be hurting people, it can lead to a great danger in our society.

The time kids used to spend playing outside in the sun have been replaced by hours in front of a computer or video game console. This change not only leads to an unhealthy life, but it is creating a whole new wave of crime that goes on behind the scenes without being seen in person. This leads to isolation and depression of young children who are victimized by groups of other students who operate undercover with the sole purpose to hurt others for entertainment.

Although most people use the Internet as a powerful and beneficial tool for communication and education – technology functions wonderfully when used appropriately with interactive learning activities – still some individuals exploit the power of the Internet for criminal or terrorist purposes. The use of the Internet for these negative purposes can be minimized by informing parents and the public of the measures they can take to protect their loved ones from the potential dangers that technology may bring.

THE CASE

When Jonathan Tyler, a thirteen year old boy, first arrived at Valley Junior High School, he really liked his new school. His teacher seemed nice and so did all of his classmates. He was put in a group with three other boys–Brandon, Jose, and Kevin. The boys immediately got along and found things they had in common like playing basketball and video games. Jonathan's parents, Mr. and Mrs. Tyler, were pleased to see their son get along with his classmates.

The following weeks after his arrival Jonathan's parents noticed a change in his behavior. He was not the same boy; in his face was a look of fear and despair. When they approached him to ask what was wrong, Jonathan simply replied, "Nothing." Mr. Tyler decided to ask the other boys if they knew anything, but they said nothing. They had begun to suspect something was wrong. Jonathan seemed isolated and depressed. They began to wonder if the move to the new school had been a bad idea, and assumed that he was simply starting to miss his old school. Both Jonathan's parents and teachers had no clue of the ordeal he was enduring.

Jonathan's nightmare started after the first week he moved to his new school. Brandon, Jose, and Kevin had asked him to become part of their group to help them do things he knew were not right. They wanted Jonathan to help them post inappropriate things on the Internet about his teacher and classmates. When he refused to do so, they began threatening him day after day over the Internet by sending him hateful messages over the Internet and PlayStation platform. As the days went by, the boys began to think of new ways to harass Jonathan and told him that if he continued ignoring them, they would take action and beat him up right in front of his house.

If it were not Jonathan's sister who discovered his ordeal, the parents were clueless about the situation Jonathan was living in. Like many other parents, they did not have any reason to believe their son was being a victim of a cyber gang right in their living room and inside his classroom.

Back in the days when Jonathan's parents were in school, it used to be school janitors and teachers who had their fingers on the pulse of underground gang activity on school grounds by the number of graffiti on the walls and other unruly behaviors.

Not knowing how to intervene, Mr. Tyler contacted Mr. Adams, who is a program coordinator for the ALERT Partnership, part of the Department of Community Safety of the city.

"Today's wannabes will be the potential O/Gs of tomorrow," Adams says of cyber gangs after hearing Jonathan's problem.

He explained that an O/G is slang for original gangster, or older street gang members who are usually in their 20s or 30s. A wannabe is often an individual seeking membership in a gang—typically youth who view the gang as a place where they could become "somebody."

Mr. Adams said that part of his job as the program coordinator for the ALERT Partnership is to educate school staff and faculty that today's potential street gang members and gangster wannabes can interact over the Web, and that means computer teachers and school technology officials are the sentinels of gang activity on school grounds. Children who might not have computers at home may try to check out illicit sites while they are at school—and school districts are taking measures to make sure those sites can't be accessed. All staff members and teachers should be on the lookout for junior high-schoolers and young teens that may be curious about gangs and checking them out on the Internet, like Brandon, Jose, and Kevin.

"Sometimes kids going on to those illicit sites are kids with great needs. By uncovering these needs adults can intervene before there is really a problem," he says.

"Since Jonathan is a new kid in the block, he becomes an easy target for wannabes like Brandon, Jose, and Kevin. We need to get to the high-risk kids early," Adams explains. "We don't need ninth- and 10th-graders turning a local school into the next Columbine," he says, referring to the deadly 1999 shootings at the Colorado high school.

Mr. Tyler was so upset that he wanted to meet in person the kids who harassed Jonathan.

"Do not take these sorts of issues into your own hands," Mr. Adams suggested.

Mr. Tyler was advised not to confront the kids who harassed Jonathan. What else can he do to help his son?

Chapter 14
Technology Integration in the Home?

Amanda Gordon
School Teacher, USA

EXECUTIVE SUMMARY

If homework assignments that require the use of a computer are given to students, should they be penalized for what their family cannot afford? In this case study, Mrs. Lincoln, who developed her course using a web-based course management system named Moodle, spent time working on her Moodle pages and posting assignments. She then explained to students how the site worked. She also spent a week in the computer lab training her students to become proficient using the Moodle application. After a couple of weeks, Mrs. Lincoln noticed that a quarter of her students were not completing their Moodle based assignments.

BACKGROUND INFORMATION

Learning how to use technology effectively can help prepare our students for the challenges they will face in the workplace. However, do all students have the ability and access to technology? Though it is great that many private schools allow students classroom-use of laptops on a daily basis, do all students have laptops to use? What kind of accommodations is made for those students who are not financially fortunate to have such technological devices? Many of the students in our schools do not have the means to technology.

DOI: 10.4018/978-1-61350-492-5.ch014

School districts know that in order for students to become well-rounded they must know how to use computer applications. Differentiated instruction allows for students to show their intelligence through computer usage. Students cannot be expected to wait until college to learn how to effectively complete a research project. Because student papers should be typed, students take a semester of keyboarding. They are *required* to do research papers and present their work with a PowerPoint presentation. Districts are spending thousands of dollars on required computer software. One such software that more districts are buying into is called Moodle. Moodle is essentially a web-based platform of learning management systems such as Blackboard. Moodle allows teachers to create a web page with assignments and notes. Through the Moodle page, students can essentially learn at their own pace. Teachers can post helpful websites and links through which students can navigate. Students can complete assignments that are posted right on the Moodle page for the teacher to grade. Teachers can post student grades on the Moodle page for student access. Moodle provides a useful and interactive medium between student and teacher. However, while students are off-campus, all Teacher-Student communication is handled through Moodle.

THE CASE

Mrs. Lincoln is a teacher at Johnson High School. Her district is fairly small and is composed of many at-risk students. Most of the students at her school are economically disadvantaged. Due to tough economic times, the district has been trying to cut back on spending and looking at ways to save dollars. At a recent professional development meeting, the district explained that teachers must fully utilize the software that has already been purchased by the district. Because all of the teachers were trained on how to use Moodle, the district told teachers that they wanted to see immediate implementation in their classrooms. Thus, Mrs. Lincoln spent time working on her Moodle pages and posting assignments. Mrs. Lincoln explained to students how the Moodle site worked. She trained them on Moodle in the computer lab over the course of a week, until all students were proficient using the Moodle course platform. After a couple of weeks, Mrs. Lincoln noticed that a quarter of her students were not completing assignments on Moodle. Due to the missed assignments, their grade was dropping significantly. This puzzled Mrs. Lincoln because these students had always completed their in-class assignments and had performed well on these assignments. Mrs. Lincoln started conferencing with these students and discovered they all shared the same problem: None of these students had computers at home and thus they could not complete the assignments on Moodle.

Mrs. Lincoln realized that many economically disadvantaged students do not have the use of computers at home. These economically disadvantaged students considered themselves lucky if their lights were on and their hot water running. Having to think about how they are going to complete their homework, especially if it is on a computer, was the least of their worries. To solve the challenge Mrs. Lincoln worked out a system where the students could arrive early to school and/or stay late after school in order to complete the assignments on the computers in her classroom. However, this raised another problem. Mrs. Lincoln's classroom had only three computers and there were numerous students who needed to use them for homework. Furthermore, some of the students struggled getting to school early and/or staying late because they had to ride the bus. Mrs. Lincoln would have to devise a rotation schedule that would allow these students to get their assignments completed. Mrs. Lincoln understood that another option would be to allow these students to write the assignments by hands, but then they would be missing out on using technology and developing the skills associated with such practice.

Chapter 15
YouTube in the Classroom?

Alison Horstman
School Teacher, USA

EXECUTIVE SUMMARY

Among Mrs. Grant's 22 first graders, ten are English language learners, while another two are autistic and have special needs. One of the autistic students is physically and verbally aggressive. Mrs. Grant realized that the classroom had many obstacles to overcome before becoming an emotionally and physically safe place for all the students. Mrs. Grant played a video explaining the importance of classroom rules. She showed another YouTube video showing students following their classroom rules.

BACKGROUND INFORMATION

Classroom climate can make or break a student's ability to be successful in school. It is the classroom teacher's responsibility to establish a positive learning environment. This environment should be physically and emotionally safe for all students. However, with the influx of special needs students into the regular education classroom, the challenge of providing a positive classroom climate is greater now than ever before. Students who do not feel physically and emotionally safe will find it impossible to focus on academics or relationships with others. Teachers need a deliberate and specific plan to teach and foster respectful and caring behavior. Helping students to develop these quality attitudes will result in greater academic

DOI: 10.4018/978-1-61350-492-5.ch015

achievement. It will also result in learners being able to get along with each other in school now and later in the work place. Helping students understand traits such as respect, integrity, safety, and effort, will have a lasting impact on their lives. Researchers find that high quality schools are characterized by supportive school climates. Supportive school climates promote resilience–the ability to rise above at-risk factors–in students.

Teachers must reach out for resources that will speak to the students of today and incorporate those resources into the classroom. Video which supports positive, caring and respectful behavior is one resource that can help a teacher establish the positive classroom climate she knows her students need.

Video is available to classroom teachers through sites like TeacherTube and YouTube. YouTube offers a great selection of educational videos and YouTube videos stream faster than the TeacherTube videos. Founded in 2005, YouTube is the main provider of online video in the United States. A downside of YouTube video is the advertisement that plays ahead of the video. Additionally, some of the advertisements are not appropriate for student viewing.

Another video resource is Discovery Education streaming, which was created by the Discovery Channel. It is a dynamic video resource which offers education videos to students of all grade levels.

TeacherTube is a video sharing website whose main goal is to provide an online community for sharing instructional videos. It was launched in 2007 by Jason Smith, a Texas school superintendent, along with his wife Jodie Smith and brother, Aaron Smith. As of October 2010, TeacherTube has over 725,000 educational videos. It has been enjoyed by educators for whom YouTube content has been blocked by campus firewall and other filtering systems or who work for a campus that does not own a subscription to Discovery Education streaming or other video archives.

THE CASE

Mrs. Grant has a class of 22 first graders. Ten of the students are English language learners, while another two are autistic and have special needs. One of the autistic students is physically and verbally aggressive. The class has 13 boys and 8 girls. She realized that the classroom had many other obstacles to overcome before becoming an emotionally and physically safe place for all the students.

During the first three weeks of school the aggressive autistic student screamed, dumped books from student baskets, poured water on the student tables and student work, and ran from the room to escape correction. Mrs. Grant was advised by others in her school that the relationship building activities she had planned for the class would not work with this student. In addition, there were several instances of sexually inappropriate touching and speaking from a male student to several female students. There was fighting when students were asked to line up. There were incidents of name calling, hitting, pushing, and pinching by two male students. Mrs. Grant took a firm hand in her classroom and at the same time she began to implement character education instruction and related activities.

Mrs. Grant began the relationship and character building activities immediately. She taught the meanings of respect, integrity, safety, and effort. She modeled respect to all of the children. She recognized students who were showing these traits. She had children work in cooperative groups on a regular basis. And from the very beginning Mrs. Grant incorporated character education videos from TeacherTube, YouTube, and Discovery Education. She played and replayed many times, a video respect song that portrayed students getting along and helping one another. Students in Mrs. Grant's class soon learned the song by heart and sang along as they viewed the images. She played a video that showed students following their classroom rules. It depicted students who were happy and safe. Another YouTube video about classroom rules produced by Harry Kindergarten became a favorite of Mrs. Grant's class.

Mrs. Grant's class has come a long way since the beginning of the year. The classroom climate is generally positive and supportive. Students work hard and exhibit respectful behavior. It is a safe and fun place to be. Mrs. Grant continues to model and teach respect and she continues to supplement her teaching with educational videos.

However, the school district's academic standards for first grade are very rigorous and it can be a real challenge planning extra time for watching a video that inspires students to care about others. It also requires a good deal of effort to search for and find quality videos.

Chapter 16

Technology and the Substitute Teacher

Chelsea Bruner
Future Teacher, USA

EXECUTIVE SUMMARY

A great deal goes into ensuring a smooth-running classroom when a teacher is absent. Mrs. Truman, a substitute teacher, highly recommends pre-regulated set-up and training in technology for substitute teachers.

BACKGROUND INFORMATION

What follows is a true account experienced by substitute teachers facing unfamiliar technology. While names have been changed to protect the innocent, the facts remain the same. Sickness, injury, pregnancy, and conferences happen. Regular teachers have to be out of the classroom yet learning must continue. Although most teachers realize that a substitute teacher's knowledge varies, not all teachers think about this variance in terms of technology integration. And despite most substitutes teachers being able to turn on a computer and take roll, not every qualified substitute can handle much more than this. Even the most technologically savvy substitute teacher can encounter trouble with unfamiliar technology. Precious class time can be wasted trying to get these technologies to work. A whole class period, a whole day, can evaporate into inactivity if the machine(s) are never figured out.

It is true that most schools have at least one dedicated technical support person. But this person is not always available. Other teachers can sometimes be implored

DOI: 10.4018/978-1-61350-492-5.ch016

for help, but sometimes the most readily available teachers can be as technologically unfamiliar as the substitute. The notable confusion of the authority figure and resulting inactivity of students can lead to an atmosphere of chaos. This problem and possible fixes will be addressed in what follows.

THE CASE

Ms. Truman is aware that a great deal of planning goes into ensuring a smooth-running classroom when a teacher is absent. Substitute teachers like Ms. Truman take on a great deal of responsibility based on high-expectations; or at least the good ones do. The school is counting on these substitutes to succeed. The administrative staff do not need to be called into every substitute-run class everyday with complaints that the students are out of control. To keep the students under control, the substitute teacher must show a high degree of *withitness* and regulation. In order for this to happen the substitute must know what he or she is doing and how they will handle what the teacher expects of them.

From her substitute teaching experiences from school to school during the past two months, Mrs. Truman highly recommends some form of pre-regulated set-up or training in technology for substitute teachers. Here's why.

The following is a note left for Mrs. Truman by Mrs. Madison, the regular classroom teacher, who needs Mrs. Truman to cover a class for one day:

Mrs. Truman,

Thank you for sub'ing for me today. My students know the rules. Tell them I expect them to follow them or there will be consequences when I come back.

All I need you to do today is show them the video I left under this note. Take them to LGI 4220. It is down the hall on the right. To get the video started all you need do is turn on the computer, set the toggle switches on the computer stand to video not forgetting to adjust the sound on the computer, computer desk, and projector, set up the projector with the gray (not black) remote in the room, get the electrical screen pulled down (use the black remote for this), and don't put the video in the computer DVD player it does not work, the DVD will become stuck, put it in the DVD/VCR player below the computer in deck 2 (it should be marked) for the DVD to work you will need to make sure that the DVD/VCR is plugged into the computer and that it is set to computer mode. This last part should be preset, but we have been having meetings in the LGI all week, so settings could be off. This shouldn't be too hard.

Technology and the Substitute Teacher

If you need help try to find Mrs. Tech, our technological support genius. Make sure the students take notes and no one sleeps.

Again, thank you so much,

Mrs. Madison

At this point most any substitute teacher would be a little worried. While computers are pretty basic devices employed by most everyone in the United States, projectors and linked devices are not as common place. For substitutes that are retired, between jobs, or just learning computer technology like Mrs. Truman, the directions in the teacher's note are not very helpful. There is a good deal of information left out. Cord types, plugs go in where? Where to find Mrs. Tech? Is deck 2 counted from top or bottom, and even which buttons to push on the TWO separate remotes?

Walking in to a new classroom, Mrs. Truman may have to face a room not properly prepared and the possibility that Mrs. Tech cannot be found. Something must be done about this. Mrs. Truman wishes that either a system at the school could be set up whereby a technology person comes in to setup the room as the teacher expects; or substitute teachers like her could be given training on the most common technology devices they will encounter in their various classrooms.

For either of these outcomes, a system must be implemented. While putting these systems into place may require some extra funds at the onset, the benefits would extend to the students and school. With one or both of these proposed systems for technology use preparation in place, regular classroom teachers could leave instruction of any kind with the security of knowing technology-related problems are less likely to arise. Administrative staff can rest easier knowing they will not have to deal with rebellious classes bored from the chaos of non-functioning technology. In all, these programs can produce a smoother running day.

Just as with most any endeavor undertaken in the educational system, the most daunting challenges come from much-needed time and money. Time has to be made for people to setup technology within those schools employing dedicated technology staff. Otherwise, if schools do not have dedicated support staff, time will have to be made for training substitute teachers in the use of technology. Money has to be spent on extended technology hours, necessary training equipment, and technology focused professional development courses for substitute teachers. Mrs. Truman understands that these are not easy challenges to overcome, especially in an economy struggling from deficits. However, she feels that an effort has to be made since technology use in schools is growing so rapidly.

Chapter 17

Video Games in the Classroom:
A Success or Game Over?

Anabel Vallejo
School Teacher, USA

EXECUTIVE SUMMARY

Mrs. Long's integration of video games in the classroom is a work in progress. She has observed how video games are a great way to motivate and engage students. On the other hand, she has observed how video games can lead to behavior and academic problems.

BACKGROUND INFORMATION

As we look around classrooms, it is impossible not to notice the effect technology is having in education. A typical classroom no longer consists of desks in rows and a chalkboard in the front. Movies are no longer shown using filmstrips. Cassette tapes and floppy disks are a thing of the past. The Net Generation grows up with modern videos, games, animations, music, and so much more virtual interactions than we previously imagined. The increase of the presence of technology in the classroom challenges teachers to rethink how they plan lessons and the techniques to use to optimize learning for the maximum number of students in the shortest possible time.

Like other abuses of technology among tweens that have been the subjects of frequent media attention, computer game playing among tweens has also become

DOI: 10.4018/978-1-61350-492-5.ch017

a controversy due to the depiction of graphic violence, sexual themes, profanity, and drugs in some games. Criticisms also include "excessive Internet use linked to depression", "game addiction similar to drug addiction", "increased the risk of attention problems", and "risk of attention problems in children and young adults". "Video game censorship" is a controversial subject. Proponents and opponents of censorship are often very passionate about their individual views. Does it sound right to modify students' computer game playing behaviors with more computer games?

If you think stand-alone video games such as DS and Game Cube are high-tech, wait until you hear about the latest Internet-enabled version. In the next 10 years, camera-based technology and tracking are going to bring in even more evolutions in electronic gaming. Some game designers coined the term "Gamepocalypse" to indicate the moment when every moment of life is actually a game.

Educators explained that the faster-paced shows increased the risk of attention problems because when playing computer games, students prime the mind to accept that pace. Real life or class work does not happen fast enough to keep attention.

Despite criticisms, why do sixty-three percent of parents still believe games are a positive part of their children's lives?

THE CASE

Mrs. Long is a third grade teacher. Her classroom contains five student computers, a document camera, projector, telephone, CD player and Internet access. The majority of her lessons contain some type of technology component; for example, a video, an electronic presentation, a website, or an online game.

One component of technology that has begun to integrate into her lessons is video games. For years, video games have targeted children. Children enjoy the constant challenge of the game and the sensation of victory after succeeding at a challenge. Since video games are so popular outside the classroom, Mrs. Long thinks that maybe it is time to seek the potential benefits they may offer *inside* the classroom. Video games are able to motivate and engage some students in a way that a teacher may never be able to accomplish. Video games are able to present information in a variety of ways that suits the need of different types of learners by using animation, graphics, sound effects, and the high level of engagement provided therein. Video games allow students to create and progress at their own pace. They provide a controlled learning environment where children can learn through making mistakes. With video games providing so many learning benefits for children, wouldn't it be a disservice to our students to ban them from the classroom?

Brad is nine years old and in Mrs. Long's third grade classroom. He has been retained once and maintains a C average in Mathematics class. He has a lot of potentials but his behavior gets in the way. He struggles with talking during class, controlling his anger, and following directions. If Brad does not get his way, he becomes very upset and shuts down. When he is upset, he will not do his class work or listen to anybody. Many times Mrs. Long has had to call his mother at work and have her talk to him to get him to finish his class work and get back on track. One thing that Brad loves is playing video games.

One afternoon, Brad had finished his Mathematics assignment early and since Brad had stayed on task and followed directions, Mrs. Long decided to reward the entire class with computer time. While on the computer, Brad played a video game called *Multiplication Attack*. The object of the game is to rescue a princess that has been trapped in a stone palace. The princess in guarded by monsters and traps. The player must navigate through the palace, escape the traps, and defeat the monsters by using mathematics. If players are able to answer a group of multiplication facts quickly and accurately, they defeat the monster and move forward to the next challenge. The game reinforces multiplication facts, which are a large part of the third grade math curriculum.

For the next few weeks, Brad was allowed to play *Multiplication Attack* several times a week. Many of Mrs. Long's students enjoyed playing the video game and were improving their memorization of multiplication facts. One afternoon, as Brad was playing *Multiplication Attack*, he was becoming frustrated with himself because he was not answering the multiplication facts fast enough to move to the next challenge. The student on the computer next to Brad was playing the same game and was answering the math challenges quickly and accurately with ease. The student told Brad that he should study his multiplication facts so that he would be faster. Brad did not appreciate the suggestion and pushed the student, along with the keyboard, resulting in dropping the mouse on the floor.

Another student in Ms. Long's class is Travis Arthur. He was very outgoing and intelligent. Travis loved to learn and had always been an A student. His parents had always encouraged him to do his best and were very involved in his learning. Within the past year, as Travis had taken up the hobby of playing video games, but this had created a problem in his academics.

It was Friday. Travis arrived home from school around 4:00. As he walked through the backdoor, his mother greeted him. They began to talk about the day and Travis' mother, Ms. Arthur, asked, "Did you learn a lot at school today? What kind of things were you all learning about?" But Travis answered a different answer than usual, and replied, "Oh. Not too much, something about Math." This was not a normal response for Travis, and Ms. Arthur began to become concerned. "Do you remember what you learned in math class?" His mother asked. "No, I know we played Jeopardy!" Travis replied. Travis then abruptly changed the subject, "Ok, well, I am going back to my room!" Ms. Arthur was taken back by his comments and allowed him to run off to his room.

Ms. Arthur continued to think about what he had said, and tried to think of what the problem could be. A few days later, Travis's report card arrived in the mail. His mother was astonished by the grades that were on his report card, C's. This was very uncharacteristic for Travis and his mother knew she had to examine the problem more closely to find out the real issue that was affecting Travis's academics. Attached to his report card was a note from Travis's teacher, Mrs. Long. The note read:

Dear Ms. Arthur,

I have recently noticed that Travis is becoming less engaged in our classroom activities. Travis has always done his best in class and his love for learning has always shown through by his constant interest in the content being taught. For the past few weeks, Travis has failed to complete all of his class work or turn in all of his homework. I just wanted to express my concerns about Travis's involvement in our class. Please let me know if there is anything that I can do to improve Travis's participation and interest in his academics.

Sincerely,

Mrs. Long

Ms. Arthur began to pay more attention to his behavior and procedures both academically and in his everyday lifestyle. As she observed, she realizes that most of his free time was spent playing video games. When Travis tells her that he was doing his homework, she used to just accept the answer with no questions asked. But this time, when he told her, she decided to peek into his room just to confirm that he really was doing his homework. What she finds him doing was not his homework, but playing video games. Ms. Arthur leaned over to him and asked, "Travis, why aren't you doing your homework? That was what you told me you were doing?" Travis shrugged. "Travis, I cannot allow you to play your video games anymore this week," said Ms. Arthur. "For the next few days, we will work on your homework together to make sure that you keep your grades up."

The next day, Ms. Arthur proceeded to contact his teacher, Mrs. Long. When his mother asked Mrs. Long about his involvement in class, Mrs. Long told her that his involvement had been declining within the past few weeks. Mrs. Long had attempted to engage Travis in learning in through many different approaches but had been unsuccessful. Mrs. Long and Ms. Arthur began to discuss ways that they could make Travis interested in school again. Mrs. Long asked Travis's mother what he enjoyed doing in his free time, as Ms. Arthur replied, "He loves playing video games most of all, but he also loves playing baseball and playing with his brother." Mrs. Long replied, "Maybe that's it!, Maybe if we could involve video games into our classroom activities, then Travis will become more interested and engaged in what we were doing!"

Mrs. Long had heard of incorporating video games into the classroom instruction to motivate the students and was interested to try it for all students since most students this age did enjoy playing video games.

The next week, Mrs. Long came to class prepared with a math lesson incorporating a video game called Time Engineers. This was a game that not only teaches math, but could help with science and history. This game involves time traveling through 3-D virtual environments. Students travel in an interactive time machine to three different time periods and encounter typical engineering problems to be solved in order to build pyramids, irrigate farm land, command a WWII submarine, raise and lower medieval drawbridges, and much more. This game allows them to do something that they enjoy and are interested in and it differentiates the instruction for Mrs. Long class without having to differentiate the curriculum.

Mrs. Long came up with two ways to incorporate this game. One way was to allow the students to take turns playing the game throughout the class time and throughout the week. The second way that she incorporated the game was through whole class involvement. Mrs. Long projected the game onto the big screen projector to allow all of the students to see. She then brought up the problem on the screen and allowed the students to write down the problem, and work individually or in groups to solve the problem.

During class, Mrs. Long saw that Travis loved the game. He was involved and adding in his answers and was actively engaged in the lesson. When he came home from school, Travis expressed his excitement to his mother, explaining that they were having the chance to play video games in school. Ms. Arthur was so relieved to see that Travis was back into involvement in his academics. As time passes, Travis's motivation and grades in school began to return to normal.

Ms. Arthur realized that she also needed to be more aware of when Travis was playing video games. She decided that limiting Travis's video game playing time at home would be best.

Many parents might argue that video games in a classroom setting may not be appropriate or that schools should not encourage the use of video games. Some parents worry that students will focus less on their schoolwork and focus more on the video games. Another concern discussed in published literature is that video games may encourage violent or aggressive behavior. Some students may become frustrated or upset with the game. Other students may have an unhealthy reaction to losing. Mrs. Long conducted her own research on integrating video games in classrooms and found that although students may benefit from playing video games in the classroom, there are some negative consequences.

Mrs. Long's integration of video games in the classroom is still a work in progress. She has observed how video games are a great way to motivate and engage students. On the other hand, she has observed how video games can lead to behavior and academic problems. She feels the need to consider both the positive and negative effects of video games.

Chapter 18

How Do We Close the Gap between Technology Innovation and Available Funding?

Christian McGlory
School Teacher, USA

EXECUTIVE SUMMARY

Roosevelt School District, a small urban elementary school district, is trying to find a way to purchase new digital technology for campuses. The bases of this case study are to develop a plan for how the district can pay for new technology.

BACKGROUND INFORMATION

Today, in the United States approximately $520.2 billion dollars of federal money is filtered directly to the states. That may seem like a huge amount of money but when all states and districts are competing for the same pot of money, it really is not.

Where does all the money go? The cost of educating children in America has become very expensive. Costly government programs initiated by the federal government make it difficult for school districts to provide what students and teachers require. Some government sponsored programs include: "No Child Left Behind", Title I programs, standardized testing, bilingual education, nutrition programs, early childhood programs, school vouchers, dropout prevention, and teen pregnancy

DOI: 10.4018/978-1-61350-492-5.ch018

programs. When all the bills are paid, there is just not enough money to go around. Therefore a huge majority of the burden of the cost of educating students has now fallen on the states. The school district receives revenue from three different sources: federal, state and local taxes.

THE CASE

Roosevelt School District is a small urban elementary school district facing a problem. The district is trying to find a way to purchase new digital technology for its campuses. Over the past two years the teachers in the district have been attending workshops, reading articles, and receiving information in the news about how the latest software innovations and digital media can have a direct impact on students' academic success.

And here is where the journey begins. The school district needs to purchase laptops for teachers, acquire smart boards, color printers, scanners, document cameras, and computer workstations for classrooms. As a result, teachers created a "technology wish list" and submitted it to school district administrators for review.

The teachers are excited about the possibility of purchasing these technology tools. Teachers understand that in order for students to be successful in the real world, learning how to use new technology is required. Today however, financial problems and the need to reduce spending in school districts has narrowed teacher concerns to purchasing the bare essentials. What is the best way for a relatively small urban school district to fund the purchase of new digital technology? Let's investigate this issue.

According to the 2010-2011 state report, 34.9% of Roosevelt School District's population is economically disadvantaged. Twenty-four percent of the population is Hispanic, and 15.8% of the population is labeled as Limited English Proficient students. As the economy continues to be uncertain, a number of houses have been foreclosed in the area serviced by the district. As a result, the district anticipates the number of economically disadvantage, Hispanic, and Limited English Proficient (LEP) students to continue to grow in the year 2012-2013 school year.

The bases of this case study are to develop a plan for how the district can pay for new technology. The teachers first decide to put an action plan committee together to look for sources of money to pay for the needed technology. The committee will meet bi-weekly and will be made up of administrators, teachers, parents, and high school students.

The committee's first order of business will be to look at all possible grants and monies for which the district could be eligible. The committee will also consider any award programs that local companies or corporations may be sponsoring.

Next, the committee decides to contemplate the possibility to let a small number of schools at each grade level be allowed to purchase the proposed technology and then compare those schools with similar populations but without the technology, to see if the technology actually increases learning. If so, the committee will recommend the district starts acquiring the technology in groups of 13 schools–one school for each grade level from Pre-K to 12–per year until all schools are equipped.

Lastly, the committee will discuss other options for budget reductions in order for the district to be able to pay for the new technology. The committee came up with a long list of suggestions which includes:

1. Eliminate all staff raises for the coming school year.
2. In the area of transportation, expand bus pickup/drop-off points of students to the State minimum of 2 miles
3. Reduce Summer School to the backbone
4. Consolidate administrative positions at Central Office, specifically in Curriculum and Instructional Services
5. Suspend Recruitment Budget (hiring freeze)
6. Eliminate Superintendent's personal assistant
7. Eliminate two area Superintendent positions
8. Eliminate newly created Parental Involvement Department
9. Remove one academic intervention specialist per campus instead of cutting teachers and/or increasing class sizes.
10. Centralize the programs for special children so that schools do not pay for 1 teacher and 2 paraprofessionals for a very small number of special needs children
11. Consolidate administrative positions at Central Office, Public Relations, and C & I department.
12. Reevaluate Bilingual Program
13. Work a 4 day work week

The committee's suggestions for budget reductions would save the district a total of \$700,190,000. The teachers have decided that there are areas that will require extra funding. The areas will include:

1. Teachers will need training on how to fully and successfully integrate technology in the classroom and to understand Internet safety.
2. Teachers will also need a technology support assistance department.

However, by and large, teachers feel that classroom use and school adoption of more laptops and more software integration will allow students to be able to increase academic success, build technology skills, and meet the state mandated curriculum guidelines. The number one goal should be to ensure **all students**, no matter what their family income or status level – are treated fairly in having access to all purchased digital media.

After much discussion, the current plan for Roosevelt is to petition the state government to allow the school district to apply for the "Tech Works I Grant". This state grant is provided based on student needs. In other words, if the school serves a certain number of low income students, the school may be eligible for funding. The district could receive approximately one million dollars of tax-free money to purchase the items on the "wish list".

Chapter 19
Technology and Traditional Teaching

Sina Andegherghis
School Teacher, USA

EXECUTIVE SUMMARY

Despite recent online learning inroads in schools, many professional educators and administrators remain hesitant, reluctant, and even resistant to teaching with technology. The cause of resistance to technology is often misinterpreted. Teachers do not resist the technology itself. Teachers resist what the technology may represent - change, confusion, loss of control, and impersonalization. As long as these concerns remain unaddressed, technology adoption in any organization will be an uphill battle.

BACKGROUND INFORMATION

The world is changing so rapidly that it should be expected the state of education will change with it. Technology is quickly becoming an integral component of the curriculum and a very important tool in the educational advancement of students today. Research shows the benefits of using technology in the classroom includes motivating and exciting young minds. The days of using paper and pencil to instruct our children are long gone. There is no longer a question of whether or not technology should be used in the classroom but *how* it should be used. The interactive whiteboard, document camera, and Internet are just a few items of a growing list of technological advances that provide students a new way to collect, analyze, and

DOI: 10.4018/978-1-61350-492-5.ch019

learn new information. It is imperative that educators be able to meet the diverse learning styles of all students. Most teachers are making changes in their instruction according to the technological advances of the new generation, but there is a resistance among some faculty to keep up with the evolving times.

Preparing a person to become a future teacher is an enormous task. There are many required courses and components of the education degree that are vital for the success of future teachers. Nowadays, students who enroll in a teaching certification program are required to take a technology course to complete the program due to the important role that it plays in the classroom today. Some twenty years ago the programs were not as strict about taking courses in technology because technology played a smaller role in education. In the evolution of technology it has required that educators become equipped with knowledge and the understanding to make good use of the available tools for effective teaching.

There can be resistance among teachers to incorporate technology for a variety of reasons; bad experiences before, feel "too old" to learn new things, not enough time to master, lack confidence to ask for help. Technology trainings and experiences are key to helping build the connection between the new generation of students and society. The educator having proficient skills in technology alone does not mean that they can skillfully prepare a lesson plan which integrates the components of technology. Such skill requires a learning process.

THE CASE

Mountain View School District's (MVSD) Technology Department sent a survey to all teachers asking about technology use in the classroom. Through the survey, over 45 percent of the teachers admitted they did not use computers as part of instruction. MVSD was looking towards setting up required workshops for all teachers to go through a computer training and implementation program. The program was designed by grade levels to help teachers structure a plan to ensure students were getting ample experience with computers and other equipment. Positive school experiences help students foster a lifelong love of learning and technology use. In the urban schools at MVSD, they found that though the students may lack the resources at home for exposure, it is important they receive it at school.

The push for classroom technology has generated a mixed feeling of excitement and fear among teachers. Most educators are able to identify with the relevance and application of technology within the classroom, but there's still a sense of resistance among the remaining teachers. This resistance may be due to the rapid changes and advancements that have occurred within the field of technology. These rapid changes have lead to a lack of confidence and knowledge awareness.

The process of integrating technology and learning is often ignored; perhaps due to its associated complexities or social resistance. Instructors know teaching and technology has incredibly "cool" tools to assist in connecting students with each other and with content. However, these two worlds don't seem to mesh easily.

Smith Elementary School is a part of MVSD. Ms. Monroe has been teaching there for over twenty years and is very content with her job. At the beginning of the school year, she was called by the district to visit the central administration office and go through a professional development incorporating a new, computer-based, Gifted and Talented (GT) differentiation tool required for all GT students. The next phase of the program dissemination will be on the campus level. Last week, she was charged with the task of serving as a campus technology leader. Her role is to be a liaison between the district differentiation tool trainer and other twelve GT teachers on her campus who are learning the new technology tool. The teachers being trained were told that the district expects the differentiation tool be fully implemented eight weeks prior to the state mandated exams. Unfortunately, a number of GT teachers told Ms. Monroe they were resistant to the change because of frustrations trying to learn the new program and not feeling adequately trained.

Ms. Monroe discussed the resistance with the district differentiation tool trainer, Mr. Cunningham, who came to Smith Elementary to train the GT teachers. "I think the teachers feel a little embarrassed; they're not experts in this field. And it may be the first time they've not been an expert at something," said Ms. Monroe.

"It all starts with how you communicate with teachers," said Mr. Cunningham, the district differentiation tool trainer. "We can position technology as, 'This is what it does', and that's fine; but when we say, 'You must use it,' that's where the resistance comes. And when we impose a deadline, it becomes another compliance matter rather than a way to enhance learning. Unfortunately, the district does give us a deadline to meet."

"I suggest that we do not try to cram it down everybody's throat," Ms. Monroe said. "I suggest we position the technology tool not as merely voluntary, but as something that will actually make the GT teachers' jobs more interesting."

"That's right," said Mr. Cunningham, "With many teachers, the way a technology is introduced into the academic environment can mean the difference between adoption and abandonment. If teachers believe they are being forced into using it, they may resist—especially if you don't show them what value it will bring to their classroom."

"One way to avoid scaring teachers off is to allow them to learn a technology gradually," said Ms. Monroe, "That approach worked well at Smith Elementary School last year when it implemented the new digital classroom learning management system."

Ms. Monroe recalled that the teacher adoption of the digital classroom learning management system the previous year was high because the technology accommodated incremental learning. Incremental learning allowed the teachers to start using the system immediately after learning the basics, and return to receive additional training on the other components that were useful but not necessary while getting started.

"We did have some who were fearful, but the nice thing about the digital classroom is you don't have to utilize everything at once, and that put a lot of teachers at ease," said Ms. Monroe. "It was challenging–the depths to which you could use the system–but the fact that you didn't have to learn it all at once made the difference. People didn't feel overwhelmed."

"Indeed, the feeling teachers can have of being overwhelmed by a new technology if they are not given enough time to learn it may be the biggest inhibitor to adoption," said Mr. Cunningham.

"It takes time to learn new tools and software, and with everything else teachers are asked to do, technology integration is often last on the list," Mr. Cunningham said, "Some teachers still feel teaching is a craft. The old method is the way they've done it for 20 years. Why change now?"

"The lack of a firm grasp of the technology–and consequently the prospect of looking bad in front of the GT students–can put the brakes on adoption," Ms. Monroe added, "GT Teachers' biggest fear is that students are ahead of them technologically."

Mr. Cunningham agreed: "There is nothing worse than a teacher having to take a product and show it to a group of digital-native students and have them know more than the teacher. Teachers don't want students to have the upper hand."

The solution, both agreed, was comprehensive training with follow-up professional development activities by the district. And although there is no standard on how much training should be given, most agree that at least one day of on-site professional development followed by various "catch-up" sessions throughout the course of the school year is the minimum a district should provide when introducing a new technology.

"We have discovered that with any new educational program, schools need to focus on ensuring proper professional development," said Mr. Cunningham. "When we work with schools on implementation, we start with one full day of on-site training, but have found that the initial professional development, when providing teachers with new and different tools, is not sufficient. In an ideal situation we offer a number of follow-up activities where our trainers go into the schools to mentor and coach in the classrooms."

Mr. Cunningham said sometimes it was unable to provide a full day's training because the school year had already begun. Instead, the trainers had to do two half-days. To their surprise, the condensed schedule worked just fine. "It was enough but not too much, so teachers could do some of the essential things and not get overwhelmed," he said.

"One of the biggest reasons we face resistance is because so many times we give instruments to the teacher with no follow-up or no training," said Mr. Cunningham. He said a lack of support could result in a negative experience with technology change agents like the GT differentiation tool, which turned teachers off. "I don't think fear is the right word. Some teachers have been burned by technology in the past. They used it and found it was either not great or incomplete, or whatever, and so they are not interested in trying anymore."

Ms. Monroe's new role will be as an on-site curriculum support specialist to supplement the training and professional development of teachers. Her role is critical in making sure teachers have a good experience. "What has made other program implementations so successful is the fact that there is a support specialist on-site," she says. "You can offer what the teachers need – one-on-one training, group professional development, grade-level professional development – with the whole curriculum."

"However, you won't find a good curriculum support specialist or an equivalent position at most school districts," Mr. Cunningham continued. "The next best thing may be a kind of peer-to-peer mentoring program, wherein one teacher becomes expert at a particular type of technology and remains on-hand to assist fellow teachers as needed."

The district had some success with one previous technology change agent using the expertise of the five teachers who had piloted the technology tool for a year prior to help the new users become proficient with the system. Mr. Cunningham said the experience led the district to consider implementing a mentoring program with each school that adopts its new technology. "We are keenly aware that teachers-teaching-teachers is the best way to go."

When all else fails, districts could consider offering the teachers incentives for learning and adopting new technology. Mr. Cunningham recalled that it was just such a tactic the district employed when it realized its classroom technology wasn't being used to the fullest extent. Rather than let it collect dust, the district decided to incentivize teachers to learn and use it. For instance, a middle school in the district offered a stipend to teachers who took classes on how to use interactive whiteboards (IWBs). The teachers had the IWBs in their classrooms for two years but were only using them as projection screens. "When the IWBs were installed," Mr. Cunningham recalled, "the school provided three hours of training but people used them only if they had the time and the capability to learn more on their own. There were some teachers who resisted, claiming they could work faster in PowerPoint."

The district recognized this dilemma of having an under-utilized technology on which it had spent a lot of money. But rather than punish teachers for not using the technology, the district decided to reward those who *did* use it. "They wanted a way to get staff to use it, so they came up with the stipend idea. It seems like more people are using the whiteboards. The program is working," said Mr. Cunningham.

"As with anything new, "Mr. Cunningham advised, "there will always be early and eager adopters of technology and those who wade into new waters, one toe at a time. The key is to encourage the spreading of the excitement of the small cohort of early adopters. "Their motivation creates a viral effect in a school community so teachers begin to explore the possibilities of new ways of learning."

"Sometimes," Ms. Monroe added, "all it takes to convince a teacher to take the leap is seeing how using technology impacts the students. Students should be the driving force of instruction. They keep teachers motivated to incorporate new strategies because they are learning one hundred times more than they would be if they were just sitting in a row listening to a lecture."

At the end of the busy school day, Ms. Monroe summarized her conversation with Mr. Cunningham and came up with these seven key ideas for successful implementation of technology training on campus:

1. Incremental Change
2. Shared Success Stories and Best Practices
3. Training and Development: Just-in-Time Support
4. An Atmosphere of Sharing
5. Awards and Incentives
6. Modeling
7. Mentoring and Coaching

The cause of resistance to technology is often misinterpreted. People do not resist the technology itself. People resist what the technology may represent—change, confusion, loss of control, and impersonalization. As long as these concerns remain unaddressed, technology adoption in any organization will be an uphill battle. It is hard to admit that as adults we do not know how to do something, but if we can get our teachers trained in a friendly environment, many positive things will emerge. It is important that educators have a desire to teach students about educational technology and through research and data, such a desire can be supported.

This case study is based on the article originally appearing in the 03/01/2009 issue of THE Journal.

Chapter 20
Technology Use
on My Campus

Diana Ramirez
School Media Specialist, USA

EXECUTIVE SUMMARY

Ms. Gonzalez, librarian/media specialist of an urban high school, is asked to prepare a presentation to explain the results of her study of the current status of technology use to a panel of campus stakeholders. The goal of the presentation is to inform the panel of stakeholders so they can develop a plan to further implement the use of technology as a teaching and learning tool on campus.

BACKGROUND INTRODUCTION

Many publications on the use of technology in K-12 schools refer to computers as simply a tool to be used in instruction. Yet as observed by many campus technology and media personnel, computer technologies are no longer simply a tool, but are teachers' present reality destined to play an increasingly important role in the future. The purpose of this case study is to gain an understanding of how technology is being used at Hamilton High School, an urban high school campus.

DOI: 10.4018/978-1-61350-492-5.ch020

THE CASE

As the librarian/media specialist at Hamilton High School, Ms. Gonzalez is responsible for the upkeep and checking-out of 10 and a half computer carts, as well as oversee a computer lab within the library. She is asked by the school principal to present the results of her study of the current status of technology use to a group of stakeholders which includes district administrators, district IT staff, PTO members, and campus administrators. The goal of the presentation is to present the results and use the information as a basis to develop a technology plan that will increase the use of technology as a teaching and learning tool. As a school leader, Ms. Gonzalez will share the survey results with the leadership team and the administration for further review.

After a brief welcome and introduction, Ms. Gonzalez focuses on the core of her presentation as follows:

Sample

The sample for this current study consists of the 43 teachers who used the computer carts and/or computer lab during the Fall semester. Of the 154 teachers on the campus, 43 teachers – 28% of the staff – used computer technology at least once during the Fall Semester. The number of actual usage ranged from two teachers who used computers 25 times, to four teachers who only used computers once. Of the 43 teachers who used computer technology, 32 (74%) responded to the technology usage survey.

Methodology

The first data collected for this study came from the teacher sign-up forms located in the library. Teachers who want to use either a computer cart or the computer lab must sign up on the check out binder located on the counter. The forms are available for two week periods, and teachers sign-up accordingly. After gathering this data, a survey was sent out to the 43 teachers via e-mail (See Appendix A). An incentive of a homemade treat was offered to anyone who responded to the survey. Teachers then responded either electronically or in person. The researcher attempted to get additional participation by visiting room by room and encouraging participation. Fifteen of the thirty-two respondents participated without any prompting other than the initial e-mail message.

Figure 1.

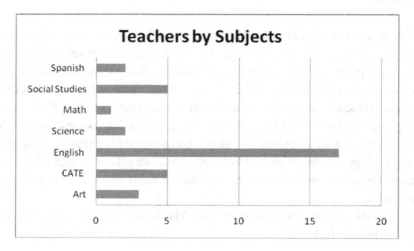

Results

The subject area results are in Figure 1.

Looking at the chart we can see that the majority of teachers who use computer technology are the English Teachers with 17 out of the 32 surveyed teachers (see Appendix B for raw data). All other subject areas fell between 1 and 5. As the media specialist, Ms. Gonzalez is a member of the English Department, yet she does not feel this is the reason more English teachers are using the computers. This clearly points out the need to expand computer usage to other subject areas.

TEACHER EXPERIENCE RESULTS

These results (Table 1.) are very interesting because the number of new teachers and experienced teachers is very similar. As is pointed out in the literature, it is important to note that not all younger teachers–as digital natives–are automatically

Table 1.

1-3 years	12
4-6 years	5
7-9 years	6
10 or more years	9

more proficient with technology. Another point made in the literature is that teacher preparation programs will need to be modified in order to prepare future teachers to successfully integrate technology into the classroom. This is also very interesting when looking at teacher-technology confidence levels. Of the three who responded with *so-so* for their confidence level, two possess the 1 to 3 years of teaching experience and only 1 was in the 10 or more years category.

GRADE LEVEL USAGE

Grade level data (Table 2) was not really useful in the investigation. As can be seen, technology use is somewhat consistent across the four grade levels. Many of the respondents teach all four grade levels or a combination thereof. Regardless, it is good to see that all grade levels are using computer technology evenly.

PURPOSE FOR USING COMPUTERS

The fact that the majority of computer usage is for either Research or for writing essays, points to the need to teach the use of online resources and of using Word processing programs more efficiently. As the librarian/media specialist Ms. Gonzalez must make sure all students are introduced to the online resources and are familiar with word processing skills. However Ms. Gonzalez was saddened by the results of her research. The data (Figure 2) shows that the school had spent thousands of dollars to provide a web-based reading incentive program called Reading Counts. Yet only four respondents–*of which one clearly stated she is not really using the program this year but intends to use it more next year*–identified Reading Counts as a purpose for using the computers.

Table 2.

9th Grade	21
10th Grade	13
11th Grade	15
12th Grade	16

Figure 2.

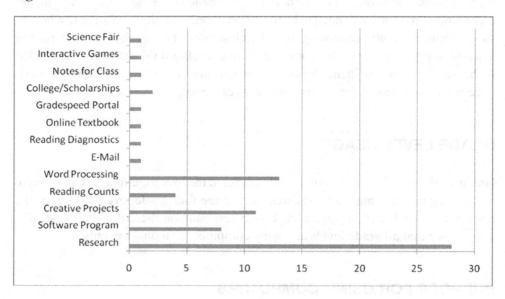

TEACHER TECHNOLOGY CONFIDENCE LEVEL

Familiarity with the National Educational Technology Standards (http://www.iste.
org/standards.aspx) and confidence in technology use and instruction were identified
as two factors vital for technology implementation. Although Ms. Gonzalez did not
survey the teachers concerning their knowledge of the NETS, the survey (Figure 3)
does clearly show that teacher technology confidence plays a very important role
in computer usage.

DISCUSSION

At the end, Ms. Gonzalez reminded the audience that the survey results point to
the need to encourage more computer use among the entire faculty and staff. The
fact that teachers are mainly using computers for research and for Word processing,
points to their lack of awareness of the many other resources available to teachers for presentations and for assigning students online activities other than merely
researching and writing reports. A very telling fact is that 29 of the 32 respondents
self-identified as either confident or very confident in their technology usage.

Ms. Gonzalez's final question to the audience is, if schools expect more teachers
to use the available technology, what else should be done?

APPENDIX A

Case Study Survey

1. What subject area are you teaching when you use the computers?
2. How many years have you been a teacher?
3. What is the grade level of students using computers?
4. What would you say is the main purpose in using the computers?
    Research, Software Program, Creative Projects etc.
5. What would you say is your confidence level concerning your technology ability?
    a. Very Confident
    b. Confident
    c. So-So

APPENDIX B

Data

Table 3.

Teacher	Number of Times Using Computers	Subject Area
1	25	CATE Health Science
2	3	Spanish
3	7	French
4	5	English
5	14	Social Studies
6	5	English
7	16	ESL
8	14	English
9	14	English
10	25	English
11	11	Art
12	19	CATE – Home Economics
13	6	English

Table 3 continued on following page

Table 3. Continued

Teacher	Number of Times Using Computers	Subject Area
14	7	Science
15	12	College Preparation
16	5	English
17	8	Houston Community College
18	5	English
19	14	CATE – Internet
20	10	English
21	2	Social Studies
22	8	Houston Community College
23	8	CATE – Health Science
24	6	English
25	2	Science
26	6	English
27	7	English
28	9	English
29	1	Art
30	1	Art
31	6	Social Studies
32	7	English
33	4	English
34	2	Math
35	2	Special Ed. Resource
36	2	Spanish
37	2	CATE- Agriculture/Horticulture
38	4	Social Studies
39	1	Social Studies
40	2	English
41	1	Spanish
42	2	Health
43	4	English

Chapter 21
A High School Librarian's Participation in Supporting Information Literacy on Her Campus

Diana Ramirez
School Media Specialist, USA

EXECUTIVE SUMMARY

The ability to navigate the web and to use technology effectively and efficiently is no longer an option but a requirement in schools and in the workplace. Information literacy is widely accepted as embracing rapid advances in technologies and recognizing the multiple literacies required of students living and learning in this century. Information literacy has grown to include traditional literacy, computer literacy, media literacy, and network literacy. School library media specialists in the twenty-first century face both challenges and opportunities in the recent high expectations of information literacy. Among the challenges is keeping up with changing technologies and taking the necessary steps to ensure students and teachers have appropriate access to resources and instruction. Opportunities include the chance to transform today's library into a resource center of the future where information literacy can be easily obtained. Welcome to the world of Ms. West, a middle school teacher turned high school librarian, and see how she ponders upon her new role as being the instructor/specialist of information literacy skills on the campus, a reading advocate and provider of reading materials, as the manager of the resources both information and library resources, and lastly being a collaborator with teachers concerning information literacy issues.

DOI: 10.4018/978-1-61350-492-5.ch021

BACKGROUND INTRODUCTION

Information literacy has been defined as a set of abilities requiring individuals to recognize when information is needed and to have the ability to locate, evaluate, and use information effectively. Information literacy has grown to include traditional literacy, computer literacy, media literacy, and network literacy. The significance of information literacy on high school campuses has become increasingly important in the last few years. The ability to navigate the internet and use technology tools effectively is becoming a vital necessity to prepare students for higher education and as they prepare to enter the business world. In order to help students and teachers, librarians–also known as library media specialists–are gradually expected to become active disseminators of technology usage, attitudes and the perceptions of information literacy on their campuses. The librarian of tomorrow will be required to provide the resources and instruction necessary to keep up with changing technology demands.

Teachers need to possess information technology abilities in order to prepare students in these skills. Libraries and librarians are central to making this a reality.

THE CASE

Meet Ms. West, who is the new school librarian at Carter High School. A previous middle school language arts teacher, Ms. West went through trainings and recertification processes to become a high school librarian.

Since she has taught middle school for over 10 years, working on a campus is not new to her. What is daunting to her is her new role and new identity as the school librarian. More than ever, students of all ages are expected to be able to perform using computer technologies. Teachers must be able to use the technologies to input attendance, grades, and to present lessons in the classroom. And school staff members are expected to be able to find the right information, organize it properly, and display and communicate that information through various media such as newsletters, portals, Web sites, wikis and blogs.

This is especially challenging when facing the high-schoolers who are called "the Internet Generation". The Internet Generation is the first to grow up with the Internet, providing a number of resources from downloading music to blogging. Cell phones are also in wide use, along with other gadgets such as electronic games. The Internet Generation takes the Internet for granted, accepting the utility of services such as Google, online chatting, online shopping, e-mailing, Wikipedia, MySpace, Facebook, and streaming videos.

However, interacting with technology on a daily basis does not mean that all students are effective and efficient users of technology. To her surprise, Ms. West found that some students who belong to the Internet Generation took a long time to find useful data over the Internet, did not know how to narrow their search results, could not differentiate quality information versus poor information, had not heard of the need for "data triangulation", did not know how to cite information sources properly, had no clue they needed to verify information found through the Internet, and many other problems.

Understanding the importance of information literacy in the world today leads to the conclusion that the educational system is the catalyst for introducing and establishing information literacy competency and the school librarian plays a particularly important role in making this a reality. To Ms. West, there is no question that librarians and school library programs are the heart of education and as such, play a vital part of bringing information literacy standards to the forefront on their campuses. The roles she identified include being the instructor/specialist of information literacy skills on the campus, being a reading advocate and provider of reading materials, being the manager of both the information and library resources, and being a collaborator with teachers concerning information literacy issues.

Librarian as Instructor

The librarian as an instructor is a feasible concept in that the teacher-librarian sees the big picture–the school as a whole–and has knowledge of the entire curriculum. The literature further addresses the need for information skills to be taught, acknowledging that they are not learned through osmosis. Yet who should actually be teaching these skills, is still debatable. Research has shown that information literacy skills need to be taught in context, and not in a one-time library lesson. The librarian, then, becomes more of a collaborator, working with the classroom teacher in providing information literacy skills to students. Another added task of the librarian is as an instructor to the faculty. The school librarian's role on campus has become even more critical in the digital age with teacher librarians increasingly acting as professional development providers of digital literacy skills.

Librarian as Reading Advocate

Another role of librarians, identified in the literature, was that of encouraging reading amongst the student population. This has been considered the main role of librarians for centuries–to provide students with a variety of appropriate and up-to-date reading materials. In 2009 an AASL study found that reading for enjoyment, curiosity and perceived competence (confidence in one's abilities) was found to contribute to both information literacy and digital literacy. This can be considered as common sense in that a student who likes to read is more likely to be successful in all areas, not just information and digital literacies. However this connection between reading and information literacy is important in that the one thing most librarians have control over are the reading programs available on their campuses. Programs such as the Renaissance Learning Accelerated Reader Program™ and the Scholastic Reading Counts Program™ are found throughout many campuses. These programs, although somewhat controversial, are used to improve student reading ability from the elementary level through the high school level. Many librarians believe it is more important to love reading than to be rewarded for reading. Yet if the research is showing a connection between readers and their information literacy skills (and being that the research shows reading proficiency as the number one predictor of student success), it may be feasible to encourage and support the reading incentive programs already on campuses.

Librarian as Resource Manager

Among family and friends, Ms. West sometimes jokingly called herself the CIO of the organization responsible for ensuring and providing information and technology facilities, resources, and services. After all, she manages a complex and expensive support system for the school community. Librarians need to keep up-to-date not only with syllabi and the curriculum on campus but with the publishing world and educational developments in order to purchase relevant materials. The librarian also needs to be alert for technological innovations which may have an impact on learning resources, and lastly she should keep an eye on educational funding to make all these things possible. In short, the librarian needs to be actively involved in what is happening in technology and what role is needed in keeping the library updated and relevant. Further, Ms. West noted an important advantage of the librarian's position on the campus is the cross-curricular and cross-hierarchical contribution to the educational purposes of the school and lack of attachment to any clique or power-base in the school. Whereas all these points were looked upon as advantages, they could also be considered disadvantages.

One problem in a large public school with many different departments would be keeping up with the curriculum for every department. This would be an exhaustive and time consuming activity which in most cases a sole librarian would not be able to achieve. Using surveys, in relation to teacher technology usage, could help provide a necessary connection between the teaching staff and the librarian, concerning curriculum and planning.

To deliver information and have her voice heard by as many students and faculty as possible, Ms. West also identifies an additional role for the librarian as that of maintaining the library website. In today's world, libraries and their resources are expected to be accessible not only when the library is open but after hours and on weekends as well. In order for this to be an actuality, a library website which is current and consistently maintained is very important. Feeling that a library website affiliated with the school homepage may take a long time to update and disseminate information, and looks too formal to the Net generation, Ms. West is learning how to create a library blog to tell students more about popular books, survey students' favorite titles, share fun facts, and recommend future reading. The task of maintaining a website and social network sites such as blogs, is a new role for librarians and one that many may not possess the skills necessary to implement. After teaching herself how to do all of these, Ms. West feels like more advanced training in website management and many other technology issues will be of the essence for her to be the librarian of the future.

Collaboration and the School Librarian

Ms. West understand that as librarians are at a critical moment in their profession, they need to seize this moment to collaborate with their learning communities as leaders in interpreting and teaching information literacy. However, librarians alone cannot be the sole providers of information literacy on a campus.

The most effective way to ensure that students are acquiring information literacy skills is for teachers and librarians to model collaborative information literacy during instruction. Ms. West recommends that teacher education candidates are educated to believe in collaboration between teachers and librarians so that they would promote the benefits of universal information literacy thereby enabling information literacy to become a self-sustaining and generative process. This concept of teaching the importance of information literacy skills through collaboration–although invigorating–has not happened yet. A disconnect between teacher education programs, librarian programs, and technology departments, still exists at the college level and as a result, also exists on the high school and other public school settings. If change were to occur on the college level, implementation of collaboration would no longer be an issue but a standard procedure for presenting information literacy skills. Until then it is imperative that the members of any school campus work together to achieve technology related goals. A friendly collaboration between the teachers and the librarian will definitely enhance information literacy skills.

Problems with Librarians as Information Specialists

Ms. West realized that the importance of human relationships in developing partnerships is crucial and will most likely be the biggest challenge in the sharing of information literacy skills. Due to budget cuts in many schools, librarians are not being replaced when they leave or retire. While research is confirming the importance of librarians in advancing schools into new technological arenas, the economy is saying the complete opposite. To make the librarian's role more visible on campus, Ms. West made a point to become actively involved in providing and presenting new technology that is available for both teachers and students. It is also important that librarians make their presence known in matters that are both relevant and necessary on campus. For instance, conducting studies, interpreting results, and presenting to faculty, staff, school administrators, as well as the community and PTO, are ways that librarians can help schools improve.

Time is another obstacle many librarians must deal with. High school libraries are often open before school, during lunch, and after school; and as such require the librarian's presence. In most public schools there is only one librarian per campus. The amount of time available to spend working with teachers and students is quite limited.

The last and perhaps most important obstacle to information literacy issues is that not all librarians are created equal. Librarians may or may not have the necessary technology background to assist in the implementation of information literacy skills.

After a period of soul searching, Ms. West gradually clarified an ideal role for librarians in the 21st century; a role which encompasses many different aspects of connecting students and teachers to technology. The librarian's role in making this a reality will be essential in the process of bringing about information literate students and teachers on a campus.

Chapter 22
Social Networks:
Education beyond the Classroom?

Ngochoai Tran
School Teacher, USA

EXECUTIVE SUMMARY

Mr. Taylor, a new and techno savvy teacher, stays connected by maintaining his own social network pages. However, after seeing that other students were using his social network page as a medium for negativity, gossip, inappropriate conversations, and unsuitable remarks, he questioned its continued use as a helpful teaching tool for those utilizing it appropriately.

BACKGROUND INFORMATION

This generation of teenagers is growing up in the technology age. Many students have personal web pages and an account with a social network due to peer incentives to stay connected or even due to peer pressure. These networks enable subscribers to find friends, interest groups, and affiliations to which they can belong. Even many businesses are using this free service of social network applications as promotion to targeted groups of customers.

Hence, even though there are some negative concerns regarding privacy and predators, there are many positive attributes offered by these social networks. Within social networks, students are more motivated to read and write posts, record status updates, and socialize as an alternative to just playing video games or watching television. Some schools are taking advantage of these social network services to

DOI: 10.4018/978-1-61350-492-5.ch022

connect with students and incorporate their use into curriculum standards. However, with this new, uncensored territory, what is the teacher's role on social networking outside of the traditional school setting? There are several differing perspectives on this social networking revolution; all of them changing the way this generation stays connected.

According to Wikipedia, a social network is a group of people tied together by sharing something in common. For generations there have been social group gatherings to discuss interests, occupations, relationships, and all things shared in common. Throughout human history, social groups of all sizes have formed ranging from those as small as a partnership, to those as big as a country or large organization. They communicated through personal meetings, phone calls, letters, or notes and memos in order to stay connected. Today's technology generation has evolved, thanks to the Internet's social networking ability to share information at incredible speeds. Though today's Internet-based social networking groups are still relatively small, there are a few social groups and services dominating today's society. With the rising popularity of social network groups, some educators are utilizing this tool in an educative way and stay connected to students and other peers. Even advertisers are turning toward the popularity of these social networks.

THE CASE

Mr. Taylor is a new teacher at Harrison Woods High School teaching geometry. He believes technology is the key to reaching and engaging students of this generation. Mr. Taylor is extremely techno savvy and up to date with all the new technologies introduced to education as well as stays connected by having his own social network pages.

Mr. Taylor was an engaging and popular teacher. His students quickly located his social networking pages and added him as a friend. Despite the warnings of his peers, Mr. Taylor expected no harm staying connected with his students via this popular new electronic platform. He had nothing to hide nor any personal things posted on his social network page. As he began befriending more students, his network began to grow and more students began adding him, even students who were not in his class. Mr. Taylor viewed this trend as a great opportunity to reach out to his students. He began to post school review sheets on his social network page and even used his page to converse with any students who had homework questions.

Mr. Taylor continued on with all this technology both in class and after work. He felt that social networking really helped connect him and his students and strengthened the student-teacher relationship. Mr. Taylor was very cautious and kept his page very professional.

A few months later, as he was skimming through his friends' updates, he noticed a student posting about brownies with a drug connotation. He was uncertain how the post got there. Any number of things may have happened. Perhaps the student's profile was hacked into. Perhaps it was a joke made to get someone's attention. Regardless, he was faced with a decision to make: Would he report this? And if so, to whom would he report it? Around the same time the brownie post appeared, Mr. Taylor noticed inappropriate discussion topics between some of his students. The topics varied, ranging from gossip to insults. And even though social networking is a great tool for sending messages and helping students, Mr. Taylor now found himself in a difficult situation.

In the end, Mr. Taylor decided to wait until the following day to talk to the student, and observe for any changes or differences in that student before he reported the situation. He noticed the student was behaving quite normal so he opted for a heart-to-heart discussion with the student instead of reporting the incident. As a result, Mr. Taylor began to question whether he should continue the use of his social network page as a teaching tool to help those who were utilizing it appropriately, after seeing that other students were using it as a medium for negativity, gossip, and inappropriate conversations or remarks. Even though teachers are encouraged to use technology and the web, Mr. Taylor discovered there were few established guidelines teachers could follow in times of making decisions with moral concerns and possible legal consequences.

Social networks have become extremely popular and even though they try to censor sexual content, should they extend that censorship to include references to drug use, cyber-bullying, and other social concerns? If so, how would oversight of such a big organization be managed?

Section 2

Chapter 23
Using Online Collaborative Tools to Foster Middle School Students' "Public Voices":
Payoffs, Perils and Possibilities

Nick Lawrence
East Bronx Academy, USA

Joe O'Brien
University of Kansas, USA

EXECUTIVE SUMMARY

Digital participatory media offer urban social studies teachers a unique opportunity to foster students' civic skills and public voice while enhancing their understanding of social justice within a democratic society. This case study addresses how an 8th grade U.S. history teacher in a New York urban school, when using wikis and online discussion with his students, came to realize that "what [technology] users need in order to take charge of their own online decision making is at best an art and, more often than not, a series of trial-and-error solutions" (Lankes, 2008, p. 103), while operating within two constraints identified by Bull et al (2008): "Teachers have limited models for effective integration of media in their teaching; and, only limited research is available to guide best practice" (p. 2). While using digital collaborative tools enabled students to develop collaborative and communication skills and begin to learn social justice oriented content, the teacher faced challenges related

DOI: 10.4018/978-1-61350-492-5.ch023

to technology integration, curricular alignment, selection of appropriate digital tools, and fostering online academic norms among students. This chapter focuses on a teacher's three-year journey from his first day of teaching to his connecting the use of technology to relevant curricular content to promote his students' use of online public voices for social justice.

BACKGROUND INFORMATION

While digital participatory media in the classroom no longer is a revolutionary concept, practitioners and researchers still are searching for best practices for how to use such media to further student learning. This case study addresses the experiences of a teacher in one of America's most urban areas who over the course of two years and in planning for his third year has sought to integrate technology into his classroom so as to better align students' academic experiences with their social, online experiences.

In order to achieve this aim his students have used digital participatory media not only for academic purposes and to develop online social skills, but also to explore social justice themes. The latter has served as a way for the teacher to tie together the curriculum at the urban school and to support a collaborative effort by his students with students in a Midwestern suburban classroom. The case study opens with the teacher's first and second years in the classroom wherein he began with smaller attempts to integrate technology into his curriculum and then gradually integrated more use of the technology as his management skills and confidence improved. The case description then discusses how the use of technology in the classroom and curriculum has been set up to support not only an expanded use of the technology in the third year, but also has set up this teacher and a colleague to explore in more depth the theme of social justice and to cultivate students' online public voice, the art and skill of persuading "other people—beyond one's closest friends and family—to take action on shared issues" (Levine, 120).

ORGANIZATION BACKGROUND

The students attend a Title I new small school with grades 6-12 in a large city in New York where more than 90% of them receive free or reduced lunch. The school is working toward a 1:1 student to laptop ratio. Grants support much of the school's technology, which are used both to sustain current technology and to invest in new forms of technology. The hardware in the school consists mostly of over a dozen carts that contain full class sets of laptops and netbooks. The administration's vision for the school centers on an online, mostly-paperless school where technology drives instruction. In addition to establishing the technology infrastructure, achieving this vision depends upon professional development, teacher interest and skill level, and a curriculum conducive to technology use.

Since the school's teachers lack adequate, formal preparation in the use of technology, the administration does not expect teachers to use the technology in a specific way, but simply that they use it as best they can. This allows for a lot of flexibility for the teachers, but also provides for a lack of direction. Professional development opportunities are given periodically within the school and many are offered by the city outside of the school, but a lack of regularity and follow up mean their impacts are really only felt in a handful of classrooms. A few teachers utilize the technology on a daily basis and put their entire curricula online, while others rarely use it. For many teachers their use, such as replacing an overhead projector and television with an LCD projector, simply reinforces old pedagogical methods where they are the focal point of teaching and learning. The technology represents but an instructional tool, rather than an opportunity to redefine how students learn. Given this, the administration formed a committee in the fall of 2009 and provided the members with three charges:

- to explore the use of technology in the school;
- to design a specific technology curriculum; and,
- to investigate how technology can play a larger role in each content area.

During the 2009-10 academic year the committee designed a vertically aligned set of skills for grades 6-12. The school will start implementing this curriculum during the 2010-11 academic year, the teacher's third year of teaching. The curriculum should provide teachers more guidance on how to incorporate technology into their instruction. Individual teachers are tasked with determining how to integrate those skills into their respective content area, which creates a unique opportunity to build upon prior work on how to foster students' civic skills and public voices.

SETTING THE STAGE

The use of digital tools to develop a public voice on social justice themes is becoming more and more critical for middle school teachers since a troubling effect of No Child Left Behind is the decline of instructional time for elementary social studies (Center on Education Policy, 2008; Vogler, Lintner, Lipscomb, Knopf, Heafner, and

Rock, 2007; and, Van Fossen, 2005). This situation is particularly acute for those in high poverty districts (Befiore, Auld & Lee, 2005), which means the students most in need of learning how to become civically engaged are the ones least likely to do so. Urban middle school teachers must discover and exploit ways to use online social media, which according to Rheingold (2008) consists of "blogs, wikis, RSS tagging and social bookmarking, music-photo-video sharing, mashups, podcasts, digital storytelling, virtual communities, social network services, virtual environments, and videoblogs"(p. 100), to foster students' public voice. One way is for students to address social justice issues in an 8th grade U.S. history course as they interact with each other and with students from a Midwestern suburban district via a wiki and an online discussion board. Challenges though include: how to align social justice themes with relevant state standards; how to incorporate digital tools into instruction, particularly since the state developed the standards prior to the advent of social media; and, how to enable students to transfer their skills and experiences with online social media to an academic setting.

INTEGRATION OF TECHNOLOGY AND INSTRUCTION

The New York Learning Standards for Social Studies only address the use of technology in the stated 1990's manner, i.e. to retrieve information as if from a digitized textbook. New York wrote the Learning Standards when the Internet was just beginning to make an appearance in schools and when few teachers had access to a computer. As a result, the standards offer little guidance either on what skills related to technology the students are expected to demonstrate while learning U.S. history or how to seamlessly weave such skills into student learning. Given the nature of online social media and the proliferation of digitized archives of primary sources, today's students cannot attain the intent of the state's standards without making use of such technologies. Since the school's teachers are not prepared to use these technologies in their classrooms, they are left on their own to discover how to use them. While professional development sessions offer a few hints and tricks for engaging students online, they hardly offer the training necessary for most teachers to implement these technologies in a way that utilizes their capacity and takes advantage of the students' every-day technology skills. The lack of training prevents teachers from taking the leap out of hard-copy images into the digital age.

While many teachers shy away from instructional use of social media, adolescents are avid users with 78% of adolescents, for example, playing online video games and 65% using social network sites (Anderson & Rainie, 2008). Social media attracts adolescents for several reasons: interest driven participation (Horst, Bittanti, Boyd, Herr-Stephenson, Pascoe & Robinson, 2008); user agency (van Dijck, 2009);

content generation (Shuler, 2007); and, sharing & socializing. Contrast what draws adolescents to social media with their experience in a typical history classroom, one characterized by teacher directed delivery of factually oriented material as students work independently. Little wonder that students confront a "digital disconnect" when they enter a history classroom, yet also little surprise that teachers, who are relatively inexperienced with social media, hesitate trying to use such media and thus compete with students' social use of it.

CONNECTION TO AND IMPLEMENTATION OF THE U.S. HISTORY CURRICULUM

The New York 8th grade curriculum is very content driven and student performance is assessed through the New York Regents Exam. The content centers on United States and state history after the Civil War. The 8th grade curriculum in the Midwest state similarly focuses on state and U.S. history, but starts in 1800. The New York social studies curriculum is traditional, yet unique. Traditional features include a focus on the political history of the United States and on great historical figures, most notably presidents. Statements such as the "meaning and morality of slavery" (The University of the State of New York, Social Studies Resource Guide with Core Curriculum, 1999, p. 60) and "Conscription as a factor in racism" (p. 64) suggest a broader and deeper exploration of social justice issues than found in most state U.S. history standards, but since racism and slavery, for example, never are paired, this suggestion is questionable. Unique features include the two years devoted to U.S. and state history in middle school and the placement of U.S. history in a hemispheric and global context. Students are to demonstrate skills such as the ability to "explain the significance of history evidence" and to "weigh the importance, reliability, and validity of evidence" (Learning Standards for Social Studies, The University of the State of New York, 1996). Addressing this standard requires the intense use of primary sources, which represents another unique feature, one supported by the inclusion of document-based questions (DBQ) on the Regents Exam. The amount of curricular time devoted to middle school U.S. history and an emphasis on primary sources offer an opportunity to explore social justice issues by drawing upon the thinking of key historical figures, such as Frederick Douglass' 4th of July speech that he delivered in Rochester in 1852. Investigating speeches not only could offer students models of those exercising their public voice in pursuit of social justice, but also could allow them to explore the context in which such people did so. Developing students' public voice would complement the Civics, Citizenship and Government Standard to "develop and refine participatory skills" (Learning Standards for Social Studies, p. 27). To meet the standard, students need to "respect the rights of others in discussions and classroom debates" and to "participate in negotiation and compromise to resolve classroom…disagreements" (p. 27).

STUDENTS

Prior to entering the 8th grade, these students typically had little or no experience with using technology to interact online in academic ways, though they had widely used the available technology for social-networking purposes. While experienced using digital media to socially interact, the students struggled interacting with each other in the classroom. The teacher faced the challenge of how to acknowledge the "informal learning that occurs in the context of participatory media," since such experiences "offer significant opportunities for increased student engagement in formal learning settings," so as to connect their "experience with communication technologies" to sound "pedagogy…content…[and] learning objectives" (Bull et al, p. 6). This was important for his students for several reasons. First, "mobile devices will be primary connection tool to the Internet for most people in the world in 2020" (Anderson &Rainie, 2008, p. 2), yet very little pedagogy is geared toward such devices. Second, "civic engagement includes the production of culture, at least insofar as cultural expression shapes norms & priorities" (Levine, 2008), which means that students' use of social networking sites and the creation and uploading of videos to sites such as YouTube represent nascent forms of civic engagement. Yet, as Levine (p. 129) recognized, how do we encourage students "to create— and…make products with public purposes—rather than use the Internet to get access to mass-produced culture"? Third, when using social networking sites and video games, youth follow a "learn to do" so as to "learn about" model of learning, whereas schools typically follow a "learn about," and then possibly a "learn to do" model (Thomas & Brown, 2009). In many respects moderate and high end users of social networking technologies, no matter their socio-economic status, are more primed to learn than their predecessors so long as teachers are willing and able to meet them on common ground.

The teacher's students though generally had less-developed academic skills in areas such as reading and writing than their average counterpart nationwide. They oftentimes were not taught many collaborative skills in school because of discipline concerns. During his first year in the classroom the teacher's colleagues advised him against using group work altogether as they considered it next to impossible with his students. To say that the students lacked communication and collaborative skills though is a bit misplaced as many of these same students used technology to create elaborate webpages on social networking sites whose primary purpose is to generate interesting content, generally about themselves. While many students had mobile devices, since students were not permitted to use them in schools, students used them for social, not academic, purposes.

TEACHER

The teacher began working at this school as a first-year teacher in 2008-9. He believed that learning how to effectively use online collaboration and communication tools to enhance student learning was an essential part of the first-year learning curve, which distinguished him from most of his colleagues and therefore made him receptive to the administration's initiatives. That said, his use of technology was very much a trial and error effort, oftentimes simply learning what not to do in the classroom. As a K-12 student in the 1990's, he only occasionally used instant messaging even for social purposes and used the Internet in school primarily to conduct research and download written work. Even in college technology still largely was used to deliver information, much as it had been through a textbook, but online. There was little instruction on how to use online social networking platforms to support student-centered learning, let alone to cultivate students' public voices and engage them in discussion about social justice.

SYNTHESIS

If urban educators possess a unique responsibility and challenge to help their students learn how to become civically engaged, then such teachers need to recognize the distinctive nature of the online setting. If as Levine (2008) notes, "democracy requires broad and diverse cultural creativity" and the "new digital media…offer opportunities for individuals and voluntary groups to create their own cultural products and to use a public voice" about matters of personal interest and social importance, then teachers must foster a disposition among their students "to make products with public purposes" (Levine, p. 129). As Rheingold (2008) concluded: "Moving from a private voice to a public voice can help students [or anyone else] turn their self-expression into a form of public participation" (p. 101). As will be discussed, accomplishing such is an incremental, multi-year process.

THE CASE

Fostering an online public or civic voice among middle school U.S. history students in an urban school required addressing four matters:

- using online collaborative tools within a school and between schools;
- integrating use of such tools within daily instruction while supporting an existing curriculum designed by the state;
- transferring students face-to-face and online communication and collaboration skills to an academic setting; and,
- growing into teaching with technology to 8th graders.

This resulted in the teacher's two year and, as yet, incomplete journey, as he heads into year 3 as outlined in Table 1.

OVERVIEW

The teacher used online collaborative tools in three ways. First, during year 1 he used a wiki with a small group of volunteer students in an after-school setting; to foster collaborative skills among students whose interpersonal skills were limited; to prepare students to complete a DBQ for the New York Regents Exam; to experiment with a wiki as a means to develop students' voice in a group setting; and, to prepare to use a wiki in a large class setting. Second, in year 2 he used a wiki for intra-school, inter-class collaborative group projects, which built upon the above purposes and what he learned during year 1. Third, during years 1 and 2 the teacher and his students worked with a colleague and her students in a Midwestern, suburban school on interstate online projects.

His first year's experience with a targeted group of students where the wiki was used for a specific purpose provided the teacher with the confidence, data, and experience necessary to move to a whole class setting. Whereas, for example, during year 1 the students primarily used the wiki to work on a specific written product, during year 2 they explored the collaborative features of a wiki in more depth and engaged in discussions about the substance of what they wrote. Unlike during year 1 where the written work was the end, now students were realizing how to use the wiki as a means to engage in thoughtful discussion. He selected topics meant to pique students' interest and promote discussion and thoughtful responses. The topics were generally current events, such as the use of cameras in schools and virtual crime, loosely tied to the curricula of the two states in which the students lived. The process the students went through was an exploration of the issue and then an application of fundamental ideas of citizenship and social justice. The premise was simple, if students were provided an online platform that enabled them to discuss substantive civic matters of interest to them then they were likely to develop and to use online civic or public voices.

Table 1. Teacher's two year journey

Project Description	Integration of Tech &Instr	Implementation of Curriculum	Students	Teacher(s)
Yr. 1 Focus on use of wiki with small, volunteer group of students & limited use of discussion board to prepare for DBQ on state exam.	While a wiki was chosen to foster collaboration, the academic task was more teacher than student centered & did not draw on wiki's potential.	Having students analyze primary source document from old DBQs directly connected to state standards.	Students were assigned partners and worked in groups of 2 or 3. Lack of civic voice- students simply answered questions from a state test.	Teacher created the wiki and posted most of the DBQ material on it, much like he did when using paper documents in class.
Yr. 1: Use of discussion board between urban & Midwestern class so students could learn about each other.	Teachers used a secure discussion board. Students & asked each other questions about themselves and where they lived.	Little to no connection to curriculum.	Students worked in small groups. Initially curious, but their interest quickly waned.	One of their first experiences with a discussion board for both teachers. Unsure of how to organize and implement online discussion.
Yr. 2 Use of discussion board between the urban & Midwestern class so students could learn about each other & discuss current events.	A wiki and secure discussion board were used to increase students' comfort with using the participatory media in the classroom	Discussion board used to address contemporary social issues that are not explicitly in the curriculum, but which had loose ties to it.	Each student is assigned a partner in her/his school and in the partner school based on ability and personality. Students post their opinions on current issues assigned by teachers.	Teachers posted material articles &links to videos to wiki pages as prompts for students' discussion, as well guiding questions and responses to students' questions.
Yr. 2 Use of wiki & discussion board between 2 classes within urban school to discuss life after high school.	Integrated use of discussion board to edit wiki pages. Students did online research and decided what to include on group's wiki page.	While topic of project interested students, there was little connection to the content of curriculum.	Students in two classes collaborated to create a wiki site. Their collaboration improved over time as groups able to contribute equally. They knew each other before project began.	Teacher's instruction based in skills, not content. Teacher acted as a guide for students as they did research online, posting questions to make sure they stayed on track.
Yr. 2 Use of wiki& discussion board between 1 class in urban school & 1 in Midwestern school	Integrated use of discussion board to edit wiki pages. Students did online research and decided what to include on group's wiki page.	While the teachers determined the content of this project was important, the standards provided by their respective states were not used over the course of this portion of the work.	Students collaborated to create a wiki site and used discussion board to learn about each other. Urban class period was 15 minutes longer than Midwestern class.	Teacher's instruction based in skills, not content; teacher acts as guide for students as they do research online, posting questions to make sure they stay on track

INTEGRATION OF TECHNOLOGY AND INSTRUCTION

Year 1

Uncertain of how to integrate instructional technology into all of his classes, the teacher created an after school project for academically proficient students interested in preparing for the Document Based Question (DBQ) portion of the New York Regents 8th grade social studies exam. In a DBQ students use a collection of primary and secondary sources to answer an essay question. The teacher took several DBQs from an old exam and posted them to a series of wiki pages. While each student individually worked at a computer, they reviewed and analyzed the documents and composed and revised possible answers to the essay question on the wiki as pairs or in groups of 4 or 5, depending upon the task. The teacher created the after school project for two reasons. First, as a beginning teacher he struggled with classroom management so that implementing a class-wide online project in all of his regular class periods seemed beyond his ability and experience not simply with instructional technology but with teaching in general. In short, self-preservation was the motivating factor for starting with a small, after school project with interested and motivated students. Second, he lacked any guidance or solid examples of technology use in an urban school. Recognizing this as an opportunity for professional growth, the teacher set up an action research project to explore how to make the best academic use of the technology and whether such use might affect how students personally interacted with each other.

The teacher chose a wiki because he and the students could post images and text to a single page and students could interact via a discussion board. Since a wiki was new to the students and relatively new to the teacher, their use was very limited and proved problematic. For example, while the students were working collaboratively through the wiki, initially two or more students simultaneously would edit the same wiki page, which meant that the edits were not saved. Lacking experience with a wiki caused the teacher to provide instruction once a problem emerged and he had determined a solution through "trial and error." This resulted in many technical difficulties, causing the students much frustration.

The teacher also used the wiki during this year to experiment with online communication and interaction as students used the wiki's discussion board to discuss their editing, even though they sat only two or three seats away from each other. His students often struggled with face-to-face discussion, yet interacting via the wiki pages seemed to have an ameliorating effect on their behavior since they were less likely to taunt each other online than they were when face-to-face offline. While this was an improvement in how they collaborated with one another, the students did not demonstrate a dramatic improvement in their ability to work together to complete an academic task. This may have been due in part to the fact that they knew the use of the wiki was unnecessary to complete the academic task.

During the first year the teacher and his Midwest colleague made a small attempt at collaboration, though several factors worked against their success: the teacher's after school group was much smaller than his colleague's classes; the teacher overly concentrated on his students in-school collaborative skills at the detriment of fostering the online discussion; and, the approaching end of the school year. The most important factor though was both teachers' inexperience with using a discussion board. As a result, they were unsure how to nurture and sustain an online discussion. After a series of sporadic interactions, the board went silent. This work though planted the seed for their collaboration during year 2 as they realized that their students could interact online without any catastrophe occurring. Heading into year 2, the teachers realized that rather than assuming a discussion would naturally emerge once the students started interacting online, they needed to decide upon the purposes of the online discussion, as well as how to initiate, maintain, and bring closure to one.

Year 2

The teacher focused on refining his use of technology and reducing the number of problems so as to streamline instruction and minimize student frustration as he moved from the small, after school group of students to each of his classes. Several steps he took serve as examples. First, since he now was more familiar with how to instructionally use a wiki, students were specifically shown how to edit wiki pages and to use the wiki's discussion feature. Then, each group of students worked together online to edit a wiki page on some aspect of preparing for life after school. Second, he sought to better integrate the wiki's editing function with the discussion board. During the first year, use of one feature was not instructionally dependent upon the other and students responded accordingly. Third, combining both features into one academic task meant starting the students with small, relatively simple tasks and, as they became more proficient, to increase the complexity of the task.

The first project the teacher undertook was between two of his classes. Since he intended to follow the same instructional model with the project between one of his classes and a Midwest class, this allowed him two trial runs for each activity. By making the instructional decisions on his own and becoming familiar with the questions that students posed as they encountered problems with the technology, the teacher gained enough confidence to work collaboratively with his Midwest colleague. Just as importantly, he felt more comfortable with his students collaborating with his colleague's students.

As the teacher and his Midwest colleague planned their second year of collaboration, they unknowingly gravitated toward features of social media mentioned earlier by allowing the students some choice in what to discuss and to use the discussion board (Figure 1) as an opportunity to socialize with students from another state. The students had the opportunity to post to a discussion board their opinions about current events such as the use of security cameras in schools. The teachers then designed a collaborative online project where the students; worked in inter-school groups to find online resources related to preparing for life after high school; posted resources to a wiki page and left comments about the resources; and, provided feedback about material for one another on the wiki page's discussion board. All communication was public and observable by all students, not just the teacher. Based on the first year's experience, the teacher realized the importance of building good offline pedagogy into the online project's design: students were put into larger groups with specific roles so as to provide students with extra peer support: only one student, the "editor," edited the wiki page at a given time, thus minimizing the likelihood of the loss of data; and, the group leader could edit the wiki but only the editor could push the edit button. Finally, they purposefully built in a beginning, middle and end to the discussion. Since both teachers wanted students to engage in an online public or civic discussion, prior to exploring the current events they asked their students to think about different types of citizens. They wanted their students not simply to explore the current events, but to realize these events related to public policy issues of importance to them as students and as citizens. Once the stage was set, groups of students researched and discussed a current event. The teachers brought closure to the discussion by asking the students to post their thinking about each event and what should be done about it. The result was more online interaction between students and an improvement in the each group's written work, but little connection to the state curriculum.

CONNECTION TO AND IMPLEMENTATION OF THE CURRICULUM

Year 1

The students' use of the wiki to work on the DBQ was an instructional means to a curricular end, i.e. practice in using primary sources to answer content specific questions in preparation for the end of year state exam. As a result, the students displayed no public voice nor did they explore anything related to a social justice theme in history. Instead they responded as best they could to a question meant to analyze a historic document, but which had a prescribed, low-level answer (generally characterized by simply copying something from that document) and which promoted very little critical thinking. The teacher's struggle to seamlessly weave

Figure 1. 8th grade civic discussion

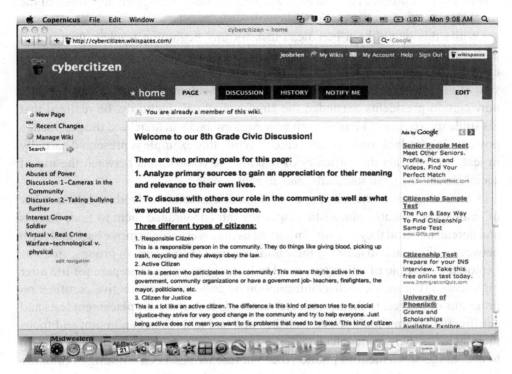

together the content, primary sources and use of the wiki reflected the lack of guidance in the state social studies standards on how to integrate technology into the use of primary sources to learn historical information.

Year 2

While he better integrated use of social media into his instruction, which resulted in better online communication between his students and laid the groundwork for the cultivation of their public voice, the teacher overlooked curricular content. While the students' online researching and discussion of current events and their consideration of different types of citizenship were loosely connected to the curriculum, the teacher was not yet experienced and versatile enough with curricular content to make direct, relevant connections. In defense of the teacher, Torney-Purta and Lopez (2006) concluded that history curricula and textbooks seldom offered explicit examples of civic participation by individuals other than political leaders and that teachers tended to avoid addressing controversial social issues. Thus, the responsibility fell upon the teacher to identify relevant parts of the history curriculum to connect to the current events so as to enable students to recognize how those of the past might have exercised their public voice.

While this would be a herculean task for any beginning teacher, this proved particularly problematic for the teacher given his students. While his students discussed how the schools' use of video surveillance potentially illustrated an expansion of governmental authority and the state curriculum required students to learn how certain presidents expanded the chief executive's authority, he realized that his students would not identify with how Andrew Jackson increased the president's powers, despite Jackson's colorful career. While this example is presented partially in jest, it highlights the difficulty of making the connections between the use of social media, the state standards, and current events.

Combining use of the wiki pages with the discussion board reduced the number of students' automatic, simplistic responses and encouraged them to find, discuss and defend material they felt was important as they were able to move back and forth between editing and discussing their thinking with their peers. In groups, students explored a subtopic of what steps need to be taken in order to prepare for life after high school (Figure 2), such as information on colleges or alternative certification programs of interest to them, retrieved materials to prepare for placement tests and certification exams, and located websites that had tools to help pinpoint and focus their interests. This content had no direct connection to the curriculum, but did help to encourage an element of public voice the teacher had been working to promote for two years, as his students worked to persuade their Midwestern counterparts to edit their shared page in a particular way. That said, the effort to learn how to use the technology in the second year did lack strong connection to the curriculum.

STUDENTS

While initially students were disengaged when using technology for academic purposes, they steadily became more engaged as they received more opportunities to create something with a public purpose. The students progressed from using technology to complete test-prep materials in basically the same way they would on paper to real-time collaboration with another class across the country. Over the course of that work they expanded their understanding of the potential of collaborative online platforms and showed signs that they were beginning to understand the potential for learning in that environment. During Year 2 the teacher worked on switching from the model of education wherein they learned about so as to learn to do to a model wherein they learned to do so as to learn about.

Figure 2. Life after high school

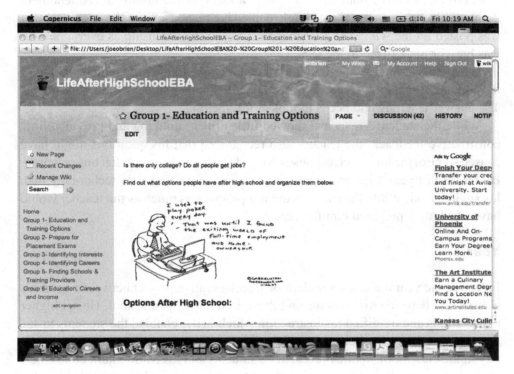

Year 1

Using a wiki to prepare for the DBQ part of the state exam was of limited importance to students, particularly since they had done DBQs without using technology. As a result, they resisted using a new, somewhat complicated medium to complete a task with which they were already familiar, often asking to complete the work on paper since they were comfortable doing the task that way. From the students' perspective the technology was not necessary and therefore served no real purpose. There also was a lack of development in online academic behavior. Their responses were short and lacked depth and any display of critical thinking.

While their ability to collaborate improved when working online, the improvement was limited. They still used text language, for example, and there was no evidence that they incorporated the feedback they received from other students into their answers, which might illustrate the need to establish an audience and public purpose for such work. While students read each other's answers, they were not expressing their own opinions and only were giving prescribed answers, which prevented them from owning the work and thus providing more constructive feedback.

For example, when responding to a prompt about how the Fourteenth Amendment defines citizenship, one student simply copied her response from the document that was posted on the wiki: The 14 Amendment defines citizenship as everyone who was born or naturalized in the U.S.

While answering the question, the student demonstrated little understanding of the content. A common response by a student to another student's initial post was: The answer is wrong and needs to look at the spelling.

While the student's response showed little critical thinking and provided little constructive feedback, the teacher also recognized that his questions might have caused some of the low level responses. Most discussions stopped after one response. By the end of year 1 the teacher learned more about using wiki technology than his students did. While the students did not progress as much as the teacher would have liked, they prepared him for Year 2.

Year 2

In the second year the teacher undertook a collaborative project between two of his classes and between his students and those in the Midwest school. He set higher expectations and modified his instruction which better enabled the students to see a connection between their own social use of technology and the use of technology in the classroom. While the teacher's students and his Midwestern colleague's students began collaborating during this year, it became evident that their varied academic and social abilities were less important than their ability to provide real feedback to their group and to contribute to the group's effort.

The teacher and his Midwest colleague used the wiki to engage their students in a discussion about current events. The teachers posted current events on wiki pages and their students interacted with each other via the wiki's discussion board. While the students' responses were short and reactive, they were posting comments on matters that piqued their interest. The students still struggled with providing very little potent feedback so their collaboration with each other was muted, although there were more responses posted that could help another student's thinking than there were in the first year of the study. Initial use of the discussion board found students simply agreeing or disagreeing with their classmates. For example, the following exchange took place when students responded to a prompt about whether or not cameras should be put in schools:

Natalie: I Think Cameras Should Be Allowed In School. Not At All Places Like Bathrooms Or Classrooms. It Shouldn't Because People Has Their Own Privacy Especially In The Bathroom.

Beth: Cameras shouldn't even be allowed. They make children insecure and it's basically an invasion of privacy. If the teachers don't see anything with their own eyes it's their fault and they should have been their to catch someone in the act.

After the original posts were put onto the discussion board, students responded with posts such as:

Edward: I think you are right.

As the work with the discussion board progressed, students began offering feedback that promoted more critical thinking but which did not promote further discussion. Examples of these responses given by students to their classmates who answered a prompt about identity theft began with "i agree because identity theft is more harmful…," and "I agree with allayas because its more harmful of someone stealing your identity…" These showed students were thinking about their classmates' responses more than the students demonstrated during the first year of the study with the initial use of the wiki. As the use of the discussion board progressed, some students went still further in analyzing their classmates' posts. An example of this was a response to a post written by a student when given a prompt about the use of new technology in combat:

Sasha: How would they be prepared? In what way? What would they be able to know before their enemies attack them? I agree with you in your second and third responses, it is true that every year there is new technology coming up or ready to be introduced.

While the teachers better integrated the technology since the inter-school discussion depended upon it, students still perceived what they were doing as akin to reading a hard copy of a news article and using pencil and paper to answer questions. Still, the students were more engaged than during the previous year, as they were using the technology to express their own opinions about topics of interest to them rather than using technology to complete academic work with completely prescribed answers.

Several factors possibly contributed to this change:

- the work they were doing seemed to have more of a public purpose;
- the students had a much more responsive audience; and
- the teacher's instruction changed to a more student-centered, skill-based approach.

The students capitalized on a desire to interact more directly with their counterparts across the country. Four classes collaborated on two wikis: two of the teachers' classes worked together on the project, while one of the teacher's classes worked with one of his Midwestern colleagues' on the project. The differences seen in the work these students did, reinforced the notion that the three factors listed above affected the students' engagement and understanding of how to use the technology in an academic way.

Having the students collaborate via the wiki to explore life after high school proved highly motivating. Rather than immediately moving into this academic task though, the students initially used the technology to learn about each other. The teachers set up secure email addresses for each student and had them email back and forth as digital pen pals for several weeks. The students were fascinated by everything from one another's names, which reflected the differences in their ethnic backgrounds, to what their ePals did on the weekends. Students were encouraged to ask questions about where their digital partners lived, what their school was like, and what their hobbies were. One student in the urban setting actually went so far as to exchange information with a student in the Midwestern setting so they could play xBox live together outside of school. By the time the academic collaboration came around, the students were practically out of social questions to ask!

The students' fascination with one another carried over into the opening interactions of the academic work of editing wiki pages and using the discussion board. The students couldn't wait to see what their trans-continental counterparts would post on their shared wiki page, regardless of their assigned topic. This continued until the students reached a logistical glitch, which discouraged the urban students. The Midwestern students' classes lasted about 40 minutes, while the urban students' classes were 60 minutes. As the students in the urban school realized they were posting more work over time, their initial enthusiasm waned as they wondered if their Midwest counterparts were upholding their end of the academic work load, a common concern when working with any group.

Conversely, the teacher's online collaborative project between two classes started out slowly. Since the students already knew each other, they immediately were immersed in the academic task. The students initially struggled though since they were not used to doing group work. Over time the interclass group partnerships flourished as their interactions increased. As their work came together, the collaboration between the urban and Midwest students stalled. In the end, while the students initially desired to interact socially online, they eventually became invested in the collaborative academic work.

Working with students outside of their class or school motivated the students, i.e. having an audience mattered to them. During year 1 the students gave one another comments on the answers they posted on the wiki about DBQ documents, but did not incorporate that feedback into their answers. When the discussion board was used by itself the students sometimes saw interesting or helpful feedback but also failed to incorporate that information into their work. When the two functions were combined the students communicated back and forth for a solid week, incorporated feedback into their work, used one another's ideas, and expected that their own ideas would be read and potentially used. Their posts were further advanced from the original reactive, prescribed responses of the first year's wiki use as well as the more analytical responses seen on the discussion board earlier in year two. The students really wanted to give one another feedback that was useful in editing their respective pages. As the work progressed, so did their feedback, moving from simple suggestions to asking questions to offering guidance and feedback on multiple aspects of the tasks. For example, responses posted to a page about preparing to take placement and certification exams were:

Sasha during the Initial Responses: They should add information to the page site. Chaz after Initial Respones: What should we do with our organization? Sasha during Later Responses: GOOD but you should add more information on what to do for like a specific exam.

While initially they complained about having to post a certain number of comments on the discussion board, students in both the Midwestern/Urban classes and the Urban/Urban classes actually began to complain that they needed more interaction, feedback, and contributions from their digital counterparts. Their desire to increase this kind of communication demonstrated in part that they understood the value of peer feedback and that they were willing and able to incorporate feedback given to them using this platform.

Toward the end of the school year the students completed a short questionnaire (Table 2) posted on Survey Monkey regarding their use of the wiki and discussion board. In answering the open-ended questions their responses included; the "comments helped us to edit our pages," "working as a team got things done faster," "the information was useful," and "working in a group (online), we learned from each other." Since over 85% of the students put either A or B for the first questions, they seemed to realize that using technology to complete collaborative projects was part of their future. 75% of the students preferred using their cell phones, IM or a social networking site to express their opinions. While possibly reflecting their inexperience with wikis and discussion boards, a more likely explanation is not that students were more adept at and comfortable with their phones and Facebook, but such platforms are more user friendly and versatile than wikis and discussion boards. Just as e-mail became the new snail mail, so too are wikis and discussion boards becoming so "last generation."

Table 2. The *questionnaire*

Questionnaire
1. Based on where you see technology going in the future, do you think that this assignment is:
A. More reflective of what I'll be asked to do in the future
B. About the same as the type of projects I'll do in the future
C. Less reflective of the type of projects I'll do in the future
2. I'm able to express my opinions more easily with:
A. A social networking site (MySpace, Facebook, etc.)
B. A wiki
C. Pencils and papers
3. I collaborate (work in a group to achieve something) more easily:
A. Using a wiki
B. Working offline, with pencil and paper
C. Using some other kind of technology
4. What are the benefits of using a wiki and discussion board? (Open-ended)

TEACHERS

Year 1

In spite of a certain level of comfort using technology to communicate with peers and colleagues, the teacher mostly knew how to deliver instruction with more traditional methods, so his use of technology supported those methods. While initially approaching technology as a "collection of tools" (Berson, Lee, &Stuckart, 2001, p. 210), the teacher recognized the need to expand beyond his overhead projector-style use of technology, which resulted in the after school project described earlier. When conducting this project he confronted challenges related to:

- the use of hardware and software;
- the management of the technology and the students;
- aligning the use of technology to the state curriculum; and,
- transferring the students' knowledge of social networking sites and handheld communication devices to the classroom.

He first encountered hardware problems with the laptops, since they were several years old and many lacked functioning batteries or the ability to connect to the Internet in a reasonable amount of time. Fortunately, with such a small group of students, a classroom set of computers was sufficient, which highlighted the advantage with starting with less than a full class of students. The software challenge proved more problematic since he quickly learned there was a wrong way to use many online collaborative platforms. Also, the poor Internet connection and the wiki's limited functionality made discussions via the wiki site very cumbersome. If nothing else, the teacher became much more proficient at trouble shooting hardware and software problems while teaching.

The teacher's design of the students' project worked against their experiences with online social media, which created barriers to the students transferring their skills using such media to the classroom. When the students used social media, for example, they autonomously generated their own content, yet the teacher generated nearly all the content in the project so as to align with the state standards. By removing those elements from their online collaboration, the teacher was essentially ignoring the students' informal, prior experience with online social media. The teacher realized that he needed to learn more about the students' prior abilities and how to capitalize upon them in the classroom; he needed to learn how his students operated as young adults. These students were aching to use technology as much and as often as they possibly could. Every single day the students were plugged into their iPods, used their cell phones in the classroom to socialize with whomever was on the other end, itched to post their latest pictures to their MySpace pages, and to generate content about their lives online. Putting pen to paper to complete the test-prep style instructional pieces given them in class every day, proved as appealing as dental surgery, highlighting the digital disconnect. Learning what really motivated them to use the technology as well as how they used it was clearly important in determining how to bring that motivation into the classroom to support instruction.

Managing the students' use of computers was a significant concern during the teacher's first year. The teachers in his school told him tales about how students would treat the laptops and what their online behavior was like. Even in the small-group, after-school setting several students were off-task on numerous occasions, flipping back and forth between the task that was given them and whatever it was they'd found online to entertain themselves. This, in part, demonstrated the existence of students' interest-driven use of technology, as well as a tendency to multi-task while online. Thus, when the teacher and students encountered hardware and software problems, students quickly turned to what had caught their attention online. Addressing this concern was not as easy as developing the troubleshooting skills, particularly since students were not used to focusing on a single task while using social media.

Due to the end-of-year exam the teacher during this year was very concerned about sticking to the curriculum, a feeling reinforced by his colleagues. Thus, using a wiki to help students deconstruct and practice DBQs seemed like a sound instructional means to connect the use of technology to the state standards. Once he started the after school project though, he came to realize how his use of the wiki's collaborative functions proved superfluous to completing a DBQ, which demonstrated that simply using technology not only can fail to transcend the digital disconnect, but potentially can reinforce it. While mindful of the curriculum, he lost sight of the students.

Truly cultivating students' online public voice was almost entirely absent during his first year though he had set out to do so. His ambition and idealism exceeded his experience and skill-set, while feeling he had accomplished little, he actually had learned a lot. First, chopping up and posting a DBQ to a wiki, while environmentally sound, was not any more motivating to students than using a pen and paper. The lack of user agency, the inability to generate their own content, an ineffective way of sharing their opinions and discussing the questions posted and a lack of interest in the test-prep material all contributed to students' lack of engagement and motivation. Technology was not a panacea. Second, while initially seeming at odds with the prior point, he spent most of that year coming to the simple, yet difficult realization that the students' desire to use technology trumps many other forms of instructional delivery. During his second year the teacher was challenged to incorporate the features of social media into academic tasks in a way that promoted civic engagement and students' use of online public voices.

Year 2

Whereas in the first year the teacher worked to figure out how to use hardware and to determine the logistics of using computers with students, the second year was devoted to determining how to increase student engagement in the online academic setting and shift the use of the technology from a teacher-centered approach to a student-centered approach. Moving in this direction allowed the teacher and students to just begin to tease out a social justice theme in the curriculum as the students began to develop a public voice.

Many of the hardware issues that the teacher faced during year 1 were alleviated by the purchase through a grant of enough new netbooks to create a 1:1 student to laptop ratio. While Internet connectivity continued to plague their work, the teacher had learned enough to trouble-shoot these issues with his students either by using one of the extra working netbooks or by reconfiguring a netbook's wireless settings. The implementation of a grade specific behavior management plan for the use of technology greatly improved the students' online behavior and their care of the netbooks. The school also purchased computer-monitoring software that allowed the teachers to view and control each laptop in the room.

During year 2 as the teacher shifted from teacher-centered online instruction to student-centered online instruction, he incorporated features of social media into an academic project. The teacher also was more purposeful in fostering students' online public voice, such as allowing students to select a topic that piqued their interest, to use the wiki as a forum to post their opinions, and to give feedback to each other's viewpoints. As Levine (2008) noted, an important motivating force in the development of an online public voice is "the belief that one can reach other people: an audience" (p. 129). Learning more about the students' intense desire to use technology, how they wanted to use it and then determining how that could be put to use in the classroom were major parts of this year. Surveys were given to determine just how the students utilize social networking sites, as well as their thinking about using a wiki and discussion board. Student engagement also went up as the digital disconnect was decreased with a shift to student-centered online research and content creation. From the process, the teacher learned what student-centered education could be, given more training and experience on his part.

The teacher's comfort level with using technology in his regular classes increased dramatically as he increased his overall knowledge and skills and ability to manage his classes. Since survival no longer was his paramount concern, toward the end of year 2 he began considering how to integrate his use of technology with the state curriculum and how to develop students' public voice on social issues. His success with a wiki-based student project showed him how the technology should be used which was in direct contrast to the previous year and which offered him insight into what he needed to do as he planned for year 3.

CURRENT CHALLENGES

Curricular Alignment

This challenge is threefold. First there is inter-district and/or the interstate alignment of curricular content. The two U.S. history curricula discussed in this chapter, for example, while taught chronologically, begin at different points in time. Second, while use of social justice themes might serve as one way to address the first challenge, neither set of state standards is organized thematically. Third, while states are beginning to incorporate 21st century skills into standards, such as those articulated by the Partnership for 21st Century Skills (http://www.p21.org/documents/ss_map_11_12_08.pdf), neither state has integrated such skills into the content standards. Aligning curricula requires the teachers to engage in an interstate, online collaboration to thematically conceptualize their respective state standards while considering how to integrate the use of social media with them. While possible collectively, this requires the teachers to have a rich understanding of the content area and of what Shulman (1987) terms pedagogical content knowledge, a facility with social media for personal and professional use, and a willingness to take risks, traits that are not necessarily highly valued in schools concerned about AYP.

Selection of the "Best" Online Collaborative Tools

Student-friendly; stable; secure; school accessible…the list goes on as to what a teacher needs to consider when considering how best to integrate use of such tools. With so many tools out there and a lack of solid literature and recommendations from others in the field, it can be a daunting task to decide which tools will be best for a certain group of students. Given the amount of time that must be devoted to familiarizing students with a given platform before they can use it fluently enough to exercise their online public voices, versatile yet stable sites are of paramount importance. Such sites though typically are commercially based, which raises interesting questions about the use of private sites to foster students' public or civic voices. In turn, if students in high-risk schools are the ones most in need to such civic preparation, what are the implications of educators indirectly marketing certain digital tools to such students? While recognizing all the facets of this challenge, the teacher himself needed stability and security, which created a dilemma for him—continue using a simpler, easy-to-use, yet limited platform, or move to a more complex, versatile site.

Creation of Online Groups and "Audiences"

The dynamics of online groups are distinct from those of face-to-face groups, which highlights Lankes' observation about the trial and error nature of this work. In turn, establishing inter-class or inter-school groups within a district, let alone between states, poses a different set of challenges. Included in this list is being familiar with students' abilities in both offline and online settings in order to best match each student to a counterpart on the other end of the Internet line. Another major challenge is being able to work with and trust the other educator to establish a working environment on their end of the collaborative effort that will best compliment her or his students. The research and the teacher's experiences though, illustrate the importance of students publishing their work for people other than those in their immediate class. Audience matters.

Carving out Instructional Time for Online Public Discussion of Social Issues

Teachers typically avoid discussing controversial social issues. State standards seldom address social issues. Schools block access to numerous social networking sites due to legitimate concerns about cyber bullying and privacy. State standards often do not lend themselves to developing and assessing students' online communication skills. Schools and teachers continually play catch-up as IT personnel try to ensure sufficient bandwidth to handle emerging uses of Web 2.0 technologies. Teachers try to stay no more than one generation behind the latest online digital tools. Ironically, while the teacher encountered several of these challenges, several other instructional challenges–related to fostering students online public voices about social issues and simple day-to-day teaching–while much more mundane, were equally problematic. For example, the teacher struggled with finding age appropriate online material, figuring out how to transfer effective offline pedagogy to an online setting, and simply keeping 30 students at a time on task while online. When placed within this context, finding instructional time for what seemed like such an esoteric goal almost was an insurmountable task.

Academic/Civic Norms vs. Social Norms

While students typically have had extensive experience with online social media, they are much less experienced with use of social media for academic or public purposes. Thus, in the process of cultivating students' online academic and public voices, the teacher realized the need to address the norms associated with both. This becomes particularly important when working between schools with students from vastly different backgrounds. He needed to help his students distinguish between social and academic or public speaking, such as the use of text language or personal idiosyncrasies when communicating online with other students about current events. One student, for example, struggled all year with how to use his academic or public voice. When responding to a prompt about military technology of the future, he wrote: "How do you think that using technology that helps identify location is harmful if it would be helpful...." He reasoned that his online communication should reflect the fact that he was very loud in real life. While very appropriate for his personal voice, what the teacher helped him to realize over time was how an online speaker was more limited in her or his ability to express a range of thinking and feeling than an offline speaker. His constant use of capitalization robbed him of a means to highlight an aspect of his thinking. The teacher was very conscious of the writing skills the students needed in a system so oriented toward test preparation. While the student's incredible offline decibel level did not diminish over the course of the year, he began make better use of online communication to convey his thinking, which also seemed to translate into his pencil and paper writing. Harking back to the prior challenge though, as an urban educator responsible for his students' performance on the Regents exam, how could he justify making this an instructional priority?

Supportive Infrastructure

Addressing all of the above is for naught unless the administrative and technological infrastructure is in place to enable teachers to engage in such teaching. Schools and districts, for example, routinely block access to social media sites and many administrators are moving teachers to scripted curricula. While working within the constraints of a much larger school system, the administration at the urban school gave a great deal of freedom to the teacher in the classroom as one of the school goals was to implement more technology in the classroom and he was one of the only teachers willing to take large steps to experiment with technology that was available.

The availability of the technology was incredibly important. The administration was dedicated to providing working technology to teachers who were willing to use it. The grade-wide rollout of the teacher's inter-class and inter-school projects only was possible with a mobile lab of recently purchased netbooks, easy and widely available Internet access, and a technology support staff. The creation of the long-term technology committee also kept the use of technology near the forefront of the school's effort to improve its instructional delivery. By working on the committee and helping to establish standards for the school, the teacher promoted the use of participatory media in the classroom as a way of supporting social studies education in general and more specifically the development of public voice and a richer understanding of social justice.

SOLUTIONS AND RECOMMENDATIONS

Curricular Alignment

So as to address the lack of chronological alignment between the 8th grade U.S. history curriculum of the two states, the teacher and his colleague settled upon equality and its application today and in U.S. history as a common theme for their collaboration during year 3. More specifically, they plan to focus on African-Americans' quest for economic, political and social equality from the establishment of the U.S. Constitution to the civil rights movement. They anticipate that the Midwest students will become the experts on the pre-Civil War history related to this theme and that the urban students will become the experts on post-Civil War history. In turn, they intend to link what students are learning about the history of equality to contemporary issues, which are drawn both from the national level, such as the ongoing debate over immigration, and the local levels, such as the issues the urban students confront in their communities. From a curricular perspective they realize that their use of social media will serve as a means to an end since neither set of U.S. history standards integrates skills related to social media into the content.

Creation of Online Groups

Cultivating online groups, particularly between schools, is a long-term, ongoing process, though different from offline groups in several significant ways. First, given the social nature of groups and the fact that online groups interact via social media, the teacher and his colleague realize they first need to establish social groups before moving them into academic tasks. While this is necessary for offline groups, the lack of face-to-face interaction and the fact that the two sets of students are from decidedly different backgrounds requires the teachers to spend more time and to be more purposeful in socializing their students with each other. As they learned during year 2, the 8th graders' natural curiosity about each other aids in this socialization. Second, when forming groups either between classes or between schools, the teacher recognized the need to consider the makeup of each online group, as well as the offline groups. He and his colleague have planned to discuss their students with each other prior to creating the online groups. Finally, the teachers are planning ways not simply to build online groups, but to encourage their own students to consider their colleague's students as an audience or public.

Selection of Online Collaborative Tools

The teacher and his colleague have chosen the more complex, yet more versatile, option. During year 3 they plan to use the Ning platform (http://www.ning.com). Ning is a social networking site and therefore is more robust than a wiki. Since many of his students are familiar with social networking sites, the teacher hopes that students will not need any more time to familiarize themselves with use of a Ning than with a wiki. On the other hand, he realizes that they are more versatile with handhelds than computers so they will need direct instruction on using the computer to navigate the Ning. The Ning's additional tools, such as a blog, potentially will strengthen the students' collaborative effort and increase individual and group participation, as well as to better enable the teachers to differentiate instruction. With the wiki, students were able to write responses to one another back and forth, but had to wait a full day in order to utilize feedback from the other half of their group. Given the option of speaking in real time, the sheer volume of interactions should increase and, if the students have developed the appropriate skills, they should complete more work in less instructional time. Unlike with the wiki where they only could write and copy/paste material from other websites, the Ning will enable students to interact and present via several forms of media.

Academic/Civic Norms vs. Social Norms

The teacher came to realize that while he could depend upon Thomas & Brown's learn to do approach as students learn the use of new platforms, developing academic/civic norms still required starting with learn about. Since students habitually used participatory media, they already had internalized that media's social norms. The teacher lacked the instructional time—and the students the motivation—to learn about academic norms while engaged in online academic tasks. The teacher and his colleague realized that rather than simply reacting to students' reliance upon social norms, such as using text language when conversing with each other online, they needed to directly teach academic norms and expect students to act on them. In some respects, this simply entailed translating good offline pedagogy into an online environment. For example, during year 3 they plan to post guidelines for engaging in an online discussion and making clear what is expected of them as participants.

Supportive Infrastructure

His colleagues' and administrators' support was critical to the success of his and his students' online collaborative work. His first year experiences, for example, illustrated the importance of functioning hardware and easy, widespread Internet access. The administration's success at securing a grant to purchase several classroom sets of netbooks helped to make possible what the teacher and his colleague did during the second year. In turn, the development of school-wide policies on use of the networks also helped with classroom management. As he and his colleague move into their third year the support needs to shift from technology and management, to curriculum, instruction, and professional development. As the teacher began during his second year, this requires him to move out of his classroom into the larger school setting and to assist with helping to shape the future curricular and instructional direction of his school. In the end the teacher recognizes the importance of his students becoming prosumers, i.e. producers and consumers of participatory or social media, which he considers as a stepping stone to becoming active and responsible citizens in off and online settings. Achieving this though, requires a school-wide effort; one where student-centered learning supported by technology becomes part of the school culture.

CONCLUSION

The development of students' online public voices is an incremental process, one where students need to develop a skill using different forms of participatory or social media and learn how to engage in thoughtful, helpful, and enriching online discussions in ever larger group settings. For the teacher the process has proven painful, yet productive. Since models for how to do what the teacher strives to achieve are only beginning to emerge, he is seeking to learn from his trial and error solutions on how to foster student voice on matters of social justice via online collaborative tools. Since "21st century, participatory media education and civic education are inextricable" (Rheingold, 2008, p. 103), then developing such models is itself a matter of social justice if he hopes for his urban students to develop into 21st century citizens. For the teacher and his colleague, as they explore how to merge participatory media with local and state curricular content and relevant contemporary social issues, such an instructional and curricular model slowly is evolving, a prospect fraught with payoffs, perils, and possibilities.

REFERENCES

Anderson, J., & Rainie, L. (2008). *The future of the Internet III*. Washington, DC: Pew Internet & American Life Project.

Befiore, P., Auld, R., & Lee, D. (2005). The disconnect of poor-urban education: Equal access and a pedagogy of risk taking. *Psychology in the Schools*, *42*(8), 855–863. doi:10.1002/pits.20116

Berson, M. J., Lee, J. K., & Stuckart, D. W. (2001). Promise and practice of computer technologies in the social studies: A critical analysis. In Stanley, W. (Ed.), *Critical issues in social studies research for the 21st century* (pp. 209–229). Greenwich, CT: Information Age Publishing.

Bull, G., Thompson, A., Searson, M., Garofalo, J., Park, J., Young, C., & Lee, J. (2008). Connecting informal and formal learning: Experiences in the age of participatory media. *Contemporary Issues in Technology & Teacher Education*, *8*(2). Retrieved from http://www.citejournal.org/vol8/iss2/editorial/article1.cfm.

Center for Educational Policy. (2008). *Instructional time in elementary schools: A closer look at changes for specific subjects*. Retrieved February 19, 2008, from http://www.cep-dc.org

Ito, M., Horst, H., & Bittanti, M. boyd, d., Herr-Stephenson, B., Lange, P., … Robinson, L. (2008). *Living and learning with new media: Summary of findings from the Digital Youth Project*. Chicago, IL: The John D. and Catherine T. MacArthur Foundation.

Lankes, R. D. (2008). Trusting the Internet: New approaches to credibility tools. In Metzger, M. J., & Flanagin, A. J. (Eds.), *Digital media, youth, and credibility* (pp. 101–122). Cambridge, MA: The John D. and Catherine T. MacArthur Foundation Series on Digital Media and Learning.

Lenhart, A., Ling, R., Campbell, S., & Purcell, K. (2010). *Teens and mobile phones*. Washington, DC: Pew Internet & American Life Project.

Levine, P. (2008). A public voice for youth: The audience problem in digital media and civic education. In Bennett, W. L. (Ed.), *Civic life online: Learning how digital media can engage youth* (pp. 119–138). Cambridge, MA: The MIT Press.

Rheingold, H. (2008). Using participatory media and public voice to encourage civic engagement. In Bennett, W. L. (Ed.), *Civic life online: Learning how digital media can engage youth* (pp. 97–118). Cambridge, MA: The MIT Press.

Shuler, C. (2007). *D is for digital: An analysis of the children's interactive media environment with a focus on mass marketed products that promote learning*. Retrieved June 14, 2010, from http://www.joanganzcooneycenter.org/pdf/DisforDigital.pdf

Shulman, L. (1987). Knowledge and teaching: Foundations of a new reform. *Harvard Educational Review, 57*(1), 1–22.

The University of the State of New York. (1996). *Learning standards for social studies*. Albany, NY: New York State Department of Education.

The University of the State of New York. (1999). *Social studies resource guide with core curriculum*. Albany, NY: New York State Department of Education.

Thomas, D., & Brown, J. (2009). Why virtual worlds can matter. *International Journal of Learning and Media, 1*(1), 37–49. doi:10.1162/ijlm.2009.0008

vanDijck, J. (2009). Users like you? Theorizing agency in user-generated content. *Media Culture & Society, 31*(1), 41–58. doi:10.1177/0163443708098245

VanFossen, P. J. (2005). Reading and math take so much of the time.. .: An overview of social studies instruction in elementary classrooms in Indiana. *Theory and Research in Social Education, 33*(3), 376–403.

Vogler, K. E., Lintner, T., Lipscomb, G. B., Knopf, H., Heafner, T. L., & Rock, T. C. (2007). Getting off the back burner: Impact of testing elementary social studies as part of a state-mandated accountability program. *Journal of Social Studies Research, 31*(2), 20–34.

Chapter 24

Digitally Capturing Student Thinking for Self–Assessment:
Mathcasts as a Window on Student Thinking during Mathematical Problem Solving

Sheri Vasinda
Texas A&M University-Commerce, USA

Julie McLeod
University of North Texas, USA

EXECUTIVE SUMMARY

The continuing improvements and access to digital technology provide opportunities for capturing student thinking never considered or available in the past. Knowing the importance of thinking processes and understanding children's resistance to writing them down, mathcasts were used as a way of supporting students during their problem solving. Mathcasts are screencaptures of students' work and thinking as they write and talk about their thinking during mathematical problem solving. Viewers of the mathcast gain unique insight into the students' problem solving process, thinking process, and mathematical conceptions or misconceptions. The authors found screencasts to be a good technological match with mathematical problem solving that provided a more powerful opportunity for both self-assessment and teacher assessment that was not available with traditional paper and pencil

DOI: 10.4018/978-1-61350-492-5.ch024

reflection. When students can revisit their verbal thinking several times throughout the year, they are equipped to self-assess in new, powerful and more reflective ways.

BACKGROUND INFORMATION

Powerful Technology and Strategy Matching

While exploring the possibilities and influences that technology has on education, our work has involved matching traditionally strong, evidence-based teaching or learning strategies with a complementary technology application and examining the possibilities these pairings afford. We have followed Kozma's (1991) lead by selecting technology that is uniquely suited to the learning project at hand while maintaining the integrity of the original learning strategy. While exploring portfolio learning paired with podcasted reflections and digital scans of learning artifacts (McLeod and Vasinda, 2009), Language Experience Approach with wiki's and blogs (Vasinda, McLeod & Morrison, 2007), and Readers Theater paired with podcasting (Vasinda & McLeod, in press), we have discovered that the multidimensional nature of these technological pairings have afforded new opportunities for learning by both teachers, students, parents and other stakeholders. In this case we will describe our latest pairing: screencasting with UPS-Check, a four-step mathematical problem solving process. We refer to this new paring as "mathcasts" an idea first used by Tim Fahlberg (Fahlberg, Fahlberg-Stojanovska, & MacNeil, 2006; Fahlberg-Stojanovska, Fahlberg, & King, 2008). (To view mathcasts, navigate to http://math247.pbwiki. com/). When considering a powerful technology and assessment strategy match, our first consideration is maintaining the integrity of the learning strategy while also creating something that was not there without the technology. In other words, we believe it is important to maintain the elements of any strategy that have proven effective through research and practice, whether a literacy strategy, problem solving strategies or those involving students in self-assessment. Then, we look for technology affordances that highlight the strategy strengths while adding a dimension that was not possible without the technology so that the combination creates positive changes in the learning environment that were not possible without this pairing (McLeod & Vasinda, 2009b).

Setting the Stage

The problem for this case was students' resistance to showing their thinking, or work, for math word problems. One of the ways to assess problem-solving is through analyzing students' written response to the word problem. Even when students do show all of their work, it is an incomplete or limited window into their thinking. Often the teacher still has to ask, "What were your thoughts here?" in order to better understand the thought process that went into the problem and solution. The learning strategy for this project is the problem solving process known as UPS-Check, or Understand, Plan, Solve, and Check (Polya, 1957, 2004). The technology match is screencasting. The element that was not possible without the technology in this match was the ability for students to self-assess their problem solving.Screencasts do not prescribe a single technology. Indeed, there are many ways to digitally capture students thinking and writing. In our situation after many trials and errors, these math problem solving screencasts were most easily facilitated through the Livescribe Pulse Pen. Because of the mathematical context of these screencasts, we use the idea and term, mathcasts, first coined by Tim Fahlberg ((Fahlberg, Fahlberg-Stojanovska, & MacNeil, 2006; Fahlberg-Stojanovska, Fahlberg, & King, 2008). Working like a traditional pen, the Pulse Pen records student written work on specially designed paper and any words the students says on a built in voice recorder. The problem solving can then be uploaded to a computer and played back like a movie rather than just a still shot of the finished product. As they finish their work, students can also listen to their thinking immediately using the playback features on the special paper. When the pen is docked to the computer, the mathcast can be uploaded to a website. It has proven to be easy and natural for students. This digital capture of student thinking provides additional ways not only for the teacher to assess a student's thought process, but for student self-assessment as well, thus bringing a new dimension to assessment.

Assessment's Transformation

The role of assessment is undergoing a transformation as we move from myopic 20th century political views of measuring outcomes for sorting, tracking, including and excluding to a view of assessment as part of the the learning process. Since the middle of the 1980s and into the first decade of the 21st century, assessment that commands the attention of schools and parents has been relegated by state and national policy to a one-dimensional end-of-year multiple choice test measuring outcomes with high stakes accountability including grade placement or graduation. This one-dimensional view of assessment omits the potential instructional and learning benefits of assessment and the learner's process of becoming a self-assessor. Although assessment has been identified as a crucial part of the learning process in teaching and learning cycles (Davies, 2007, Guskey, 2007; Pollock, 2007), this type of assessment has been overshadowed by standardized assessment during the last century. Removing assessment from the learning process takes it out of its intended context. As with most things taken out of context, assessment removed from the learning process has limited value. Stiggins' (2005) defines assessment as "the process of gathering evidence of student learning to inform instructional decisions." With ongoing and sometimes competing concerns of performing well on standardized testing as well as knowing that the results often are not used to inform teaching, many educators seek more formative assessments that help both the teacher and the student "gather evidence of student learning." When assessment is varied and used holistically, it is a powerful tool for teachers and students to successfully navigate the learning process (Pollock, 2007; Stiggins, 2005). Formative assessments, or assessments for learning, give students and teachers a window into the thinking during the learning process rather than relying solely on summative assessments or evaluations at the end of an instructional unit which can leave all stakeholders frustrated when results are disappointing (Davies, 2007). Davies advocates a three-part process to utilize assessment for learning. First, teachers must analyze the curriculum objectives and standards to develop and describe their own understanding of what students are to learn. This may include reviewing work samples to determine what evidence of understanding looks like at the particular grade level. Second, teachers must bring students into the assessment process through discussing the learning, reviewing samples of what the evidence of the learning looks like, co-creating criterion for learning, and how evidence of learning might be collected. This process includes opportunities for self-assessment, peer assessment, goal setting and self-collecting their own evidence of learning. Finally, the teacher must also provide time, opportunities, and structures for student-sharing of work and thinking, to others to gather feedback. This process is a continuous cycle of clarifying learning targets, setting and resetting goals, co-creating criterion, collecting evidence, and getting feedback that partners teachers and students in assessment for learning. Involving students in the process of their own assessment supports them in examining their own thinking and creates a shared vision of expectations. Indeed even the simple act of sharing the learning target with students is a step toward sharing both wisdom and power (Stiggins, 2005), equipping students to be active agents of their own learning. When students understand the learning objectives and their own thinking and learning processes, they are in a better position to be successful learners and help each other assess. Creating this deeper understanding offers more and more opportunities for assessment during the process of learning. Creating structures for this to happen also ensures that students have the time and opportunity to use work samples to practice the assessment. Using Davies (2007) process of involving students in assessment and pairing screencasting with math problem solving, we found another opportunity to make a purposeful match of a proven, research based strategy with complementary technology tools (Vasinda & McLeod, 2008, McLeod & Vasinda, 2009, Vasinda & McLeod, in press). In this case we investigate pairing a widely used four step math problem solving strategy, UPS-Check, with screencasts, or mathcasts, as we refer to them herein. Our continued goal is to maintain the powerful aspects of the traditional strategy that existed prior to the technology introduction while also creating something not possible without the technology. With this case, self-assessment was the new element that was not there without the technology. Ultimately we believe the combination to be more powerful than either part alone. As with other cases we have explored, we found that students naturally self-assess when technology provides unique opportunities to revisit their work repeatedly.

THE CASE

The Context

The setting for this case is a Title I elementary campus in a North Texas metropolitan area where 60% of children receive free or reduced lunch. This campus serves the district bilingual students from pre-kindergarten to grade two as well as the district Head Start program. The thirty-seven year old elementary campus has had several renovations over the years, including wireless hubs installed in some areas of the school during the 2008-2009, and school-wide in 2010. Philosophically, this campus has made a commitment to focusing on formative assessment practices to develop a clear vision of instructional targets. The faculty and principal have studied and implemented the use of Common Formative Assessments (Ainsworth, 2007; DuFour, DuFour, & Eaker, 2008) and some are utilizing assessments that are co-created with their students (Davies, 2007). This project began in Julie McLeod's (coauthor) sixth grade math class where her intentions included a classroom for the twenty-first century that incorporated technology as a set of integrated tools that are part of the regular rhythms of the classroom rather than a once a week trip to the computer lab, as well as equipping students to become involved in the direction and assessment of their learning. The sixty sixth grade students are departmentalized into three blocks, a language arts block, a science and social studies block, and a math block. Julie works with three sections, or blocks, of math students each day: one advanced and two heterogeneously mixed with on-level and struggling students. Mathcasts are just one project in this classroom.

Students Resist a Powerful Problem Solving Strategy

In this sixth grade mathematics classroom, as typical in mathematics classrooms across the nation, students are asked to solve word, or story, problems using the mathematics concepts under study. Teachers ask students to document their thinking in writing using the "show your work" mantra. By doing so, teachers gain access to students problem solving process that allows for targeted instructional adjustments when students do not understand or have misconceptions. Students in this case have used a process titled UPS-check for problem solving (Polya, 1957, 2004), which provides a structure for novices to slowly adopt the thinking process of experts. Students as early as Kindergarten are introduced to this process of Understanding the problem, Planning how to solve, Solving and Checking the solution. By sixth grade, students are frustrated by the UPS-Check process because they consider the work required from the process to be out of proportion compared with the benefit of the disciplined thinking. In a reflective interview early in the school year, one student noted that the UPS-Check process was "too much writing." Another student felt that the process "slowed me down too much." One student even believed the process was "invented so teachers could torture students!" While experts certainly understand the benefits of this thinking process, novices must come to their own conclusion about it before it will be assimilated into their own thinking and working process.

Getting Started

Julie had seen Tim Fahlberg's work on mathcasts and knew the potential was great for this technology to aid in problem solving. After many attempts to find the best combination of tools for our district and our students, she found the LiveScribe Pulse Pen. The pens were rather expensive so she wrote a local grant to obtain a set for use the following year. While originally thinking this tool would aid in successful problem solving processes, during the 2008-2009 school year, she began to see the power of this process as an assessment tool. As she observed students listening to themselves, she noticed they self-assessed informally on their own. To take advantage of this natural occurrence of self-assessment and to strengthen it, she knew she and the students would need to co-create learning target criteria. During the 2009-2010 school year, the Criteria for Strong Mathematical Thinking was co-created with students using the four-step process for setting and using criterion (Gregory, Cameron, & Davies, 1997; Davies, 2007). To begin this process to co-create the Criteria for Strong Mathematical Thinking, students watched and listened to several mathcasts from previous years' students. They brainstormed the aspects of the mathcast that were strong thinking and the aspects that could have been stronger. This brainstorming led to a list of criteria that are important for both strong communication of the mathematical thinking, as well as the mathematical thinking itself. The students then analyzed the list and grouped similar aspects together. Julie synthesized the lists from all three math blocks and noticed that the categories were well aligned with state problem solving standards with one difference. The Criteria for Strong Mathematical Thinking is included as Table 1.

Table 1. Student co-created criteria for strong mathematical thinking

Communicating Mathematically	
Written Communication	Verbal Communication
Showing work, Showing work, Documenting what he knows–showing work	Clear voice, Voice–clear and energetic, Clear voice, High energy
Neat	Ways to keep yourself on track (noises)
Organized work	Knew what he was saying, he didn't stutter
Labeling the work, Used a key – tool he built	Not nervous when messing up
Documenting important information	Keeping the viewers interested
Not just talking, not just writing – doing both	Not just talking, not just writing – doing both
	Described with his words what was going on in the problem, Explained in his own words what the question was about

Thinking Mathematically		
Using Strategies	Persistence	Justifying Thinking
Connecting to content/classwork (objective) – organization of knowledge, Connecting to content/classwork (objective) – organization of knowledge, Connection to content/classwork (objective) – organization of knowledge	Knowing what you are saying – finding your own mistakes and fixing them	Not just picking a letter – justifying your answer
Using mathematical strategy, Problem solving strategies, Identify your strategy ahead of time, Identifying the best way to solve a problem	Sticking with the question – persistence, Don't stop even if you mess up, He figured out what he needed to do and then he was able to do it	Checking your work, Checked his work
UPS-check, Used pieces of UPS-check		Step by step, He knew where to begin, Identifying when you are done
		Thinking, "push the save button"
		Thorough
		Pause to think
		Remembering what he learned from all the units, Used background knowledge - schema
		Chose one option to solve the problem instead of doing all the options
Key:Block 1	Block 2	Block 3

Criteria for Strong Mathematical Thinking

The difference in the student created Criteria for Strong Mathematical Thinking and communication was that the students identified persistence as one of their criteria and the state standards do not address persistence. During class the next day, Julie and the students reviewed the synthesis of all the blocks criteria and discussed the alignment with the state standards. They also discussed the persistence aspect that they identified but the state had omitted. Interestingly, persistence in solving difficult problems is an important consideration for asking students to continue learning higher math even when they may not directly use the content (Souviney, 1994, 2005). The national standards written by the National Council of Teachers of Mathematics also omit persistence in their problem solving strategies (NCTM, nd). The classes decided that a very important aspect of problem solving had not been addressed by state and national mathematical experts. Through their comparison of their own findings with state and national standards, the students felt powerfully equipped to evaluate their own thinking, but the problem still remained that novices struggle to solve a problem and evaluate their own thinking in the midst of that same problem solving.

The Process

Students were partnered with a peer, taking turns solving a word problem, while writing and explaining their thinking and work to their partner. Each pair used a Pulse Pen with its special notebook, two math problems, an interview protocol, or script, and their Criteria for Strong Mathematical Thinking that we had co-created. Because of our previous successful experience with interview protocols within student digital portfolios, Julie created a similar interview script (McLeod & Vasinda, 2009). The interviewing peer used the interview protocol to support the problem solving peer with probing questions designed to scaffold the problem solver through the UPS-Check process. By having students talk out their thinking and digitally record that talk instead of writing it, an opportunity exists for more dialogue during the problem solving as well as afterward. Further, talking is a natural way for students to think (Vygotsky, 1978) and work out problems (McLeod & Vasinda, 2009). The interview protocol is included in Table 2.

The student partnerships found a place around the room for their problem solving documentation and assessment to begin. The students each selected one of the problems to solve and also decided which one of them would be the first problem solver. The other partner interviewed the student using the protocol and was also responsible for assisting the problem solver if necessary. The math instructional specialist for the school happened to come to the room as the students were recording their first mathcast. She noted that the students "were completely engaged" in

Table 2. Mathcast interview script

Mathcast Interview Script
Today is _____ and I am interviewing _____ as he/she solves a math problem.
1. Can you please tell us what this problem is about?
2. What do you think you will do to solve it?
3. Do you think you are ready to solve the problem now?
4. How do you know you solved it correctly?

what they were doing. Even though pairs of students were scattered throughout the small room and into the hallway, each pair was "on task and doing some great thinking." These were strong statements, particularly for the context of the classroom in which she entered. This particular class was one that struggled to be wholly on task in any activity, no matter how engaging. Throughout the years in this school, the math instructional specialist had watched these same students at earlier grade levels continue to struggle to persist and dig deeper into their work and thinking. She was impressed with the commitment to the work she observed during this unplanned visit to the class.Students problem solved and then spent time listening right away to their recording. They listened with a critical ear, sometimes worrying about "sounding funny" and sometimes worrying about whether their answers were "right." They asked others to listen to their recording and they asked Julie to listen. In fact, they spent so much time listening again and again to their recording that in most pairs, the second partner did not have time to record their turn at problem solving. Plans for the next day were revised to allow for the second round of interviews and recordings to take place. The next school day students returned to their partnership and completed the process, ensuring that all students were able to adopt the role of problem solver and interviewer. After all students had completed their first mathcast, we explored their experiences using a reflective interview. Because of time constraints, students were simply asked what they thought went well during their mathcast and what could have been better.

Findings from This Case

The first theme that emerged from the reflective interview was that the students found their own power to self-assess. Indeed, it was a natural process for these students to identify their mistakes. One student noted that the mathcast allowed him to "identify your mistakes when you listened to yourself." Because students were eager to listen to themselves and repeated the listening several times, there were many opportunities for students to identify and refine their thinking. Some students even listened to their mathcast and then re-recorded it to correct their thinking. This self-assessment brings transparency to the learning process. One student noted that "when you get feedback [by listening to the mathcast], you can see what's wrong." This student realized that she did not have to wait for the teacher or a more capable peer. She was fully capable of assessing her own thinking, and merely needed a means to record her thinking. Recording and listening to their thinking, removed the mystery and the apparent randomness that can surround assessment, making assessment an integral part of the learning process. The second theme that emerged from the interview was that students recognized the importance of using a process such as UPS-check to support their problem-solving thinking. While just a few months before, students had expressed their disdain for the process, mathcasts enabled students to find value in the process. As we studied the interview transcript, we noted that at least one student appreciated every step of the UPS-check process. During the Understand-the-problem step, students are typically asked to write phrases or sentences in their own words to describe the problem in the question. At the beginning of the year, many students noted that UPS-check was too much writing. However after the mathcasts, one student noted that he liked "putting [author's note: putting means writing down] the important things before solving the question." During the Plan step, students are asked to identify the strategy or process that they will use to solve the problem. After mathcasts, a student said that "thinking of the strategy" before solving really worked well for her. During the Solve step, students are asked to document all of their work to solve the problem. While students at the beginning of the year noted that they disliked this part of the process, after mathcasts, students noted that they "liked showing the work." Finally, the Check step asks students to check their calculations. This step is actually designed as a self-assessment step, but students view this check step similarly to editing a paper. They believe that they have already completed the work and that this step is making them repeat their work for no reason. As with editing for clarifying the writer's message, they have not found value in this self-assessment step. After the mathcasts, students realized the value of this self-assessment step as noted in the previous theme. Additionally, one student said that she "liked showing how we know the answer is correct." Overall, the UPS-check process is simply a scaffold to support novices as they learn to solve complex and difficult problems. However, students have resisted the scaffold, deeming it unnecessary and intrusive. Once students were placed in a position to self-assess via mathcasts, they began to see value in the scaffold. The final theme that emerged was that students appreciated the scaffold of the interview protocol. A partner was not just viewed as a social venue. Students relied on each other and on the protocol that their partner was using to help them. They also valued the mathematical coaching that came from their partner. Interviewing partners were not to give answers, but were to use questioning to help guide the problem solver through the question. Students noted that the "question part of the interview made you say more about the problem." They also noted that the interview questions "made" them recheck their work, which is "how I knew I did it wrong." This appreciation for an interview protocol mirrors our previous experiences with using protocols as scaffolds with children when creating digital portfolios, another form of assessment (McLeod & Vasinda, 2008).Overall, mathcasts offered students a unique opportunity to self-assess their problem solving thinking that was not available before this technology. After self-assessing, students noted their appreciation for scaffolds such as the UPS-check thinking process and the interview protocol used by their partner.

UNPACKING THE CASE STUDY

Making Thinking Visible

When students show their work, they are making their thinking visible. They become consciously aware of the problem-solving strategy they use and they learn to communicate mathematically. Yet thinking is a process and processes are not captured as well on a static medium such as paper. Technology can be utilized to more fully and authentically capture processes. For example, time-compression video more dramatically illustrates the life cycle of a plant than three sequenced photographs of a seedling, a partially mature plant and a full grown plant. The three photographs capture moments in time of the process, but they do not capture the entire process nor do they expose the students to the complexities, intricacies and nuances that can be a part of many natural processes (McLeod & Vasinda, 2009). Similarly, the thinking and problem solving processes can be better documented and assessed if we can capture not just students' written documentation, but also the evolution of those writings and the thinking that is occurring while writing. Thus, in this match of the UPS-Check problem solving process and digital capture, students' screencasts of their problem solving while working a problem offers insight into student thinking and processes that were not available without this technology. With mathcasts, students can watch their problem solving actions and revisit their thoughts through listening to their narration of their process. The audio recording aspect of the Pulse Pen affords learners the opportunity to go back and revisit their thinking through their spoken words. The video record aspect allows learners to see visual records of their thoughts in a real time sequence. Because this technology integrates both written and auditory work and can be posted to a website, it is ideal to authentically integrate technology in math problem solving, widen the audience for the students' demonstration of knowledge and maintain the integrity of the UPS-Check problem solving process. It offers the further benefit of providing a venue for student involvement in self-assessing. Further, integrating this technology into students' mathematical problem solving introduces and extends the concepts of new literacies, such as screencasting, that can be developed and learned through the use of technology. The capture of this process through video allows both the teacher and the student to revisit this thinking together and separately without having to be physically present with each other. This provides additional opportunities for assessment to determine mastery of content, for determining the instructional adjustments or modifications that should be made and to provide another communication tool between home and school. But just capturing the thinking does not equate to assessment. By providing opportunities for students to revisit, review and reflect on their problem solving process, they began to self-assess the way they approached the UPS-Check problem solving process and began to see its value as a process to improve their ability to solve problems rather than an invention of "teacher torture". It also removes the mystery of success providing them with a better understanding of how to achieve the learning targets to which they are held accountable (Stiggens, 2005). Mathcasts become an important tool for students' self-assessment because of the dynamic nature of problem solving that cannot be captured on a static media. When students are solving problems, important thinking occurs whether it is written down for later evaluation or not. Further, the structure of the thinking or the order in which students solve a problem can offer significant insights. This information is not always captured with the written work left after problem solving. However, when thoughts, words and writing are all captured dynamically and can be played back like a movie, all of these aspects are available for inspection and evaluation–repeatedly if desired.

Scaffolds

Partnering with another child to support not only the capture of thinking, but also to support the problem-solving process, makes this assessment process a learning process as well. By completing peer interviews, students can progress, over time, through the Vygotsky's Zone of Proximal Development from the sensitive stage of needing mediation from a more capable peer or the teacher so that concept development is within reach of that student. Using students' verbal thought, or talk, gives us a window into their inner thoughts, or as Vygotsky (1986) posits, "Thought development as determined by language." Verbal thought becomes a mediation tool and a formative assessment that is accessed through the digital capture. Scaffolds can be a powerful tool for novices as they explore new learning worlds. However, unwelcome scaffolds make learners feel as if the expert or teacher believes the student is not capable as a learner. Thus, learners must come to perceive the value for scaffolds on their own. For example, when the UPS-Check strategy has been a requirement for problem solving from as early as Kindergarten, without an experience (Dewey, 1997) illuminating its value as a scaffold, children view it as "teacher torture" rather than a tool to use when problem-solving is difficult; when they are "stuck." The effectiveness of any scaffold is that students know the scaffold is available and how to use it, and also that they understand the situations in which that scaffold would be useful to each individually. This discernment process can be difficult, especially when students do not have the benefit of self-assessing their own thinking process. Thus, this purposeful match of technology to problem solving has created an important opportunity that was not available without the technology.

CHALLENGES

Time

While we deemed this work worthwhile, it did have some challenges. Certainly, the most important challenge to consider is time. It is a scarce resource that must be protected and purposefully allocated. Using direct instruction for problem solving certainly uses much less time. However, the results from our students indicate that time spent in direct instruction is often squandered when they do not see any value in the content or process being taught. As noted, many students who have had years of direct instruction in problem solving see little value in the process. Of course, children who understand and enjoy the problem solving process will willingly engage in it and there are a few who will learn school's lessons without questioning the value. But it is more common for children in today's world to be searching for the value and relevancy before putting forth the effort to learn. Thus, while we certainly spent more time on problem solving with this process, students overwhelmingly found value and thus decided to put forth the effort to not just learn the process but to appreciate and assimilate it. We also argue that the time spent repeating and repeating the direct instruction of problem solving processes, may equate to the same amount of time as allowing children to come to their own realization of its value.

Logistics

Another challenge was the logistics of the process. When small groups were creating mathcasts, the process to upload the mathcast and listen to the students' thinking seemed much less overwhelming to the teacher who is stretched for time. However when all students had access to the technology and were creating mathcasts on the same day, the process of uploading the mathcasts seemed too vast. The district had not yet approved the LiveScribe software for their servers, so Julie was taking the pens home to upload all the mathcasts. Even with just sixty students, this process was daunting. In the future, we are planning to use district computers to upload the mathcasts, making it a project for students rather than the teacher. Another suggestion is to use any teaching assistants that might be available in the school to upload the mathcasts. The teacher is then freed to actually listen to the students' thinking and bring out exceptional examples for students to evaluate during class, thus deepening students' learning for the next mathcast.

Other Challenges

Other challenges might exist that we did not experience. For example, funding the technology to create mathcasts might be an issue for some teachers. Another issue could be that some administrators might not support this type of work in the classroom. Likely, the most important challenge to overcome to introduce this type of work is to have a stance that children are strong and capable learners with the ability to self-assess at least as well as the teacher. Most American educators underestimate children's capabilities to represent their thinking and the quality of their intellectual capabilities (Katz, 1998). We have found that children often are more critical of themselves when allowed to self-assess (McLeod & Vasinda, 2009b). Schlechty (2002) believes that students should be viewed as a volunteer in the classroom, even when their attendance is compulsory. In other words, students truly decide whether or not they will "volunteer" their attention and engage in the work to learn the school's lessons. Their physical presence in the classroom does not guarantee that learning will occur. This is not a stance of empowering children, although that is certainly a step in the direction of viewing children as strong and capable learners. Indeed, the term empowering means to give away power when in reality the children have the power to learn all along (McLeod, Lin & Vasinda, in press). Instead, our stance is that we equip learners with the tools and techniques they need to learn. Properly equipped, we believe children will far surpass our expectations (Vasinda, 2004). Attempting this technology match trying to gain the benefits of student self-assessment without this stance will likely be fruitless.

SOLUTIONS AND RECOMMENDATIONS

Looking for More Powerful Matches

As in past projects, we look for opportunities to match proven traditional strategies or work with a technology component that creates new opportunities for enhanced learning and thinking (McLeod & Vasinda, 2009; Vasinda & McLeod, in press). The UPS-Check problem solving process continues to be a strong problem solving strategy that has proven itself over time (Polya, 1957, 2004), but students resist its use and do not see its value as a supporting structure. In our work, we look for good solid strategies and match them with an appropriate technology to maximize and enhance the results. We know the power of UPS-Check before the technology match, but technology provided a new dynamic dimension that was not present before. As new technological applications become available, we welcome the opportunity for more powerful matching.

Recognizing Children's Power

The most difficult challenge comes without an easy solution. Technology has certainly changed our world (Friedman, 2006) and using technology in the classroom has changed many of the power dynamics present there (McLeod, Lin & Vasinda, in press). At the heart of the impact of this case is the authors' stance or viewpoint that children are strong and capable learners. Viewing children as strong and capable learners, we recognize the power they hold in the learning environment and we use technology to help them demonstrate and enhance their power. Without this stance we believe the students' work would have been relegated to "activities" designed by well-meaning teachers that fill children's school days but do little to help them recognize their full potential. Our stance is not teachable, but is a part of our philosophical views about teaching, learning, and children. While we believe that we cannot teach or force anyone to adopt our stance, we have some recommendations for particular groups of educational stakeholders. Teachers must explore their own philosophical stance, be able to support it with educational theory and research and be able to demonstrate with specific examples how they are living that philosophy. School administrators should examine teachers' educational philosophies, particularly prior to hiring or funding technological innovations. Researchers should move beyond the discussion of achievement, an observable outcome, but one that is riddled with subjective judgements about learners and their abilities. Instead, researchers could explore higher level constructs such as power, motivation, and curiosity that give students desire and purpose in their learning. Indeed, when students have that desire and purpose, we have found that they exceed experts' standards (Vasinda, 2004).

CONCLUSION

Overall, mathcasts offered students a unique opportunity to self-assess their problem-solving thinking that was not available before this technology. The process of co-creating the criteria allows students to better understand the criteria used to evaluate work. Sharing the learning target and co-creating criteria creates a collegial and more cooperative classroom environment where students share ownership of both the process and the outcome. The technology aspect offered greater opportunity for self-assessment, uncovering potential that children already have by equipping them with tools to become more purposeful learners. After self-assessing, students noted their appreciation for scaffolds such as the UPS-check thinking process and the interview protocol used by their partner. As teacher researchers we continue to find technology to be a medium that not only enhances learning strategies when carefully and appropriately matched, but also as a medium for uncovering the potential and power that children inherently possess. Teachers who believe that children are capable of directing their own learning and understanding are in the best position to take advantage of the opportunities these powerful matches afford.

REFERENCES

Davies, A. (2007). *Making classroom assessment work*. Courtenay, Canada: Connections Publishing, Inc.

Dewey, J. (1997). *How we think*. Mineola, NY: Dover.

DuFour, R., DuFour, R., & Eaker, R. (2008). *Revisiting professional learning communities at work: New insights for improving schools*. Bloomington, IN: Solution Tree.

Fahlberg, T., Fahlberg-Stojanovska, L., & MacNeil, G. (2006). Whiteboard math movies. *Teaching Mathematics Applications*, *26*(1), 17–22. doi:10.1093/teamat/hrl012

Fahlberg-Stojanovska, L., Fahlberg, T., & King, C. (2008). Mathcasts: Show-and-tell math concepts. *Learning and Leading with Technology*, *36*(1), 30–31.

Friedman, T. (2006). *The world is flat: A brief history of the twenty-first century* [Updated and expanded]. New York, NY: Farrar, Straus and Giroux.

Gregory, K., Cameron, C., & Davies, A. (1997). *Knowing what counts: Setting and using criterion*. Courtenay, Canada: Connections Publishing, Inc.

Gusky, T. R. (2007). Using assessment to improve teaching and learning. In Reeves, D. (Ed.), *Ahead of the curve*. Bloomington, IN: Solution Tree.

Katz, L. (1998). What can we learn from Reggio Emilia? In Edwards, C., Gandini, L., & Forman, G. (Eds.), *The hundred languages of children: The Reggio Emilia Approach- advanced reflections* (2nd ed.). Norword, NJ: Ablex.

McLeod, J., Lin, L., & Vasinda, S. (in press). Children's power for learning in the age of technology. In Blake, S., Winsor, D., & Allen, L. (Eds.), *Technology and young children: Bridging the communication-generation gap*. Hershey, PA: IGI Global. doi:10.4018/978-1-61350-059-0.ch003

McLeod, J., & Vasinda, S. (2008). Electronic portfolios: Perspectives of students, teachers and parents. *Education and Information Technologies, 14*, 29–38. doi:10.1007/s10639-008-9077-5

McLeod, J., & Vasinda, S. (2009a). Web 2.0 affordances for literacys: Using technology as pedagogically strong scaffolds for learning. In Kidd, T. T., & Chen, I. (Eds.), *Wired for learning*. Charlotte, NC: Information Age Publishing.

McLeod, J., & Vasinda, S. (2009b). Electronic portfolios: Perspective of students, teachers and parents. *Education and Information Technologies, 14*(1). doi:10.1007/s10639-008-9077-5

National Council of Teachers of Mathematics. (n.d.). *Appendix: Table of standards - Process standards*. Retrieved August 1, 2010, from http://standards.nctm.org/document/appendix/process.htm

Pollock, J. E. (2007). *Improving student learning one teacher at a time*. Alexandria, VA: Association for Supervision and Curriculum Development.

Polya, G. (1957). *How to solve it*. Princeton, NJ: Princeton University Press.

Polya, G. (2004). *How to solve it: A new aspect of mathematical method*. Princeton, NJ: Princeton University Press.

Souviney, R. J. (1994). *Learning to teach mathematics*. Columbus, OH: Merrill Publishing Company.

Souviney, R. J. (2005). *Solving math problems kids care about*. Tucson, AZ: Good Year Books.

Stiggins, R. (2005). *Student-involved assessment FOR learning* (4th ed.). Upper Saddle River, NJ: Pearson.

Vasinda, S. (2004). *Reinventing Reggio through negotiated learning: Finding a place for voice and choice in an American standards-based elementary classroom*. Unpublished doctoral dissertation. Texas A&M University-Commerce.

Vasinda, S., & McLeod, J. (2011). Extending readers theater: A powerful and purposeful match with podcasting. *The Reading Teacher, 64*(7). doi:10.1598/RT.64.7.2

Vasinda, S., McLeod, J., & Morrison, J. (2007). 1+1=3: Combining language experience approach with Web 2.0 tools. *LEA SIG (of the International Reading Association). Newsletter, 38*(1), 6–10.

Vygotsky, L. (1986). *Thought and language*. Cambridge, MA: MIT Press.

Chapter 25
Educational Technology in a Novice Science Teacher's Classroom

Selcen Guzey
University of Minnesota, USA

Gillian Roehrig
University of Minnesota, USA

EXECUTIVE SUMMARY

Why do some science teachers successfully integrate technology into their teaching while others fail? To address this question, educational researchers have conducted a growing body of research focused on technology integration into classrooms. Researchers are studying everything from teachers' philosophical approaches to teaching that influence efforts at technology integration to classroom-level barriers that impact technology integration. Findings indicate that while some teachers fail in utilizing technology due to the personal and classroom barriers they experience, others eagerly work to overcome the barriers and achieve technology integration. In this case, Mr. Bransford, a novice science teacher who has incorporated technology into his classroom practices within his first five years of teaching, is discussed. Mr. Bransford teaches 8th grade Earth Science using a range of educational technology tools. The barriers he has faced, his strategies to overcome those barriers, and his technology enriched classroom practices are presented.

DOI: 10.4018/978-1-61350-492-5.ch025

BACKGROUND INFORMATION

Teaching science with technology has been widely addressed in many recent educational reforms (e.g., NRC, 1996). It has been documented that when used appropriately educational technology tools improve students' content knowledge (Lei & Zhao, 2007) and scientific inquiry skills as they collect and analyze data to answer scientifically oriented questions and share their findings with others (Hug, Krajcik, & Marx, 2005). Furthermore, the use of learning technologies in science classrooms also enhances students' attention, engagement, and interest in science (Van Lehn, Graesser, Jackson, Jordan, Olney, & Rose, 2007). In spite of the substantive body of research demonstrating the efficacy of technology to enhance science learning and attitudes toward science, the vast majority of science teachers either do not use technology tools in their teaching or only employ technology in ways that replicate traditional instructional strategies (U.S. Dept. of Education, 2003).

In order to successfully use technology as an instructional tool, science teachers need to know about educational technology tools and make informed decisions about what technology to use, where (in the curriculum) to use it and how to use it. Thus, teacher education programs are very influential in teachers' use of technology in classroom instruction. Today, more than 90% of teacher education programs provide coursework where pre-service teachers learn about various content specific educational technology tools and ways to integrate them into the curriculum (Kleiner, Thomas, and Lewis, 2007). Kleiner, Thomas, and Lewi's (2007) study also shows that a smaller percentage of institutions teach techniques to use technology in assessing student learning. However, some institutions offer technology courses integrated into content methods courses.

Having knowledge of and prior experience with educational technology tools can help novice teachers smoothly integrate technology into their teaching (Niess, 2005). Thus, including educational technology training in teacher education programs is critical and should be considered essential in teacher preparation. However, having well-developed knowledge on technology tools is necessary but not sufficient to integrate technology into teaching. Teaching with technology is demanding particularly for novice science teachers as they are also faced with other unique challenges during their first years of teaching (e.g., classroom management). Also, as integrating technology into the curriculum requires extra time and effort, for most novice teachers, designing and implementing technology-rich lessons is not a priority.

Various studies report on the obstacles that impede successful technology integration (e.g., Clausen, 2007; Mumtaz, 2000). These barriers include lack of financial support, time, technical support, access, experience with technology, and supportive administration and colleagues. In addition, students' comfort and prior experience with technology strongly influence teachers' technology integration efforts (Kozmo,

2003); it is easier to integrate technology if students' are technology-savvy and motivated to use technology.

Setting the Stage: Mr. Bransford's Profile

Mr. Bransford is a middle school science teacher who has received several awards for his technology rich classroom practices. He is a Google certified teacher and Active Board Lead teacher in his district. Mr. Bransford decided to become a science teacher after teaching for several years in various informal science settings. With his bachelor degree in Environmental Science, Mr. Bransford applied for a 15 month post-baccalaureate teacher education program at a public university in the Midwest U.S. His dedication to improve science learning of underrepresented students in urban schools and his well-developed content knowledge and pedagogical skills allowed him to receive a prestigious Noyce scholarship to support him during his teaching licensure and Master in Education degree. As a requirement of the Noyce scholarship, Mr. Bransford was required to teach in a high-need school for a minimum of two years. He has been teaching 8th grade Earth Science and elective technology courses at a high-need school for five years.

The school serves 900 students in grades 7 through 9. Approximately 30% of the students are eligible for free or reduced-price lunch program. 79% of students are white with the remaining student population as almost exclusively African-American. While not as diverse as many other schools across the nation, the school is becoming more racially and economically diverse each year. Providing students with high quality and technology-rich education is the priority of the school. Thus, teachers are asked to integrate technology into their teaching. In the past five years, almost every classroom has been equipped with a Smart board, portable laptops, and classroom response systems.

Including Mr. Bransford, there are four science teachers at the school. They meet regularly to talk about the science content they will teach the following week; however, each uses different teaching strategies to teach the content. Mr. Bransford is the only one who makes frequent use of educational technology tools in classroom instruction. He is also the one who frequently uses inquiry-based instruction in his classroom. Mr. Bransford always shares his successful technology-rich inquiry activities with his colleagues, but only occasionally do they implement these activities.

THE CASE

Mr. Bradford's Technology Integration Efforts

Mr. Bransford expresses that when he started teaching in his school five years ago, none of the teachers were using a Smart board or any other technology tools that were available to them. During his first year at the school, Mr. Bransford's principal asked him to try the Smart board to see if he could use it in his instruction. Mr. Bransford started to play with the Smart board and he immediately loved it. To discover innovative ways to incorporate the Smart board into his teaching, Mr. Bransford spent hours at his classroom after school. Now Mr. Bransford is very comfortable with using the Smart board and he has a very impressive repertoire of digital images, videos, podcasts, graphs, simulations and animations, virtual labs, and assessments. According to him, the use of audio and visual applications allows his students to deeply understand science. He also expresses that Smart board allows him to create a classroom environment where students are active learners. In addition to the Smart board, Mr. Bransford uses probeware and student response systems. His students join online discussions on his class website. They complete classroom projects using Google applications (e.g., Google docs and Google presentation.), iMovie, VoiceThread, etc. According to him, the application of educational technology tools makes classroom instruction more student-centered and learning more meaningful while promoting student collaboration and inquiry.

Mr. Bransford is intrinsically motivated to use educational technology in his teaching. In Mr. Bransford's case, he is using the technology without expecting any rewards from his principal or colleagues. Instead, he is using technology for internal rewards such as feeling satisfaction. Unlike many other teachers, Mr. Bransford does not fear the technology. For him, teaching with technology is easier and also more effective than simply lecturing. He believes in the importance and effectiveness of technology in student learning and he uses technology to help students to engage in their learning and to make science more interesting for them. Mr Bransford's beliefs about student learning and the positive influence of technology tools on student learning, clearly represent his classroom practices.

Seeing the effectiveness of educational technology on student learning led Mr. Bransford to help other teachers incorporate technology in their teaching. Mr. Bransford helps not only teachers in his school but also in his district. He is a Smart board lead teacher in the district. With a team of teachers Mr. Bransford designs technology integration workshops to assist other teachers in using Smart board in their classroom instruction.

Mr. Bransford completed his licensure at an institution that includes coursework in educational technology and integrates technology across their methods courses, thus allowing him to have experiences with many educational tools before he started teaching. In his program, Mr. Bransford enhanced his knowledge of various educational technology tools such as data collection and analysis tools (e.g., probeware), graphic tools, planning and organizing tools (e.g., concept mapping software), software programs (e.g, e-portfolio software), multimedia and hypermedia tools. This experience helped him gain confidence in teaching with technology. His teacher education program was also highly focused on inquiry-based teaching and Mr. Bransford had well-developed understanding and skills related to scientific inquiry on completing the program. After completing the program, Mr. Bransford continued to increase his knowledge about educational technology tools. As previously noted, he spends a lot of his own time learning about the educational applications of various technologies and designing effective technology-rich lesson plans. He collaborates with science teachers outside of his district on social networking sites (e.g., twitter) to share ideas about lesson planning. One of his technology-rich classroom activities is discussed in the following section.

Mr. Bransford's Technology–Rich Classroom Practices

Jeremy, a student new to Mr. Bransford's class, has had a hard time adjusting to Mr. Bransford's teaching style. In his previous school, Jeremy's science teachers mostly lectured and assessed student learning through formal end-of-unit tests. Mr. Bransford, on the other hand, wants his students to be active learners and engaged in developing scientific ideas in classroom activities; thus, he mostly uses inquiry-based and student-centered instruction. Instead of pouring information into students' heads, Mr. Bransford asks them to discover things by themselves through searching the Web, conducting classroom projects, and joining discussions with their peers. The vast majority of the students in Mr. Bransford's class are technology-savvy and comfortable with Mr. Bransford's teaching style. However some students, including Jeremy, are reluctant to use technology in their learning; they want Mr. Bransford to teach science in a traditional way.

When Mr. Bransford started to explain the next classroom project on water quality, the majority of the students became very interested in the project as it required them to use educational technology tools and to explore the water quality of a nearby waterfall. Mr. Bransford explained to students that they were going to work in groups of three to design and conduct experiments to answer their own research questions regarding the water quality of the waterfall. Mr. Bransford provided the students with a variety of technology tools such as probeware and Internet access for research purposes. The class practiced with probeware before going to the site and collecting water samples. Students designed their experiments after practicing with the tools. Most groups preferred to investigate several water quality variables such as dissolved oxygen, pH, nitrates, temperature, and phosphates. Mr. Bransford also asked students to enter their data into a database on their class website and to prepare a report and a Google presentation to share their findings with their classmates.

Jeremy worked with two other students who are very excited about the project. Jeremy played a passive role during the entire project and the rest of the group members seemed not to care much about whether he contributed or not. Mr. Bransford assessed student learning through evaluating the reports and presentations. He designed a scoring rubric to grade the design of the experiments and the quality of the reports and presentations. Each student in a group received the same grade. Thus, even though Jeremy did not contribute to the project he received the same good grade as the two other students in his group.

Current Challenges Facing Mr. Bransford

Technology integration is not an easy process and it takes time. During his first five years of teaching, Mr. Bransford experienced constraints in incorporating technology into his instruction. Lack of time to design technology-rich lesson plans, non-technology savvy students, and insufficient school technology infrastructure are some of these barriers. He worked hard to find strategies to overcome these barriers. For example, collaborating with other teachers has helped him decrease the amount of time that he needs to create technology-rich lesson plans. By writing small-scale grants he purchased technology tools for his classroom which were previously not available in his school. However, for Mr. Bransford, his non-technology savvy students are still the most challenging barrier to the successful use of technology in his teaching. He struggles with his efforts to find effective ways to help this group of students to engage in technology-rich classroom activities. Mr. Bransford expressed that these students' limited skills with technology also limits their content learning because in Mr. Bransford's classroom most activities require students to learn science through the use of technology.

CONCLUSION

Teachers face various challenges while integrating technology into their teaching. The complexity and the difficulty of integrating technology are different for each teacher. Having non-technology savvy students is a common challenge for most teachers and it is not easy to overcome this barrier. In each classroom there will be several students who are resistant to using technology in their learning and reluctant to become active learners. There are several recommendations in dealing with non-technology savvy students and they are discussed in the following paragraphs.

Students might eagerly complete technology-rich activities when teachers design effective lessons with appropriate educational technology tools (Roblyer, 2006). Teachers should consider students' stages of development when choosing educational technology tools to integrate in a classroom activity. For example, while a middle school student may have hard time working with a design software program, an elementary school student may struggle with conducting an experiment using probeware. Mr. Bransford provided his students with developmentally appropriate technology tools; however, this strategy was not enough to increase the interest of all his students' in learning with technology. Since students like Jeremy did not have previous experiences with the provided technology tools, they did not engage in the activity.

Giving students an opportunity to practice using the technology tools before starting the activity can help students to become familiar with the tools and decrease their fear of technology. This strategy also prevents learning the technology from becoming the task-at-hand, rather than learning the content. Thus, effective technology enhanced classroom instruction requires teachers to fully explain to students how to use the chosen educational technology tools in the assigned activity. Mr. Bransford asked his students to practice with the technology tools before starting projects. However, this strategy also seems not to work well in Mr. Bransford's classroom since the projects require students to use several technology tools in tandem. While incorporating several technology tools in an activity can increase the motivation among technology savvy students, learning it can increase the struggle of non-technology savvy students.

As teachers incorporate technology into teaching they should be aware of what their students already know and need to learn. Focusing primarily on the technology tool and missing the content to be learned, is a common mistake among teachers. This leads students to lose interest in content learning and only pay attention to technological aspects of assigned activities. Indeed, Mr. Bransford acknowledged that he focused his attention more on the technology tools than the content in the example presented in this case study. Thus, his students spent most of their time on using the many features of Google presentations and selecting pictures and slide transitions rather than focusing on content learning.

Using cooperative learning strategies in which students work in small groups might also help teachers increase students' motivation to learn with technology and create comfortable and productive classrooms (Johnson & Johnson, 1993). Through the effective use of cooperative learning, teachers can build an empowering classroom. In our case Mr. Bransford simply told students to work as a team and as noted through our observations of Jeremy, this did not ensure student learning and participation. High quality cooperation and learning depends on placing students into groups based on their content knowledge, skills, and technology comfort level.

Also, formally assigning a role to each student is very critical in helping them to understand their responsibilities. Jeremy would have performed better if Mr. Bransford had asked Jeremy to complete a specific task, possibly allowing him to focus on one–rather than many–of the technology tools.

Finally, differentiating teaching style is another possible solution. Based on their students and the topic they teach, teachers should decide on how to structure the classroom activities and what teaching strategies to use. It is important to note that teachers cannot utilize educational technology tools in each lesson. For example, assigning students to complete technology-rich inquiry projects in every unit is unrealistic.

ACKNOWLEDGMENT

This material is based upon work supported by the National Science Foundation under Grant No. 0833250. Any opinions, findings, and conclusions or recommendations expressed in this material are those of the author(s) and do not necessarily reflect the views of the National Science Foundation.

REFERENCES

Clausen, J. (2007). Beginning teachers' technology use: First-year teacher development and the institutional context's affect on new teachers' instructional technology use with students. *Journal of Research on Technology in Education, 39*(3), 245–261.

Hug, B., Krajcik, J., & Marx, R. (2005). Using innovative learning technologies to promote learning and engagement in an urban science classroom. *Urban Education, 40*(4), 446–472. doi:10.1177/0042085905276409

Johnson, D., & Johnson, R. (1993). Cooperative learning and feedback in technology-based instruction. In Dempsey, J., & Sales, G. (Eds.), *Interactive instruction and feedback* (pp. 133–159). Englewood Cliffs, NJ: Educational Technology Publications.

Kleiner, B., Thomas, N., & Lewis, L. (2007). *Educational technology in teacher education programs for initial licensure* (NCES 2008-040). Retrieved April 13, 2010, from http://nces.ed.gov/

Kozma, R. (2003). ICT and educational change. In Kozmo, R. (Ed.), *Technology, innovation, and educational change: A global perspective. A report of the second information technology in education study: Module 2* (pp. 6–18). International Association for the Evaluation of Educational Achievement.

Lei, J., & Zhao, Y. (2007). Technology uses and student achievement: A longitudinal study. *Computers & Education, 49*, 284–296. doi:10.1016/j.compedu.2005.06.013

Mumtaz, S. (2000). Factors affecting teachers' use of information and communication technology: A review of the literature. *Journal of Information Technology for Teacher Education, 9*(3), 319–341. doi:10.1080/14759390000200096

National Research Council. (1996). *National science education standards*. Washington, DC: National Academy Press.

Niess, M. L. (2005). Preparing teachers to teach science and mathematics with technology: Developing a technology pedagogical content knowledge. *Teaching and Teacher Education, 21*, 509–523. doi:10.1016/j.tate.2005.03.006

Roblyer, M. D. (2006). *Integrating educational technology into teaching* (4th ed.). NJ: Pearson Education.

U.S. Department of Education. (2003). *Federal funding for educational technology and how it is used in the classroom: A summary of findings from the integrated studies of educational technology*. Retrieved December 10, 2009, from http://www.ed.gov/rschstat/eval/tech/iset/summary2003.pdf

Van Lehn, K., Graesser, A. C., Jackson, G. T., Jordan, P., Olney, A., & Rose, C. P. (2007). When are tutorial dialogues more effective than reading? *Cognitive Science, 30*, 3–62. doi:10.1080/03640210709336984

Chapter 26
Case Study of Game–Based Learning in a Citizenship Education K–12 Classroom:
Opportunities and Challenges

Venus Olla
University of Nottingham, UK

EXECUTIVE SUMMARY

This chapter focuses on a case study that involves the incorporation of ICT in particular gaming technology into the subject area of Citizenship Education (CE), a non-traditional ICT focused subject. The case study is within the context of a K-12 classroom and it explores the processes in which a classroom teacher may have to navigate to be able to use innovative ICT within their classroom. The case highlights the main issues as relating to pedagogical and institutional considerations.

BACKGROUND INTRODUCTION

This introduction presents the research conducted as part of a larger research project which focused on the use of ICT and student voice as pedagogical tools within the K-12 classroom for the teaching and learning of Citizenship Education. The participants involved in the case study were members of a specialized educational

DOI: 10.4018/978-1-61350-492-5.ch026

program for minority at-risk youth in high school. We begin with the background of Citizenship Education CE) as the school subject.

This section provides a discussion of Citizenship Education's introduction into the K-12 curriculum in many Western countries, the contentious issues associated with CE as a curriculum subject, the different pedagogical approaches to the teaching and learning, and how game-based learning has been suggested as an adequate pedagogy for CE. The benefits of game-based learning will also be discussed as they relate to teaching and learning within today's educational systems.

This will be followed by a description of the contextual circumstances in which the case study was conducted as well as its design and implementation. Additionally, the current challenges to the K-12 classroom teacher attempting to incorporate game-based learning into their classroom will be presented. Finally, this section will conclude with recommendations and future research directions for the use of game-based learning.

BACKGROUND

Over the last twenty years (Osler & Starkey 2006), many developed democratic nations have experienced a reduction in voting during elections. Many countries, fueled in part by media anecdotes, believe there is a moral deficit and lack of civic and political engagement among young people. These observations coupled with issues of religion and state in many parts of the world, have created a perceived fear of the demise of democracy (Hébert & Sears 2001; Bennett 2008; Osler & Starkey 2003). In order to counteract these trends CE was introduced as a specific school subject through which young people could be taught how to be good citizens (Hébert & Sears 2001). The use of games in certain subject areas produce easier evaluation of assessment outcomes such as in the subject areas of mathematics, science and geography. Such use of games in those subject areas are probably easier to defend compared to subjects such as Citizenship Education which is a contested subject area already. However it is due to the complexity of the subject area of CE that I believe the use of gaming and ICT is particularly appropriate because they have the potential to allow young people to explore the different facets of CE within the classroom.

The presence of ICT in secondary education is claimed to have begun in the eighties and its presence has increased and diversified over the decades. This ranges in scope from traditional Web 1.0 uses of the world wide web as a means of accessing information from the internet (Web 1.0), to the use of Web 2.0 applications such as social networking tools to create user-generated content and software as learning tools in the classroom (Paas & Creech 2008; White 2005). This expansion of use has also been driven in part by Government policy of many Western countries such as the U.S., United Kingdom and Canada, which in the early 1990s emphasized the move from the industrial society to an information society and more recently from an information society to a knowledge society (Strong 1995). This shift in the contribution that an individual makes in his/her society has been due to the change in the expectations of an individual in society. There has been a shift from knowledge that was based on learning facts and information that could be regurgitated when needed, into having the ability to investigate and discover new and relevant data and being able to generate information from that data. This has been described as a move from the information society to the knowledge society (Pelgrum & Plomp 2005; Strong 1995).

Most ICT educational policies at the beginning of this decade had been geared towards hardware and connectivity of the schools within their educational systems. Great strides have been made in this respect for example in the US. Virtually every school in the K-12 has internet access and Mexico has given every teacher a laptop and is adapting its teacher training courses to support ICT use in schools (Patrick 2008). In Canada there is no national education department and as a result ICT educational policy has been carried out on a provincial basis and reliant on the coordination between provinces to drive connectivity. In 1997 a Federal Government initiative aimed to make Canada the most connected country in the world by 2000 (Government of Canada INformation Highway Advisory Council 1997). The policy also focused on training for citizens and enhancement of services and applications (Ramirez 2001). Canada has been described as 'one of the most internet connected countries' and so it could be agreed that it achieved its goal as being the most connected country in the world. This is also reflected in the classroom with the Government investing large sums into ICT in schools (Milton 2003).

It has been suggested that this drive for connectedness in Canada is due to the fact that ICT has the potential to help lower achievement gaps in education by improving the standard and quality of teaching and learning in the classroom. However despite this investment there appears to be a growing achievement gap between socio-economic groups (Milton 2003). It is this paradox that is calling into question the use of ICT in education, not with regards to its effectiveness but with regards to policy, school culture and structure, teacher understanding and ability with regards to ICT and the call for new pedagogies and theories that allow for the effective integration of ICT in the classroom (Milton 2003; Breuleux 2001; Paas & Creech 2008; Kozman 2005). More recently Canada has been focusing on the improvement of digital content and instruction. There has been an increase on teacher training in the area of ICT use in education and there has been an investment in online learning with more than 25,000 students in Alberta enrolled in online courses (Patrick 2008). This positive shift demonstrates a change in how ICT in education is being viewed within Governments and supports the idea that ICT may still cause a reform in educational systems by changing the way education is perceived, delivered and assessed (Pelgrum & Law 2008).

One of the main objectives of an education system is to prepare its young children to function and contribute in their society as adults and it is for this reason that education is valued as a major means to achieve the preparation of citizens for a knowledge society, due to the fact that in most western countries young people are required to obtain a compulsory education which therefore makes schools the ideal vehicle for building ICT knowledge in a society (Tondeur et al. 2006). This belief has resulted in high levels of government investment in ICT in education by many western countries and the development of educational policies to support this investment (Milton 2003; Breuleux 2001; Pelgrum 2001). Many countries have included ICT as a standalone subject in the curriculum to address ICT competency in their citizens.

ICT in education not only manifests itself as a subject in the curriculum, but also as a tool for multidisciplinary uses, for example as an information resource, for supporting classroom-based activities (as described) or distance/online learning (Paas & Creech 2008). The increased ability of ICT to allow for remote collaboration has even resulted in speculations of it driving educational reform (Pelgrum 2001; Breuleux 2001). In terms of teaching and learning, it is the idea that ICT is able to engage and motivate learners, increase the higher order thinking of students and even help teachers teach more effectively that drives the debate for its inclusion in the teaching and learning of any curriculum subject (Tondeur et al. 2006; Higgins 2003).

ICT integration into education is an evolutionary process which will progress over time and has been described as moving through a spectrum of diffusion into education. The first level of the spectrum is substitution; that is, ICT being used to substitute for traditional teaching and learning tools that are predominantly teacher centered and orientated and corresponds to educational policies that are focused on capacity and connectivity. The next level is transition in which concepts and frameworks for ICT integration and new instructional methods are investigated and implemented in the classroom and corresponds to a change in educational policy that supports teacher training that focuses on student-centered teaching and learning. The final level of the spectrum is transformation in which ICT will be used creatively, innovatively, and in completely new instructional situations in a student-centered educational environment. This level would correspond to changes in educational policy towards curriculum and assessment that no longer focuses on knowledge assimilation but knowledge production (Breuleux 2001; Pelgrum & Plomp 2005). Access has increased and there has also been a simultaneous increase in educational innovations such as online educational games which no longer require software to be downloaded (see for example www.gamesforchange.org), real-time, real-world learning such as National Geographic's Congolese trek in which participants follow an exploration of the jungle (www.nationalgeographic.com/congotrek), and virtual worlds and simulations such as Quest Atlantis and Sims City, through which students are able to live out a life and view the consequences of their actions. As a result the implementation of ICT, integration has evolved from mere internet connectivity into best practices for the incorporation of these novel pedagogical tools into the classroom such as game-based learning. However despite these major advancements in connectivity, infrastructure, and computer skills, ICT use within education has not "reached a critical level" (van Braak et al. 2004; Shapka & Ferrari 2003; Tondeur et al. 2008). However the rationale for the innovative use of ICT such as gaming will be discussed next.

There is strong evidence to support the role of gaming as an effective instructional tool based on the theory of constructivism which bases the goal of instruction on the development of a deeper level of understanding by the learner (Lim 2008; Fosnot 1996). Games have also been cited as giving students the ability to think critically (Williamson 2003). Games can help support the development of arbitrary (skills that are difficult to assess) skills, such as critical thinking, strategic thinking, communication, and group decisions (Kirriemuir & McFarlane 2004). There is also a belief that games are able to affect the cognitive functions of the participants, stimulate curiosity, and promote goal formation (Amory & Seagram 2003). Games can also help students to apply, synthesize, and think critically about what they learn through active and social participation (Colby & Colby 2008).

The main rationale for the incorporation of game based learning in the form of educational computer games in the classroom is based on their capacity to motivate and engage young people (Paraskeva et al. 2010; Marc Prensky 2001). It is a well-established notion that ICT and gaming technologies are already an integral aspect of the lives of young people outside of school (Facer 2003; Kafai 2001; Kirriemuir & McFarlane 2004; Papastergiou 2009; Oblinger 2004; Downes 1999; Harris 1999; Mumtaz 2001). It is on this basis that the potential for game-based learning has the potential to create a more relevant and student-centered classroom for young people.

There are several considerations with regards to the use of games within the classroom. There is the balance between the educational and gaming activity; the more entertaining the game the less learning occurs (Bokyeong et al. 2009). The instructional context in which games are utilized is also important, 'games are not effective in isolation but should be used in conjunction with other instructional support' and that diagnosis of student ability, clear learning objectives and appropriateness of use are all important considerations (Robertson & Howells 2008). The following subsection will discuss the link between ICT technology use and the need for acceptance of new ICT within the classroom. This acceptance needs to come from those in positions of power within educational systems so that these technologies can be used within a classroom setting.

These observations lead to the link between the innovative use of ICT such as gaming in the classroom and the role of the teacher in facilitating and leading the process. It is becoming a well-established fact that teachers are the "most powerful system influence" (Alton 2003; Darling-Hammond 2000; Nye et al. 2004; Ward & Parr 2010) and their beliefs have a direct impact on their classroom practices (Fang 1996; Haney & McArthur 2002; Tondeur et al. 2008) and there is evidence to show that teachers with constructivist beliefs are more likely to use ICT as a teaching and learning tool (Becker & Ravitz 1999; Niederhauser & Stoddart 2001). Teachers identified an inability to utilize games to address aspects of the curriculum they were teaching, time constraints of learning the new game and implementing it in the classroom, and also completing the necessary curriculum requirements, as being obstacles in the use of games in the classroom (McFarlane et al. 2002; Gros 2007; Kirriemuir & McFarlane 2004). Suggestions have been made to address the issue of teachers' beliefs being an obstacle to classroom ICT integration. Three factors are identified by Ward and Parr (2010) that need to be addressed; "perception of need" which influences motivation and "readiness to use" (Ward & Parr 2010). They suggest that multi-faceted professional development that takes into account the pedagogical aspects of ICT integration are also required in order to counter the insufficient levels of ICT integration in the school classroom (Shapka & Ferrari 2003; van Braak et al. 2004; Tondeur et al. 2008; Becker 2001; Becker & Ravitz 1999; Cuban 2001; Hayes 2007; Lai et al. 2001; Cox et al. 2003a; Cox et al. 2003b). This will increase teachers' confidence to become innovative with regards to the use of ICT tools within the classroom.

However it is not only teachers' belief that influence their teaching practices. Teachers are also operating in an assessment driven educational system and so additional obstacles with regards to innovative uses of ICT tools within the classroom is also the priority of Ministries of Education and public opinion on high scores on national assessments which poses a large problem with regards to the use of games within the educational process and classroom. This is highlighted in a report produced by MacFarlane in which both teachers and parents stated that they did not feel that 'playing games' within the classroom would be useful for producing good results in assessments (McFarlane et al. 2002).

Contextual Setting of the Case Study

The case study was conducted within the context and perspective of a lone educator attempting to introduce ICT into the CE curriculum, which is distinctly different from the current research that has been done on ICT in the classroom. Currently reports of successful integration of ICT into the classroom–or at least attempts of the integration of innovative ICT practices into the classroom–have occurred due to deliberate collaboration of education technology researchers, cognitive scientists or educational researchers with a specific agenda who help guide the process after which the perspectives of the teachers are then gathered (Gros 2007; Milton 2003). Even Lim (2008) states that 2 out of the 4 criteria for the school chosen for conducting his research into Quest Atlantis (QA)–a virtual environment for the exploration of global citizenship–were a track record of "innovative technological and pedagogical practices in the last 2 years" and "openness of the school administration to consider alternative curriculum and assessment" (Lim 2008). This evidence demonstrates that at present, successful implementation of innovative ICT integration in the classroom requires certain prerequisites within the school and administrative structures to allow for this to occur.

A case study design was employed to allow the exploration of the whole process of the investigation which falls into Yin's description of a case study as an empirical inquiry that "investigates a contemporary phenomenon within its real-life context, especially when the boundaries between phenomenon and context are not clearly evident" (Yin R 2003). "The basic case study entails the detailed and intensive analysis of a single case" (Bryman 2001).

The use of games as the ICT tool was based on the belief that they would be engaging for the students and that according to the literature, games that explored different notions of CE had been developed and could be readily accessed. Games aid the development of arbitrary skills, such as critical thinking, help with self-directed learning, and have great potential in the field of education, yet more research is needed in this area (Selwyn 2007). This research study was NOT attempting to evaluate the usefulness of gaming or ICT, but was focused on how it can be integrated into the classroom and how this incorporation affects the teaching and learning of CE in the classroom from a student perspective, which is a mixture between an exploratory and descriptive case study.

THE CASE

The case study was designed to investigate the incorporation of ICT in the form of simulation games into the CE classroom. The games chosen were based on themes generated by students' perspectives of CE. A total of 24 mixed gendered students took part in the classroom aspect of the study. The students were a mix from grades 9 to 11 corresponding to ages 14 to 17. Some of the students had taken the Grade 10 Civics course (which corresponds to the term Citizenship Education). Online games were chosen for ease of use and access. It was necessary that software did not need to be purchased due to the financial implications, or downloaded due to the need to gain permission from Board level administrators which often takes many weeks.

It was also necessary to investigate the accessibility of the games from the School network prior to the classroom sessions, as the School Board has strict internet restrictions and many educational sites cannot be accessed via the school internet portal. Prior to the classroom session, I investigated internet access to each game via the school's internet portal.

The games were accessed through the web-portal www.gamesforchange.org. Gamesforchange is a non-profit organization that designs and hosts video games to help address current social issues. The organization believes that games have a "transformative power" that can help the formation of a "just, equitable and tolerant society" (www.gamesforchange.org/ourwork). The site has games that fall into 9 categories; Human rights, economics, public policy, environment, public health, poverty, politics, global conflict, and news. Gamesforchange collaborates with organizations that address social issues to develop games. Each game falls under one of the above categories and an indepth description of each game is given, however there is no advice on how these games can be used in the classroom. Six games were chosen from the website for use in phase 2 of the research. They were Darfur is dying, Against all odds, Climate Change, Orange Revolution, Ayiit and Replaying finding Zoe.

The students were divided into six groups of four students. Each group was given the website for one of the online games and all the students within the particular group played that particular game. A class session was 75 minutes in total. The students were given 10 minutes to familiarize themselves with the game by reading the instructions.They were instructed to read how to play the game and when finished to begin playing. Students that completed their games were allowed to try a different game. Once all the students had completed at least one game, each group of students that had played a particular game–for example Darfur is dying–were asked to give a brief oral presentation regarding what they had learned about their topic. The final summative part of the classroom session was based on the question: what do you think of using games like these in the classroom? Students were put into pairs and asked to write down their thoughts regarding this question. This information was collected at the end of the session.

CURRENT CHALLENGES

The findings from the case study can be divided into two categories; pedagogical and institutional. The first category concerns the pedagogical issues associated with simulation game use in the CE classroom and includes: the degrees of engagement of the individual students involved, the lack of interaction and collaboration between the students their peers and the students and educator. This categorical challenge highlights the inability of single player simulation games to produce critical self reflection in the learning process, despite the fact that two students played the same game, though on separate desktop computers. The second category deals with the institutional obstacles that were experienced by the educator attempting to incorporate ICT into the CE classroom.

Pedagogical Issues and Simulation Game Use

There is compelling evidence that the simulation games were engaging for the participants in this study, as demonstrated in the observations made while the students were taking part in the activity, and the discussion and responses given by the students at the end of the classroom session. However, it was also apparent that a high level of engagement was not necessarily experienced by all the participants that were present. One male student displayed a high level of engagement requesting the website address for the game he was playing so he could play it at home. The next level of engagement was demonstrated by the students that played their games and then requested further attempts at the games, not to win but to find out how different decisions would affect the game outcome. The lowest level of engagement was the students that simply played the games as instructed. The assumption that gaming technology is engaging for all learners is not necessarily true and a further area of research would be to investigate the differences between engagement and the types of learners (Squire 2005; Selwyn 2008).

The simulation games as a classroom activity helped to facilitate a discussion within the classroom session. The students were able to talk about the topics for which their games had been designed; however I do not believe that this translated into a deeper understanding of the issues associated with the topics, with one student commenting that she had not felt like she had learned anything about the topic. This concern has been observed in other studies involving ICT and CE that merely adding gaming technology to a classroom environment does not result in the students' automatic engagement with the subject area and that it is possible that using this strategy could in fact result in perpetuating misconceptions and mere exchange of information rather than deeper understanding (Dixon 2000; McFarlane et al. 2002).

Unfortunately critical reflection based on the individual students' perspectives, values, and opinions did not occur and so there was low transformative learning. The games were single player games and did not permit social collaborative inquiry between the students or teacher, as is essential in constructivist and transformative learning theories. There was a degree of interaction between the students in terms of the discussion after the simulation games had been played, however, this was not collaborative in terms of the students working with each other to solve the problem or complete the assigned work for the class. The simultaneous experience of social collaborative inquiry and social interaction helps in the construction of meaning regarding concepts and issues that may arise.

Institutional Obstacles Associated with ICT Classroom Implementation

Research has shown that the teacher is a major factor with regards to the use of ICT incorporation into the classroom. The educator's experience therefore became a natural focus of the research process. The educator's perspective was also incorporated into the investigation and findings of this case study.

The preliminary work that was necessary in order to incorporate gaming technology into the case study was time consuming, but not particularly difficult. The most difficult factor was locating suitable online games for the subject area of CE. The games needed to be subject appropriate, informative, and engaging. In the situation experienced in the case study luck was a factor with regards to the discovery of the www.gamesforchange website which has an array of games that suited the CE purpose. There are many resources on the internet regarding CE such as suggestions for lesson plans or how to explore particular topics, however I was not able to find much regarding gaming technology and CE that was freely available on the internet; freely meaning that there was no subscription fee or financial purchase of software. If this situation had occurred for the average classroom educator wanting to use gaming technology in the subject area of CE, the sheer time and effort necessary to locate, research, and then include gaming technology into the classroom pedagogy would probably be a deterrent. This finding supports the research that an obstacle to the integration and incorporation of ICT into the classroom is not just the ability or confidence of the educator with regards to ICT but also the "buy in" of the educator to the needs and benefits for the classroom pedagogy by using ICT (Sang et al. 2010; Tezci 2009; Drent & Meelissen 2008). Educators also need direction to navigate through the complexities of incorporation of ICT into the CE classroom as a pedagogical tool.

My experience in this case study also showed the institutional obstacles that are currently in place which can deter or prevent an educator from incorporating ICT into their classroom pedagogy. It could not be assumed that there would be access to all online resources from the school network and I had to spend a substantial amount of time to ensure that all the games that I had chosen could be accessed from the school's internet. This notion of protection of students from the deviant information that can be accessed via the internet can also block access to desirable resources. It highlights a fear of those in authority in education towards ICT and this fear continues to prevent young people from using ICT in more ways that are relevant to young people today in education (Kendall 2000; Selwyn 2007).

The findings from this study also highlighted the importance of classroom pedagogy for CE with respect to ICT incorporation and student voice. In terms of ICT, the addition of the games did engage the students, but due to its limiting interactions was a somewhat traditional classroom activity. This shows that it is not just the ICT tool that makes the difference within the CE classroom in terms of engagement and learning experience but how the ICT tool is used in the classroom that is of significance.

CONCLUSION

This chapter presented a single case study into the use of gaming technology in teaching and learning in the subject area of Citizenship Education in the K-12 classroom. The findings from the case study, while unable to be generalized, provide an in-depth description and exploration of the pedagogical and institutional obstacles that classroom teachers face when attempting to incorporate ICT into teaching and learning. Further work needs to be done on how teachers can be supported more readily with regards to the pedagogical use of ICT in their classrooms and deeper exploration into the reasons for the barriers that are encountered within educational institutions with regards to ICT access and availability, with a focus on how these barriers can be removed.

REFERENCES

Alton, L. (2003). *Quality teaching for diverse students in schooling: Best evidence synthesis*. Wellington, New Zealand: Ministry of Education Policy Division.

Amory, A., & Seagram, R. (2003). Educational game models: Conceptualization and evaluation. *The Journal of Higher Education, 17*(2), 206–217.

Becker, H., & Ravitz, J. (1999). The influence of computer and Internet use on teachers' pedagogical practices and perceptions. *Journal of Research on Computing in Education, 31*(4), 356–385.

Becker, H. J. (2001). *How are teachers using computers in instruction?* Paper presented at the 2001 Meetings of the American Educational Research Association.

Bokyeong, K., Hyungsung, P., & Youngkyun, B. (2009). Not just fun, but serious strategies: Using meta-cognitive strategies in game-based learning. *Computers & Education, 52*(4), 800–810. doi:10.1016/j.compedu.2008.12.004

Breuleux, A. (2001). Imagining the present, interpreting the possible, cultivating the future: Technology and the renewal of teaching and learning. *Education Canada*, *41*(3), 1–9.

Bryman, A. (2001). *Social research methods*. New York, NY: Oxford University Press.

Colby, S., & Colby, R. (2008). A pedagogy of play: Integrating computer games into the writing classroom. *Computers & Education, 25*(3), 300–312.

Cox, M., Abbott, C., Webb, M., Blakeley, B., Beauchamp, T., & Rhodes, V. (2003). *ICT and attainment: A review of the research literature. ICT in Schools Research and Evaluation Series – No.17*. British Educational Communications and Technology Agency.

Cuban, L. (2001). *Oversold and underused computers in the classroom*. London, UK: Harvard University Press.

Darling-Hammond, L. (2000). Teacher quality and student achievement: A review of State policy evidence. *Education Policy Analysis Archives, 8*(1).

Dixon, A. (2000). Free blankets or depth charges: choices in education for citizenship. *Forum, 42*(3), 94–99.

Downes, T. (1999). Playing with computing technologies in the home. *Education and Information Technologies, 4*(1), 65–79. doi:10.1023/A:1009607432286

Drent, M., & Meelissen, M. (2008). Which factors obstruct or stimulate teacher educators to use ICT innovatively? *Computers & Education, 51*, 187–199. doi:10.1016/j.compedu.2007.05.001

Facer, K. (2003). *Computer games and learning: Why do we think it's worth talking about computer games and learning in the same breath?* A discussion paper for FutureLab.

Fang, Z. (1996). A review of research on teacher beliefs and practices. *Educational Research, 38*(1), 47–65. doi:10.1080/0013188960380104

Fosnot, C. T. (1996). Constructivism: A psychological theory of learning. In *Constructivism: theory, perspectives and practice*. New York: Teachers College Press.

Gros, B. (2007). Digital Games in Education: The Design of Games-Based Learning Environments. *Journal of Research on Technology in Education, 40*(1), 23–38.

Haney, J. J., & McArthur, J. (2002). Four case studies of prospective science teachers' beliefs concerning constructivitst teaching practices. *Science Education, 86*(6), 783–802. doi:10.1002/sce.10038

Harris, S. (1999). Secondary school students' use of computers at home. *British Journal of Educational Technology, 30*(4), 331–339. doi:10.1111/1467-8535.00123

Hayes, D. (2007). ICT and learning: Lessons from Australian classrooms. *Computers & Education, 49*, 385–395. doi:10.1016/j.compedu.2005.09.003

Higgins, S. (2003). *Does ICT improve learning and teaching in schools?* United Kingdom: British Educational Research Association.

Information Highway Advisory Council. (1997). *Preparing Canada for a digital world*. Ottawa, Canada: Industry Canada: Final Report of the Information Highway Advisory Council.

Kafai, Y. B. (2001). *The educational potential of electronic games: From games–to–teach to games–to–learn*. Chicago, IL: Playing by the Rules Cultural Policy Center, University of Chicago.

Kendall, M. (2000). Citizenship is lifelong learning: The challenge of information and communications technology. In D. Benzie & D. Passey (Eds.), *Proceedings of Conference on Educational Uses of ICT*. Beijing, China: Publishing House of Electronics Industry.

Kirriemuir, J., & McFarlane, A. (2004). *Literature review in games and learning: A report for NESTA*. United Kingdom: FutureLab.

Kozman, R. B. (2005). *ICT, education reform and economic growth*. White Paper for INTEL.

Lai, K. W., Pratt, K., & Trewern, A. (2001). *Learning with technology: Evaluation of the Otago secondary schools technology project*. Dunedin, FL: The Community Trust of Otago.

Lim, C. (2008). Global citizenship education, school curriculum and games: Learning Mathematics, English and Science as a global citizen. *Computers & Education, 51*(3), 1073–1093. doi:10.1016/j.compedu.2007.10.005

McFarlane, A., Sparrowhawk, A., & Heald, Y. (2002). *Report on the educational use of games: An exploration by TEEM of the contribution which games can make to the education process*. Cambridgeshire, UK: TEEM, St Ives.

Milton, P. (2003). *Trends in the integration of ICT and learning in K-12 systems*. Report for the Canadian Education Association.

Mumtaz, S. (2001). Children's enjoyment and perception of computer use in the home and the school. *Computers & Education*, *36*(4), 347–362. doi:10.1016/S0360-1315(01)00023-9

Niederhauser, D. S., & Stoddart, T. (2001). Teachers' instructional perspectives and use of educational software. *Teaching and Teacher Education*, *17*, 15–31. doi:10.1016/S0742-051X(00)00036-6

Nye, B., Konstantopoulos, S., & Hedges, L. (2004). How large are teacher effects? *Educational Evaluation and Policy Analysis*, *26*, 237–257. doi:10.3102/01623737026003237

Oblinger, D. (2004). The next generation of educational engagement. *Journal of Interactive Media*, *8*, 1–18.

Paas, L., & Creech, H. (2008). *How information and communications technologies can support Education for sustainable development: Current uses and trends*. International Institute for Sustainable Development.

Papastergiou, M. (2009). Digital game-based learning in high school computer science education: Impact on educational effectiveness and student motivation. *Computers & Education*, *52*(1), 1–12. doi:10.1016/j.compedu.2008.06.004

Paraskeva, F., Mysirlaki, S., & Papagianni, A. (2010). Multiplayer online games as educational tools: Facing new challenges in learning. *Computers & Education*, *54*(2), 498–505. doi:10.1016/j.compedu.2009.09.001

Patrick, S. (2008). ICT in educational policy in the North American region. In *International handbook of Information Technology in primary and secondary education* (pp. 1109–1117). US: Springer International Handbooks of Education. doi:10.1007/978-0-387-73315-9_70

Pelgrum, W. J. (2001). Obstacles to the integration of ICT in education: Results from a worldwide educational assessment. *Computers & Education*, *37*(2), 163–178. doi:10.1016/S0360-1315(01)00045-8

Pelgrum, W. J., & Law, N. (2008). Introduction to SITES 2006. In *Pedagogy and ICT use in schools around the world: Findings from the IEA Sites 2006 study*, (pp. 1-11). CERC Studies in Comparative Education. Netherlands: Springer.

Pelgrum, W. J., & Plomp, T. (2005). *The turtle stands on an emerging educational paradigm*. Netherlands: Springer.

Prensky, M. (2001). Digital natives, digital immigrants. *NCB University Press*, *9*(5), 1–15.

Ramirez, R. (2001). A model for rural and remote information and communication technologies: A Canadian exploration. *Telecommunications Policy, 25*(5), 315–330. doi:10.1016/S0308-5961(01)00007-6

Robertson, J., & Howells, C. (2008). Computer game design: Opportunities for successful learning. *Computers & Education, 50*(2), 559–578. doi:10.1016/j.compedu.2007.09.020

Sang, G., Valcke, M., van Braak, J., & Tondeur, T. (2010). Student teachers' thinking processes and ICT integration: Predictors of prospective teaching behaviors with educational technology. *Computers & Education, 54*(1), 103–112. doi:10.1016/j.compedu.2009.07.010

Selwyn, N. (2007). Technology, schools and CE: A fic too far? In *Young citizens in the digital age - political engagement, young people and new media* (pp. 129–142). London, UK: Routledge Taylor and Francis Group.

Selwyn, N. (2008). An investigation of differences in undergraduates' academic use of the internet. *Active Learning in Higher Education, 9*(1), 11–22. doi:10.1177/1469787407086744

Shapka, J. D., & Ferrari, M. (2003). Computer-related attitudes and actions of teacher candidates. *Computers in Human Behavior, 19*(3), 319–334. doi:10.1016/S0747-5632(02)00059-6

Squire, K. (2005). Changing the game: What happens when video games enter the classroom? *Innovate, 1*(6), 82–89.

Strong, M. (1995). *Connecting with the world: Priorities for Canadian internationalism in the 21st century. International Development Research and Policy Task Force. International Development Research Centre (IDRC); International Institute for Sustainable Development (IISD); North-South Institute*. NSI.

Tezci, E. (2009). Teachers' effect on ICT use in education: The Turkey sample. *Procedia - Social and Behavioral Sciences, 1*(1), 1285-1294.

Tondeur, J. (2008). ICT integration in the classroom: Challenging the potential of a school policy. *Computers & Education, 51*(1), 212–223. doi:10.1016/j.compedu.2007.05.003

Tondeur, J., van Braak, J., & Valcke, M. (2006). Curricula and the use of ICT in education: Two worlds apart? *British Journal of Educational Technology, 38*(6), 1–14.

van Braak, J., Tondeur, J., & Valcke, M. (2004). Explaining different types of computer use among primary school teachers. *European Journal of Psychology of Education, 19*(4), 407–422. doi:10.1007/BF03173218

Ward, L., & Parr, J. (2010). Revisiting and reframing use: Implications for the integration of ICT. *Computers & Education, 54*(1), 113–122. doi:10.1016/j. compedu.2009.07.011

White, G. (2005). *Beyond the horseless carriage: Harnessing the potential of ICT in education and training.* Australia: Education.au Limited.

Williamson, A. (2003). Shifting the centre: The Internet as a tool for community activism. In *Proceedings of the 5th International Information Technology in Regional Areas (ITiRA) Conference,* (pp. 149-155). Rockhampton, Australia: Central Queensland University.

Yin, R. (2003). Applied Social Research Methods Series: *Vol. 34. Applications of case study research* (2nd ed.).

Chapter 27
Leveraging Technology to Develop Pre–Service Teachers' TPACK in Mathematics and Science Methods Courses

Kate Popejoy
University of North Carolina at Charlotte, USA

Drew Polly
University of North Carolina at Charlotte, USA

EXECUTIVE SUMMARY

These two cases address issues related to using technology as a tool to develop pre-service teachers' Technological Pedagogical and Content Knowledge (TPACK) in mathematics and science methods courses. The chapter assumes the following scenario and overarching case study question:

You and your colleagues are the course instructors of a mathematics and a science methods course. Your pre-service teachers typically lack content knowledge in mathematics and science. Further, you must also address pedagogies and how to use technology as a tool to support student learning of mathematics and science concepts. What activities can you create to simultaneously develop knowledge of content, pedagogies, and how to teach with technology?

DOI: 10.4018/978-1-61350-492-5.ch027

BACKGROUND INFORMATION

This case focuses on the Elementary Education Graduate Certificate in Teaching (GCT) program at a large university in the southeastern United States. The university has approximately 25,000 students. The program recommends approximately 350 students for their Elementary Education (Grades K-6) license each year; 100 of those are post-baccalaureate students in the GCT program. During the 2009-2010 year, the program underwent major 're-visioning', as the State Board of Education mandated that all teacher education programs reform their courses to integrate 21st Century Skills such as technology use, collaboration, problem solving, and critical thinking. The GCT program comprises 27 credits, including two courses about teaching mathematics and one course related to teaching science. This case addresses issues related to integrating technology into both the science course (taught by the first author) and the second mathematics course (taught by the second author).

Setting the Stage

The GCT program prepares candidates to earn a North Carolina teaching license for Grades K-6. Since the program's inception in the 1980's, the coursework has focused on in depth exposure to child development instruction. Prior to 2006, students in the GCT program only worked with technology during their first six credits which focused on child development, instructional design, diverse learners, and technology integration. Technology integration content focused primarily on the Microsoft Office suite and how to integrate tools such as PowerPoint presentations or word processing into the processes of teaching and learning. Most of the technology-based activities focused on teacher use of technology, and did not explore student uses. There was no technology integrated into the mathematics or science methods course prior to the implementation of these projects.

Following are the two case studies organized by introduction to the topic, technology concerns needing to be addressed, and the technology components integrated to meet those concerns.

CASE ONE DESCRIPTION: TEACHING AND INTEGRATING ELEMENTARY SCIENCE METHODS

Teaching and Integrating Science is a one semester course in which students learn about science pedagogy for the elementary classroom setting. Though not explicitly a content course, most students enrolled in the course have little preparation in science; therefore a large amount of content information is conveyed along with pedagogical knowledge. These two components are melded together in a pedagogical content knowledge (PCK) approach (Shulman, 1986). In addition, the majority of students approach science with a high degree of nervousness, many with disappointing or damaging past experiences in science classes. As this is a post-baccalaureate course, all students have a college degree; some are quite recent, while others may be up to thirty years post degree. There is also a handful of Teach for America students (who are full-time paid teachers in high needs schools) in the class each term. Each class is predominantly female, with an average of 5-10% male students. Also, the large majority of students are white, with approximately 12% of students being students of color. The class meets for 2.5 hours in the evening once a week for a semester. The majority (~90%) of students are in the last semester of their licensure program and are student teaching full time in addition to taking another evening course.

In addition to using a PCK perspective, Kate has chosen to integrate a relatively large amount of technology into the course. This has resulted in a TPACK approach similar to that delineated by Mishra & Koehler (2006), and Niess (2005). As stated by Mishra & Koehler:

Quality teaching requires developing a nuanced understanding of the complex relationships between technology, content, and pedagogy, and using this understanding to develop appropriate, context-specific strategies and representations. Productive technology integration in teaching needs to consider all three issues not in isolation, but rather within the complex relationships in the system defined by the three key elements (2006, p. 1029).

Technology Concerns

Students come to us from a wide range of technological backgrounds, with some barely able to navigate the Web or use e-mail, and others far more advanced and proficient. In addition, the classrooms in which these students are teaching (or performing the clinical component of the course if not teaching full time) cover a broad range of available technology; from having only a single computer and overhead projector, to having a laptop cart, projector and SMART Board with packages such as Discovery Education available. However, "teachers at all levels…are expected to embrace technology and integrate emerging technologies into their teaching" (Nworie & Haughton, 2008, p. 53). Higher education faculty should also apply technology in their fast-changing learning context. There are benefits to implementing technology in the classroom that might not be evident when looking at student outcomes. These benefits "include making available a wide range of resources outside the traditional classroom, making provisions for individual learning styles, providing instructional alternatives, improving student motivation, and equipping instructors with a variety of new teaching tools" (Nworie & Haughton, 2008, p. 53).

As noted in the recent report from Walden University (Grunwald, Associates, & LLC, 2010), most teachers do not feel that their teacher training programs prepared them well in educational technology. Additionally, though many of us who are involved in teacher preparation believe that newer teachers are more likely to use technology in their classrooms, this is not the case according to the same study. Lastly, "both teachers and administrators believe that technology helps them engage many different types of students, including high-achieving students, students with academic needs, and English language learners" (Grunwald et al., 2010, p. 6). With our institution's focus on the challenges associated with urban education, it is imperative that we provide our teacher candidates with all the tools they need to reach diverse student populations.

The science classroom is a natural location for technology integration as so much of science relies on technology, and to be a modern scientist, one must be conversant with computers and other technology tools (McCrory, 2008). Digital media have emerged as a tool for providing multimodal instruction, integrating pedagogy and content, and complementing instruction in science in inclusive classrooms. Podcasting and video podcasting (vodcasting) are examples of new technologies that have caught the attention of students, instructors, the news media, and the general public (Brown & Green, 2007), and continue to be explored in various classroom contexts (Plankis & Weatherly, 2008). Some authors state that technology should be used to do things that would be difficult, or perhaps, impossible to do (McCrory, 2008). However, we believe that there is also value in using technology in order to be more efficient, to engage learners in difficult subject matter, to encourage group collaboration, and to access various modes of learning in students.

Lastly, as those of us who regularly use technology in the classroom know, using something new means risking failure. Modeling this use for our students, and sometimes encountering difficulties, helps our students to see that these practices are at times challenging, but worth the trouble. Technology failure often happens in the first attempt, which can become the last attempt for a novice user of technology (McCrory, 2008). Working on technology projects in groups can lessen the nervousness felt by students. It is also important that preservice and novice teachers see that the level of effort expended and persistence in attaining goals can increase student confidence and feelings of self-efficacy (Manner, 2007).

Technology Components

In the science methods course, students use technology in a variety of ways. Of course, all assignments must be created using word processing software, and often are turned in via e-mail or Blackboard. Each student presents one science-related current event article during the term. Most use PowerPoint to do so, often containing an internet component such as a video clip. In addition, some students make use of the SmartBoard in the science methods classroom. Some students also bring their own laptops to class and we encourage their use.

Three additional assignments heavily feature technology (specifically podcasts and video podcasts, or vodcasts), the individual Science Friday Podcast Response paper, an individual science (or science education) podcast review, and the small group Coriolis Force Video Podcast project. We have chosen to use the podcast as an avenue of instruction for a variety of reasons. First, many students are not familiar with podcasts and how to find and listen to them. For example, in the ECAR 2009 (Smith, Salaway, & Caruso, 2009) report, only 5.8% of undergraduate students surveyed reported using podcasts in their classes (and we believe the number is similar for our post-baccalaureate students). Second, an incredible array of current science and education information are available through podcasts for university students, classroom teachers, and their K-12 students. (See for example, Scientific American, National Geographic, or Naked Science podcasts).

In the first assignment, students listen to a Science Friday podcast related to the Intergovernmental Panel on Climate Change (IPCC) Report (original broadcast Feb. 2, 2007). Science Friday is a weekly podcast from National Public Radio in which a wide variety of scientists and others are interviewed about their work in the field In this episode, host Ira Flatow interviews Dr. Kevin Trenberth about the IPCC report. After listening to the podcast and reading the IPCC Summary for Policymakers (IPCC, 2008), students write a short paper in response to a series of questions related to the nature of scientific research, language usage in scientific work, global climate change, the role of scientists in policy decisions, and possible usage of podcasts in their future classrooms.

In the second assignment, students search for an interesting podcast related to a science and/or science education topic. They then write a short review paper in which they summarize and critique the podcast, and then tie it to the state science standards and relate how it could be used in the classroom. The review is then placed on the class Blackboard page so that all students can explore their colleagues' suggested programs.

In the third assignment (and the main focus for this case), the first author, Kate, introduces students to the Coriolis Force via a video segment she created on a recent visit to the equator in the South American country of Ecuador. In the segment, a museum guide "demonstrates" the Coriolis Force by draining water from a basin on the equator, and approximately ten feet away to the north and south. Kate also shows a short segment from the popular media about the Coriolis Force, e.g. a Simpsons episode (Oakley, Weinstein, & Archer, 1995). Students are then challenged to support or dispute these representations. In groups, the students do their own Internet-based research about the Coriolis Force, and then produce a short video podcast explaining it. The multidimensional student goals for this assignment are to: (a) perform research on the Web about a scientific topic (Coriolis Force), (b) determine the validity of information found in this research, (c) understand the basic parameters of the Coriolis Force, and (d) present their accurate understanding via a video podcast. The vodcasts are then placed on the class Blackboard page for peers to review.

Students work in groups of three or four on the project, and use digital cameras with video capability to make their video footage. Then, using the College laptop cart of PCs, students import their video and utilize the Windows Movie Maker program to make their finished products. The requirements for the video are not complicated. The movie should be three to four minutes long, and include title and credits slides. In order to assist students in using the at times unwieldy Movie Maker program, Kate has created a specific printed tutorial and instruction sheet so that students will make the correct format of movie to be turned in. Please note that we certainly understand that the Coriolis Force is not part of the elementary science curriculum. However, it is part of the grades 9-12 (our state) Standard Course of Study (SCOS) for earth science, regarding the hydrosphere and the mechanisms for ocean currents and upwelling, specifically, temperature, Coriolis and climatic impacts. Theoretically, the elementary science methods students should have been exposed to Coriolis in their high school science classes. However, very few have ever heard of it, or if they have, it has been through (often inaccurate) media representations. So, almost all students are starting at the same point in the content knowledge. If we chose a topic from the elementary science curriculum, it is possible (though depressingly unlikely) that some students would have a thorough understanding of the content, while others would not. This assignment models a teacher encountering a science topic to be taught with which s/he is unfamiliar, doing research on the topic, and then being able to explain that topic to others.

At this point, the first author has received 37 student created movies. In the first few terms, the focus was on the students being exposed in a safe, low-pressure way to these challenges of content and technology. However, in more recent terms, a larger emphasis has been placed on the quality of the videos and accurate content being presented, with a thorough rubric given to students. The results are promising, with the majority of the videos being accurate and within the specified parameters.

The student work products have varied considerably. Some have shown a thorough and accurate understanding of Coriolis, while others have stated that the representations I have shown them are accurate and that water would indeed drain out of a basin in different directions in the northern and southern hemispheres. This reflects student use of cursory research practices. It may also reflect student trust in the first author, as the professor and person in authority, who presumably would not show students incorrect information in class. Many student groups become fixated on toilets, and make their movies in bathrooms with toilets exclusively. A few groups have interviewed other students (not in our classes) and other faculty members in a 'man on the street' format. Some have chosen to go with a news report format. The wide range of approaches has allowed students to use their creativity, and at times, dramatic flair, in the interest of science, something that may not have happened in previous science experiences.

CASE TWO: DEVELOPING TPACK IN ELEMENTARY MATHEMATICS METHODS COURSE

The elementary mathematics methods course discussed in this case is the second of two mathematics courses that students in the Graduate Certificate in Teaching (GCT) program complete. The first course focuses on number sense and some algebra, while the second course was designed to focus on other mathematical concepts, as well as the issues of differentiation and assessment in elementary school mathematics. The course is taught using a hybrid approach, in which candidates have eight to ten course meetings, and the remainder of the class meetings are online activities or projects.

Similar to the situation described in the science course mentioned in the previous case study, candidates typically are uncomfortable with their lack of understanding of concepts related to geometry, algebra and statistics. Further, candidates need experiences that also develop pedagogical knowledge related to those content areas. In this course, technology has taken on two roles. First, technology supports candidates to develop their understanding of content. Secondly, in the spirit of developing TPACK (Niess, 2005), the technologies that are used are constantly examined so candidates may consider how these technologies can support mathematics teaching and learning in elementary school classrooms.

Technology Concerns

As stated earlier, candidates in the GCT program vary in age, educational background and technological skills. While some have recently finished their undergraduate degree, and are used to using course management systems, blogs, wikis, and social networking software, a majority of the students need ample support setting up accounts for blogs and wikis, or to submit assignments via a course management system. Nearly every candidate is able to word process, build a simple PowerPoint presentation and send e-mail.

Research has found significant gains in student learning when elementary school teachers integrate technology in higher-level thinking activities in mathematics (Polly, 2008; U.S. Department of Education, 2008; Wenglinsky, 1998). However, teachers tend to resort to technology drill-and-practice mathematics activities, rather than using technology to support students' higher-level thinking and conceptual understanding (Becker, Ravitz, & Wong, 1999; ISTE, 2008; Mann, Shakeshaft, Becker, & Kottkamp, 1998). Research on developing TPACK in mathematics has found that teachers (or preservice teachers) need hands-on experiences with technology that are explicitly linked to content, in addition to classroom support, in the form of co-planning, demonstration lessons, or co-teaching (Niess, 2010; Polly, in press; Polly & Hannafin, in press). However, the development of TPACK and teachers' comfort teaching with technology requires extensive time for preparation; more than what is typically allotted in a college course or short-term professional development experience (Polly & Hannafin, in press).

Another shortcoming with which candidates enter the mathematics class is experience planning instruction for students. Preservice teachers who do not plan technology-rich instruction are less likely to integrate technology, as they lack the knowledge and skills associated with designing how technology can support teaching and learning (U.S. Department of Education, 1993). In this course, the tasks that students complete are designed to develop teachers' content knowledge (CK), pedagogical content knowledge (PCK) and TPACK.

Technology Components

Organizing internet-based resources. Early in the semester, candidates set up a Diigo account in order to evaluate and organize internet-based resources related to elementary mathematics. Diigo (www.diigo.com) is a social bookmarking site that allows students to bookmark websites, and organize them according to keywords (tags) that they choose. Diigo also allows users to set up lists of resources centering on individual concepts, and includes a social networking feature that allows for easy sharing of resources between users.

During the course, candidates are exposed to two main repositories of internet-based mathematical tools. The first repository is called Illuminations (http://illuminations.nctm.org) and features K-5 activities and games. Illuminations is sponsored by the National Council for Teachers of Mathematics. The second, the National Library of Virtual Manipulatives (http://nlvm.usu.edu) features internet-based activities and some online manipulatives that allow students to explore mathematical concepts. Candidates learn about additional resources from other Diigo users, conversations with classmates, or searching for resources about specific concepts. Through these activities candidates are also introduced to information literacy skills where they are expected to evaluate internet-based resources.

Using Technology to Support Problem Solving

During the course, candidates use calculators and internet-based technologies to support problem solving. In one course meeting, groups of students are given four different shapes of rectangular boxes and are asked how much it would cost to paint 30 of each box. Students are given rulers however the amount of space covered by each can of paint is in square feet. Since the task is focused on measurement–linear (dimensions of the box), surface area (size of each face of the box) and capacity (paint needed to paint the boxes)–a calculator allows students to focus their energy on the measurement skills and how to solve the problem. Calculator use, in this case, supports computation, which is not a focus. Therefore, candidates can hone in on the skills that are the focus–measurement and problem solving. In other activities, candidates use geometry software or internet-based activities to learn about various concepts.

Communicating Ideas about Mathematics Teaching and Learning

Candidates are expected to communicate with each other about their views of mathematics teaching and learning. As they teach lessons and spend more time in classrooms, these views tend to shift. During the course, candidates set up a blog (http://www.wordpress.com), and post weekly writings based on a variety of different prompts that are posed. Further, candidates respond to at least two classmates' blogs each week which helps ensure students stay updated with each other.

Integrating Resources into Planning

After identifying internet-based resources using Diigo, candidates are expected to integrate a few of them into lessons that they teach to a small group of elementary school students. Each candidate is placed in an elementary school classroom and charged with pre-assessing, teaching five lessons and then conducting a post-assessment about a specific mathematical concept with three to five students. In two of the five lessons, candidates are expected to integrate a technology-rich experience for students. Based on the Revised Bloom's Taxonomy (Anderson & Krathwohl, 2000), candidates must design uses of technology that demonstrate higher-order thinking skills among the elementary students, such as analyzing, evaluating, or creating. These may include internet-based activities, games, or calculators to support problem solving.

Using Technology to Examine Student Learning Data

After teaching the five lessons and collecting pre- and post-unit assessment data, candidates analyze the data using a Microsoft Excel spreadsheet. Candidates examine pre- and post-unit assessment scores, along with summative data from each lesson, and then create tables and graphs to analyze student progress across the five-lesson unit. Based on the GCT program's goal to focus on data-driven decision making, candidates examine data after each lesson and modify subsequent lessons based on that data. Further, at the end of the project, candidates create a performance report for parents based on multiple data sources. By the end of the course, students are proficient at entering data into a spreadsheet, creating appropriate graphs, and drawing conclusions about student performance based on the data and graphs.

CONCLUSION

At our institution, we enjoy relative freedom in determining the curriculum and approach for our methods courses, so long as we adhere to state-mandated standards and outcomes. This allows us to integrate technology as we so desire in the context of instruction. However, a few issues still need to be addressed.

Management and Organizational Concerns

An unintended effect of technology adoption is a widening of the gap between the technology haves and have-nots (Nworie & Haughton, 2008). Our GCT students are placed in a variety of K-6 classrooms in the surrounding area, most in the large urban district of our city, but some in more rural settings. Many of the more rural schools have less technology hardware in their classrooms, while more urban classrooms enjoy a richer technology content. All of the urban classrooms contain a greater variety of technologies as well as more computers, calculators, and interactive whiteboards; allowing some students to immediately try out some of the technologies we present in their teaching classroom. However, others in more rural settings that have little access to technology do not have the opportunity to try things out right away. We hope that students will remember these experiences later, when they eventually work in a more technology rich environment. If instruction was limited to traditional, non-technological approaches, the playing field might be more level. In addition, educational environments, when viewed through the lens of complexity thinking, are complex, dynamic, and adaptive systems (Davis, Sumara, & Luce-Kapler, 2000). Implementing technology tools to improve teaching and learning can introduce unintended effects.

Due to our College's (but not university) exclusive reliance on the PC platform, we are restricted to using the Windows-based Movie Maker application on the PCs in the laptop cart to make the Coriolis movies. Movie Maker is a bit unwieldy and less intuitive to use than other programs such as iMovie from Apple. Some students have Mac laptops and they are encouraged to bring them to class which enables some groups to utilize iMovie. However, in spite of the clear oral and written instructions, some student groups turn in a Movie Maker data file rather than a finished movie file itself. These groups then need to go back to their camera and laptop to re-do the assignment. Students are also allowed to work on this assignment out of class, though enough time is set aside in class for work to be completed.

Originally, the first author had plans to post the student Coriolis movies on the class web page, which is also accessible to the general public; in other words, make a true video podcast, that would be displayed to the world. However, many student groups have objected to this due to privacy concerns. The compromise has been to post them to Blackboard, where only students in their class can see the videos. In the future, we hope to be able to make these final productions public.

As mentioned above, students are encouraged to bring their laptops to class. At first glance, one may think that students are busily engaged in classwork with their laptops. However, we cannot always be certain that students are using their laptops in ways that we prefer. In fact, they may be using them to e-mail, surf the Web, chat, pay bills, play games, or shop! These distractions interfere with students' paying attention and benefiting from classroom activities and instruction (Nworie & Haughton, 2008).

REFERENCES

Anderson, L. W., & Krathwohl, D. R. (2000). *A taxonomy for learning, teaching, and assessing: A revision of Bloom's taxonomy of educational objectives*. Boston, MA: Allyn and Bacon.

Becker, H. J., Ravitz, J. L., & Wong, Y. (1999). *Teaching, learning and computing: 1998 national survey (Report #3)*. University of California and University of Minnesota: Center for Research on Information Technology and Organizations.

Brown, A., & Green, T. D. (2007, March 2007). *Podcasting and video podcasting: How it works and how it's used for instruction*. Paper presented at the Society for Information Technology and Teacher Education (SITE) Conference 2007, San Antonio, TX.

Davis, B., Sumara, D., & Luce-Kapler, R. (2000). *Engaging minds: Learning and teaching in a complex world*. Mahwah, NJ: Lawrence Erlbaum.

Grunwald., & Associates, L. L. C. (2010). *Educators, technology and 21st century skills: Dispelling five myths*. Retrieved November 23, 2010, from http://grunwald.com/pdfs/Educators-Technology-21stCentury-Skills.pdf

International Society for Technology in Education. (2008). *Technology and student achievement: The indelible link*. Retrieved August 3, 2010, from http://www.iste.org/Content/NavigationMenu/Advocacy/Policy/59.08-PolicyBrief-F-web.pdf

IPCC. (2008). *Summary for policymakers*. Geneva, Switzerland: IPCC.. *Climatic Change*, 2007.

Mann, D., Shakeshaft, C., Becker, J., & Kottkamp, R. (1998). *West Virginia story: Achievement gains from a statewide comprehensive instructional technology program*. Santa Monica, CA: Milken Exchange on Educational Technology.

Manner, J. C. (2007, March 2007). *Widening the audience: Using podcasting to share student work*. Paper presented at the Society for Information Technology and Teacher Education International Conference (SITE) 2007, San Antonio, TX.

McCrory, R. (2008). Science, technology, and teaching: The topic-specific challenges of TPCK in science. In Technology, A. C. I. a. (Ed.), *Handbook of technological pedagogical content knowledge (TPCK) for educators* (pp. 193–206). New York, NY: Routledge.

Mishra, P., & Koehler, M. J. (2006). Technological pedagogical content knowledge: A framework for teacher knowledge. *Teachers College Record, 108*(6), 1017–1054. doi:10.1111/j.1467-9620.2006.00684.x

Niess, M. L. (2005). Preparing teachers to teach science and mathematics with technology: Developing a technology pedagogical content knowledge. *Teaching and Teacher Education, 21*(5), 509–523. doi:10.1016/j.tate.2005.03.006

Niess, M. L. (2010, May). *Using classroom artifacts to judge teacher knowledge of reform-based instructional practices that integrate technology in mathematics and science classrooms*. Paper presented at the 2010 Annual Meeting of the American Educational Research Association. Denver, CO.

Nworie, J., & Haughton, N. (2008). The unintended consequences of the application of technology in teaching and learning environments. *TechTrends, 52*(5), 52–58. doi:10.1007/s11528-008-0197-y

Plankis, B. J., & Weatherly, R. (2008, March 2008). *Engaging students and empowering researchers: Embedding assessment, evaluation and history into podcasting.* Paper presented at the Society for Information Technology and Teacher Education International Conference (SITE) 2008, Las Vegas, NV.

Polly, D. (2008). Modeling the influence of calculator use and teacher effects on first grade students' mathematics achievement. *Journal of Technology in Mathematics and Science Teaching, 27*(3), 245–263.

Polly, D. (2011). Examining teachers' enactment of TPACK in their mathematics teaching. *The International Journal for Technology in Mathematics Education, 30*(1).

Polly, D., & Hannafin, M. J. (in press). Examining how learner-centered professional development influences teachers' espoused and enacted practices. *Journal of Educational Research, 104*(2).

Shulman, L. S. (1986). Those who understand: Knowledge growth in teaching. *Educational Researcher, 15*(2), 4–14.

Smith, S. D., Salaway, G., & Caruso, J. B. (2009). *The ECAR study of undergraduate students and information technology, 2009.* Boulder, CO: EDUCAUSE Center for Applied Research.

U.S. Department of Education. (1993). *Using technology to support education reform.* Washington, DC: U.S. Department of Education, Office of Research.

Wenglinsky, H. (1998). *Does it compute? The relationship between educational technology and student achievement in mathematics.* Educational Testing Service Policy Information Center. Retrieved September 10, 2002, from www.mff.org/pubs/ME161.pdf

Chapter 28

Issues and Challenges in Preparing Teachers to Teach in the Twenty–First Century

Susan Gibson
University of Alberta, Canada

EXECUTIVE SUMMARY

Preservice teachers need to acquire both technological skill and understanding about how technology rich environments can develop subject-specific knowledge as a part of their teacher education programs. The purpose of the research project, as described in this case study, was to examine the impact that immersion in technology-infused social studies pedagogy courses had on preservice teachers' willingness to use computer and online tools as well as how they used them during their student teaching. Teacher education students enrolled in two pedagogy courses were surveyed at the beginning and end of the courses and interviewed over the duration of the courses regarding the nature and extent of their technological knowledge and skill. Following the completion of the pedagogy courses, six volunteered to have their technology use tracked during their nine-week practice teaching experience. Findings showed that while the preservice pedagogy courses did increase the student teachers' knowledge of and skill with a variety of computer and online tools as well as their desire to use them during their student teaching, the elementary schools in which they were placed for their practicum were poorly

DOI: 10.4018/978-1-61350-492-5.ch028

equipped and the mentor teachers were not using the tools that were modeled on campus. If preservice teachers are to truly understand the benefits of learning and teaching with technology, teacher education institutions and school districts need to work together to present a consistent vision of technology integration, and schools need to provide environments that encourage and support technology use.

BACKGROUND INFORMATION

Educating our youth for the digital age requires learning experiences that are not only infused with the latest in technological tools but that also help to develop them as digital citizens who can locate, evaluate and ethically use information, think critically and creatively, problem solve, make decisions based on sound evidence, and collaborate with others from around the globe using digital resources. In order for these experiences to be a part of their learning, students need teachers who are both aware of and skilled with the latest technologies. While most practicing teachers have professional development opportunities in which to acquire these skills, it is paramount that new teachers entering the field are familiar with these tools as well. In order to prepare our beginning teachers for this twenty-first century reality, we must build wide-ranging educational experiences that encourage the use of emerging technologies throughout our entire teacher preparation program.

Setting the Stage

Traditionally most teacher education institutions have attempted to develop beginning teachers' technological knowledge and skills through a mandatory stand-alone technology course focused on learning how to use a variety of computer-based tools and programs. While such a course can assist with the development of technological skills, the research recommends that if student teachers are to be prepared to go out to classrooms and foster change, then teacher preparation programs must model the use of these technologies and provide opportunities for preservice teachers to increase their technological skills throughout their preparatory experiences, including during practice teaching in schools (Angeli, 2004; Brown & Warschauer, 2006; Magliaro & Ezeife, 2007). In addition to modeling a variety of technologies there also needs to be the ongoing discussion incorporated into all aspects of the teacher preparation program about issues and challenges related to technology use.

One way to extend preservice teachers' understandings of the potential of a technology rich environment is to model such an environment in subject-specific pedagogy courses offered as part of a teacher education program (Beaudin & Hadden, 2005;

Dexter & Riedel, 2003; Rowley, Dysard & Arnold, 2005). These pedagogy courses can provide opportunities for preservice teachers to develop deeper understandings about how to use technology in ways that engage children critically, creatively and collaboratively in conjunction with the development of subject-specific knowledge (Brown & Warschauer, 2006).

THE CASE

The study reported in this case examined the influences of technology-infused social studies pedagogy courses on student teachers' perceptions about why, when and how to most effectively infuse technology in their teaching, and their attempts at incorporating those technologies during their practice teaching in schools.

The Technology Experiences Provided

As part of a four year Bachelor of Education Program, students majoring in elementary social studies education in our Faculty of Education can take two pedagogy courses related to social studies teaching and learning. In the introductory course, technology is being used to expand students' knowledge and understanding of key social studies concepts such as citizenship and diversity, as well as teaching approaches such as constructivism and concept development. Students are introduced to examples of technology-supported best practices including videoclips of expert teachers working with elementary students (Brown, Collins & Duguid, 1989). Teacher tools such as rubric generators, lesson plan databases, and repositories of primary sources for teaching history are also investigated and evaluated in terms of their fit with the mandated curriculum and their suitability for supporting a constructivist learning environment. Student assignments introduce technology-supported modes of representing learning, supporting metacognitive thought, and deepening understanding of abstract concepts using tools such as weblogs, digital mapping, podcasts, video interfaces and VoiceThreads (Jonassen, 1995). A wiki serves as the hub for the class by providing a space to host course content as well as a collaborative environment for students to construct their knowledge and reflect on their learning.

In the second advanced social studies pedagogy course, videoconferencing technology is used to bring the realities of classroom teaching into the course (Basham, Lowrey & Jones, 2006; Lehman & Richardson, 2007). Student teachers are connected synchronously to practicing teachers and children in elementary classrooms as social studies is being taught. These videoconferencing sessions not only allow students to share a common observation of skilled teachers, which can then be discussed in class, but the students also experience an authentic example of how this technology can be used in the elementary classroom to promote collaboration and communication among learners. For one assignment students are to work in groups to design their own telecollaborative learning experience for an elementary grade. Wikis and blogs are most often used for these projects. For a second course assignment, students create an online scrapbook around a controversial issue. Student efforts are to focus on a specific elementary grade level and social studies curriculum topic. Suggested tools for creating this scrapbook are Zoho Notebook, Mixbook and Glogster.

Student Teachers' Views on the Effectiveness of Technology Experiences

Students in these two courses were surveyed both prior to and following the 13-week courses regarding the nature and extent of their technological knowledge and skill for teaching social studies subject matter. Twelve volunteers from among those surveyed were also interviewed at the midpoint of each course. The surveys identified that for the most part by the end of the courses our students were feeling prepared and ready to use technology in their teaching (88% up from 44%). Ninety-seven percent agreed/strongly agreed that after their courses, they could think of lots of ways to use computers in teaching social studies (up from 83%). They were more familiar with wikis and blogs (90% up from 28%), digital mapping and storytelling tools (74% up from 12%), audio and visual recording tools like podcasts and VoiceThread (72% up from 18%), and videoconferencing (58% up from 26%). Ninety-three percent felt more comfortable with how to locate and evaluate the quality and appropriateness of educational web sites (up from 68%). However, despite the focus on technology in the courses, half of the students continued to feel nervous about using technology in teaching.

The interview conversations with the education students clarified and brought deeper understanding to the survey responses in three areas: a) perceptions of the role of technology as a tool for supporting and enhancing learning, b) ideas for how to integrate technology into their social studies teaching, and c) concerns about using technology as a teaching and learning tool.

Perceptions of the Role of Technology as a Tool

The interview participants saw technology as a way to enhance children's interest in their learning, to make learning more relevant and meaningful, to engage students in discovery learning and exploration, to increase interaction in and outside the classroom between the teacher, the students, and the home, and to incorporate multiple perspectives on issues through easy access to a wealth of information in a variety of formats. Here are some of their comments:

I want to get the kids involved. I want them to have positive experiences with technology. [I want to use computers] to enhance student interest, provide meaningful learning experiences, and increase their sense of wonderment in the subject.

It can be a wealth of information if used correctly, students can develop their own meanings and answers to questions that don't have one right answer.

When I was in school I worked out of a textbook the entire time, and now seeing the options for making the class more interactive and everything, it's fantastic. Plus it includes the visual learners in the classroom. Having information and giving it in many different media doesn't leave anyone out.

I am perfectly willing to put the wiki up so they can go home and show their parents what they have learned. Maybe have that as a requirement once a month, you have to show your parents, and teach them what you have learned in this class. Brings accountability that way too.

You need to use technology to engage your students and have them do discovery learning and exploration.

Kids are digital learners and the technology needs to be relevant to them and interactive.

Ideas about how to Integrate Technology in Their Teaching of Social Studies

The students who were interviewed talked about a variety of ways to use technology in their teaching of social studies such as showing videos from YouTube and TeacherTube, powerpoint lectures, teacher and student research, making student productions, recording interviews, telecollaborating using wikis, Nings (social networking), and blogs, setting up Delicious accounts for keeping track of best practice websites, teaching concepts using Wordle, and using digital mapping to design a community walk. Two stated:

Social studies is a great place to incorporate technology and make it more interesting, because social is one of the least favorite subjects among students. If I were using it, it would be based on an actual culminating project or helping them develop deeper understanding. Maybe we do some blog writing, role modeling like take a historical point of view on blogs or they could use digital storytelling.

Teaching is almost going to go international—classrooms talking with classrooms in Tunisia, using email to create that inter-connectiveness. I can't wait to try it in teaching.

Concerns about Using Technology as Teaching and Learning Tools

While the student teachers that were interviewed were generally feeling more knowledgeable about the various tools and more motivated to want to use them in their teaching, they also talked about a number of concerns that they had about using technology in their teaching. These concerns included: dealing with glitches, fear of not knowing as much about the technology as the children, needing more exposure to more tools, having access to technology in their practicum school, managing the classroom, having a supportive practicum teacher, ensuring the safety of students, and feeling somewhat unprepared to teach social studies. Here are some of the students comments related to each concern:

Dealing with glitches

The thing that overwhelms me is getting something to work. If the technology goes down, how do I fix it?

[My concern is] that when you have a spectacular lesson, nothing works and you have to pull the lesson out of thin air and do it without technology. [I worry] if something goes haywire, and you totally lose the kids.

One student was already thinking about what to do when encountering these glitches:

You can expect glitches will happen. Always have a plan B, so you have things ready such as a printout.

The need to know more than the children

I would be concerned that kids would know more than me about say PowerPoint, or even a spreadsheet, or a database. I would take classes so that I know a little bit about it. If I don't feel completely comfortable with something students want to use, I do not know how I would handle it.

Others did not perceive this lack of knowledge as a concern:

I'm okay with the kids knowing more than me, because teaching is a learning process for everybody. I have no fear about saying to kids, 'I don't know how set this up, I need somebody to help me.'

More opportunity to experiment with various tools

One aspect that scares me is Smartboards, and it shouldn't. There are so many ways to use it. It is mindboggling; I don't even know where to start. I could use it, but if I was told to integrate, I could, but things are always changing, too. I could never say I know everything. I constantly have to be learning, doing the training and figuring things out.

I am not comfortable at all right now about using technology in my teaching. The only things I have been exposed to are in this [social studies] course. I don't really know much about using the Internet with elementary age students.

I'm excited, but a little overwhelmed because I know there is so much you can do. I am not confident in using technology. I need to learn where to get those resources.

Here are concerns about the availability of the equipment:

Accessibility is an issue. In my IPT I did a math unit, and we used Spy Guys math and I wanted them to work that project in pairs, but another class booked the lab. So we did it as a class in the classroom, which was fine, but I did not get to see who really understood. There was not as much individual input.

Having the resources is a concern because some schools do not have the technology I would like to have.

The need to manage student learning

I think it is hard when students have a computer in front of them. How do we know they are on task?

189

One student was already thinking about a solution:

Having students on task is my concern. I think it is quite easy to get off target. Instead of saying surf and find the Canadian government, I would have three sites on the whiteboard and those are the only sites they can go to. I think that is how I would manage it.

Another management issue was about ensuring that the tasks set out were at the appropriate ability levels for the children.

My concerns would be that the activity set out for them is scaffolded enough so that they can actually do it.

I worry the students absolutely don't get what you are trying to get at.

Some students commented about their upcoming student teaching experience:

In my practicum the school had two SMART Boards and the teachers never even touched it.

Some teachers are threatened by technology, which is so sad. If they could just realize the value in it.

A lot of my friends and family are teachers. I go home and am really excited about what I have been shown that are technology based; videos you can use, Zoho Notebooks, and the first response I get is 'that's great, but how will it work in a real classroom? We don't have the technology. How are you going to teach it if you do not have the technology?' So I feel there is some cynicism about using it in the 'real' classroom. It makes me a little bit nervous, coming out of university thinking about the great things I want to do, but will I be able to use it? You go into an environment [school] and you are so excited. And then you feel all the excitement you have about something is shot down.

I sure hope my APT (practice teaching) is in a school with a focus on technology because I have learned all these great things here about it and I hope to apply it somehow, instead of just drawing maps on the floor, traditional style social studies.

The other teachers at my mentor school had never heard of any of these tools - the Wiki, Wordle, they were all new to them. I am enjoying being able to share them with other teachers.

Here are concerns about the safety of students:

It is scary to have kids on computers. There are a lot of bad things that can result from that. How do you protect your students when they are online? How do you ensure their security on a wiki or Ning, or how do you stop them navigating some place you do not want them to go? I know that if I had a student on a chat line and something happened, I would be responsible. So it is really scary.

I would like to learn more about the safety of using it, such as protecting yourself so that students do not get into (compromising) sites.

Some felt that they were adequately prepared to teach social studies:

I worry that I would leave this university not having enough ideas or knowing where to get ideas [for social studies].

I think it's fantastic using technology, but I want more insight into how I'm supposed to have children understand what I'm trying to say and how I can be a good teacher with the units and the resources I can use to meet the different learner outcomes and understand it on a bigger basis that what I know.

I believe it would be more beneficial to focus on the Program of Studies for social.

Summary of Response Evaluations

In sum, all but one of the student teachers who were interviewed stated they believed technology is a useful tool for fostering learning and identified ways they could use it in their social studies classrooms. They all expressed concerns over their ability to handle technology glitches, accessibility of equipment, and their need for more opportunity to experiment with new technologies such as the Smartboard. Some felt that before they would integrated computers in their teaching, they needed to know more about technology than their students. And all were concerned about classroom management and student online safety when using computers. Most of the interviewees were concerned that their mentor teacher in their upcoming practicum might not use technology and therefore be unable to support them in their attempts to integrate computers with learning. A few of the preservice teachers felt their pedagogy course had provided too much information about technology and not enough about teaching social studies.

Experimenting with Technology during Practice Teaching

Six of the student teachers that completed the survey and the midpoint interviews agreed to be followed into their practice teaching settings the following term. These six were interviewed three times during the subsequent 9-week practice teaching experience to examine the impact that the modeling of new technologies in the social studies pedagogy courses had on their use of technology during their practice teaching. They were also given a laptop and a data projector to use for the duration of the practicum.

In the first interview they talked about why they felt it would be important to integrate technology into their teaching and their feelings of preparedness to use it as well as what tools they would like to try out. All except one of the six were optimistic about the idea of using technology to support and enhance children's learning. One remained skeptical about those benefits.

All six of the practice teaching schools were in smaller and, in several cases, rural school districts, and possessed limited access to technology and no wireless access to the internet in the classrooms. The only computer available in each classroom was on the teacher's desk. School labs were available in each case but scheduling was limited, internet access was slow, and many labs were outdated. All six mentor teachers were making limited to no use of computers in their teaching. While none of the mentor teachers refused to let the student teachers use technology in their teaching, they neither encouraged its use nor made suggestions for further use beyond what the student teachers wanted to try.

The student teachers used the laptop and data projector provided through the research project mostly for lesson and unit planning, to display images captured from the web, to provide students with access to websites related to topics under study, to play online games, to show videos, and for graphing, poster design and digital mapping activities. One student teacher created a class wiki. Several students were in classrooms where the Smartboard had just recently been introduced. The most reticent technology user was one of these students and he benefitted from attending workshops and learning along with his mentor teacher.

By the end of the practicum the student teachers identified the benefits for the children's learning resulting from the use of the technology as: increased excitement and interest in what was being learned; the ability to make the children's learning more concrete; the ability to extend and relate learning to the children's worlds; the ability to increase the students' feeling of controlling their own learning; increased communications between the teacher and the students and between the home and the school; and, the ability to meet the needs of visual learners. They also noted limitations regarding technology use such as the amount of preparation time required outside of classroom teaching; school district restrictions on access to the web, to email and to connecting their personal laptops to the school network; inaccessible and/or slow internet access in the classrooms and in rural homes; classroom management issues particularly in a lab setting; outdated applications, computers and data projectors in schools; the children's lack of computer skills; computer lab booking issues; and, the difficulty of getting technical assistance in the schools.

CONCLUSION

This case study acknowledges that the preservice pedagogy courses did assist in increasing preservice teachers' understandings of a variety of ways to approach the use of various technology tools in their teaching as well as their willingness to use them during their practice teaching. However, for the most part the student teachers were still nervous about using those tools during their practice teaching especially when it came to dealing with computer glitches. More emphasis in our preservice program needs to be placed on developing student teachers' troubleshooting and problem solving skills when it comes to technology use in order to increase their feelings of self-efficacy.

Current Challenges

During the practicum the student teachers were also able to experiment with some of the tools about which they learned in their courses. However, the schools presented many unexpected barriers to that use. For the most part, the classrooms were poorly equipped and mentor teachers were not using the digital tools to which student teachers had been exposed during their social studies pedagogy courses. Teacher education institutions and school districts need to work together to present a consistent vision of technology integration. All instructors teaching in teacher preparation programs need to commit to modeling meaningful uses of technology that enhance learning in their courses, and the schools need to provide environments that encourage and support technology use in tandem with our integration efforts in our preservice pedagogy courses in order for our student teachers to truly see the benefits.

REFERENCES

Angeli, C. (2004). The effects of case-based learning on early childhood preservice teachers' beliefs about the pedagogical use of ICT. *Journal of Educational Media*, *29*, 139–151. doi:10.1080/1358165042000253302

Basham, J. D., Lowrey, K. A., & Jones, M. L. (2006). Making use of the net: Internet based videoconferencing and online conferencing tools in teacher preparation. In Crawford, D. A. Willis, R. Carlsen, I. Gibson, K. McFerrin, J. Price, & R. Weber (Eds.), *AACE handbook* (pp. 1440-1444). Retrieved September 25, 2009, from ED/IT Lib.

Beaudin, L., & Hadden, C. (2005). Technology and pedagogy: Building techno pedagogical skills in preservice teachers. *Innovate 2*(2). Retrieved November 9, 2009, from http://www.innovateonline.info/index.php?view=article&id=36

Brown, D., & Warschauer, M. (2006). From the university to the elementary classroom: Students' experiences in learning to integrate technology in instruction. *Journal of Technology and Teacher Education, 14*(3), 599–621.

Brown, J., Collins, A., & Duguid, P. (1989). Situated cognition and the culture of learning. *Educational Researcher, 18*, 32–42.

Dexter, S., & Riedel, E. (2003). Why improving preservice teacher educational technology preparation must go beyond the college's walls. *Journal of Teacher Education, 54*, 334–346. doi:10.1177/0022487103255319

Doering, A., Hughes, J., & Huffman, D. (2003). Preservice teachers: Are we thinking with technology? *Journal of Research on Technology in Education, 35*(3), 342–361.

Jacobsen, M., Clifford, P., & Friesen, S. (2002). Preparing teachers for technology integration: Creating a culture of inquiry in the context of use. *Contemporary Issues in Technology & Teacher Education, 2*(3), 363–388.

Jonassen, D. H. (1995). Supporting communities of learners with technology: A vision for integrating technology with learning in schools. *Educational Technology, 35*(4), 60–63.

Lehman, J. D., & Richardson, J. (2007). *Linking teacher preparation programs with k-12 schools via videoconferencing: Benefits and limitations*. Retrieved from http://p3t3.education.purdue.edu/AERA2007_Videoconf_Paper.pdf

Magliaro, J., & Ezeife, A. (2007). Preservice teachers' preparedness to integrate computer technology into the curriculum. *Canadian Journal of Learning and Technology, 33*(3), 95.

Rowley, J., Dysard, G., & Arnold, J. (2005). Developing a new technology infusion program for preparing tomorrow's teachers. *Journal of Technology and Teacher Education, 13*(1), 105–123.

Chapter 29
Web–Based Instruction:
A Case Study of Preservice Elementary Teachers' Efficacy in Modeling and Reasoning with Fractions

Cheng-Yao Lin
Southern Illinois University Carbondale, USA

Fenqjen Luo
Montana State University Bozeman, USA

Jane-Jane Lo
Western Michigan University, USA

EXECUTIVE SUMMARY

This case study explored the efficacy of web-based instruction on preservice elementary teachers' mathematics learning. Web-based instruction is appealing to many schools in urban settings because it helps them to face the two big challenges most akin to their schools: to motivate students' interests and to meet the diverse students needs with its interactive feature and adaptive capability. Ten preservice elementary teachers were interviewed regarding their ability to model and reason with fractions after receiving web-based instruction on these topics in their regular mathematics method course. The interview transcripts were used to provide information about the strength and weakness of participants' conceptual and procedural understanding of fractions. The findings of this case study identify promises and challenges in supporting the recommendations of many national reports, such as

DOI: 10.4018/978-1-61350-492-5.ch029

the NCTM Professional Standards for School Mathematics (2000) and the National Mathematics Advisory Panel (2008), in incorporating technology into the compulsory mathematics classrooms.

BACKGROUND INFORMATION

According to National Council of Teachers Mathematics (NCTM) (2000), "technology is essential in teaching and learning mathematics; it influences the mathematics that is taught and enhances students' learning." (p. 24). Past studies on integrating technology in mathematics teaching and learning have investigated the impact of spreadsheets, and dynamic geometry software on student achievement (Isikal & Askar, 2005; Olkun, Altun, & Smith, 2005; Sinclair, 2004). The findings of the research have generally shown positive effects of computer-based instruction on students' achievement.

With the recent enormous growth of the World Wide Web, web-based instruction has, in particular, received a lot of attention from mathematics education researchers. Studies have shown that using multimedia or interactive web-based modules can increase student learning (Aberson, Berger, Healy, & Romero, 2003; Bliwise, 2005; Fletcher-Flinn & Gravatt, 1995; McNeil & Nelson, 1991). Specifically, studies have examined the effect of web-based tutorial on learning various statistics concepts (Bilwise, 2005). A study conducted by Aberson et al. (2003) found that students who used a freely available web-based tutorial on hypothetical testing performed better on a quiz than did students who completed the standard laboratory.

Setting the Stage

The purpose of this study was to investigate the effectiveness of web-based instruction in supporting preservice elementary teachers' learning. Despite web-based instruction having a strong presence in mathematics teaching and learning, the empirical research conducted on the efficiency of web-based instruction in mathematics teacher education is limited. Our understanding about the nature and strength of web-based instruction is still insufficient. For example, it remains unclear whether web-based instruction can help learners achieve a high conceptual level regarding mathematical teaching and learning.

The mathematics content that we focus on in this case study is fractions, a critical component of elementary school mathematics. Through exploring preservice teachers' efficacy in fraction modeling and reasoning, this case study will increase our understanding of the nature and effect of web-based instruction in the teacher education setting.

THE CASE

Considering many teachers lack the knowledge of how to properly incorporate technology in the classroom (Doering, Hughs, & Huffman, 2003), participants were provided with web-based training for six weeks (18 hours) in Number and Operations as part of the regular classroom curriculum in a Mathematics Content and Methods for the Elementary School Teachers course. They were introduced to several interactive web sites appropriate for elementary students such as National Library of Virtual Manipulatives (National Library of Virtual Manipulatives, 2007) and Illuminations (National Council of Teachers Mathematics, 2007). Next, they were asked to use web-based instructional software to model or reason a mathematics idea in different ways and present their work. The purpose of the web-based training is to ensure they possess sufficient knowledge and skills concerning web-based instruction. Participants were interviewed with respect to their beliefs in teaching fractions under a web-based setting.

In addition, participants were asked to describe and illustrate in detail how to model or reason major fraction ideas including the meaning of fraction numbers, equivalent fractions, fraction addition, and fraction multiplication using web-based tools. The following is a sample of the interview questions:

- What aspects of the web-based instruction in multiplication of fractions were beneficial to you? Why? Give an example to illustrate.
- What aspects of the web-based instruction in division of fractions were beneficial to you? Why? Give an example to illustrate.

Current Challenges Facing the Organization

In general, participating preservice teachers expressed positive attitudes toward learning and teaching mathematics through web-based software. They commented on being captivated by the interactive and learner-centered features of the web-based activities. The dynamic and animated tools have helped them improve their abilities to visualize and conceptualize mathematics concepts. One student Markie commented,

One of the websites was beneficial in that it clearly demonstrated the link between finding area and multiplying fractions. For example, the program demonstrated the problem $1/9 \times 1/9$. Through the interactive session, I was able to create two figures that displayed what $1/9$ looks like. Then, the program superimposed the two fractions over one another making the denominator 81. After this, I could see that out of 81 squares only one of these overlapped. Hence, the answer was $1/81$.

Figure 1. Example of student's model of fraction multiplication

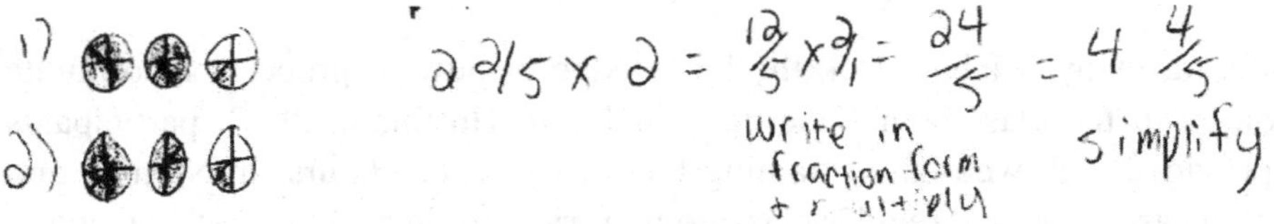

Furthermore, interviewees felt that the instant feedback they received through the programs was valuable in helping them identify the weakness of their understanding, and formulate future learning plans. Most of them felt that their conceptual knowledge as well as procedural knowledge has improved. All of them felt comfortable and confident about delivering web-based instruction in mathematics.

Like many tutorial tools, the challenges that web-based instruction faces are the breadth and depth of mathematical teaching and learning. First of all, although the web-based environment was very enjoyable and stimulating, most of the preservice teachers felt that currently there was insufficient connection between web-based instruction and real-world mathematics. They also felt that web-based instruction is not yet able to serve as a medium to teach conceptual knowledge at a deep level.

With regard to fractions, the challenges facing web-based instruction are especially amplified in the most challenging topics–fraction multiplication and division. In terms of fraction multiplication, although preservice teachers improved their fraction multiplication procedural knowledge through web-based instruction, they were not able to learn as much conceptual knowledge as was expected. For example, one student, Whitney, knew how to compute $2 \ 2/5 \times 2$ using paper and pencil. However, she did not know how to appropriately model fraction multiplication. Figure 1 is her drawing for $2 \ 2/5 \times 2$. She did not draw fiths proportionally. In addition, the final solution 4 4/5 was not derived from her pictorial model.

Similar conceptual weakness was found for other preservice teachers' responses to fraction division problems. One student, David, drew $1/2 \div 3/4 = 2/3$ as seen in Figure 2. He did not know 1/2 divided by 3/4 is the concept of how many 3/4 fit into 1/2. He simply showed his conceptual knowledge by overlapping 1/2 and 3/4.

Our analyses of the interview responses as well as the web-based activities have pointed to several sources of its shortcoming. First, the visual simulations are only available for certain models. As shown in Figure 3, for example, the visual simulations provided by the National Library of Virtual Manipulatives (NLVM) are only limited to area modeling. There is no explanation for why fraction multiplication can be simulated this way. And there is no corresponding word problem, posed to help its users make meaningful understanding of fraction multiplication, such as

Figure 2. Example of student's model of fraction division

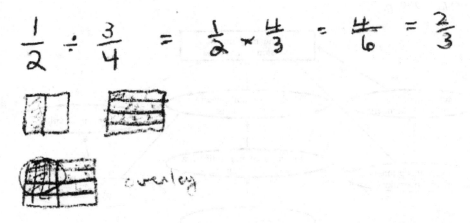

"Amy has 3/4 of a cup cake. She puts sprinkles on 2/3 of her cup cake. How much of a whole cup cake will have sprinkles?"

Another weakness about web-based software like NLML is the lack of connection between related mathematics units. For example, its virtual simulation of fraction multiplication is not related to more basic topics such as whole number multiplication and fraction addition or more advanced topics such as fraction division. Tacit transition between different levels such as from a fraction by whole number

Figure 3. Visual simulation of fraction multiplication

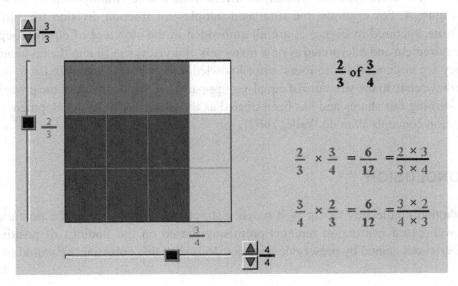

Figure 4. A knowledge package for understanding the meaning of division by fraction (Ma, 1999, p. 77)

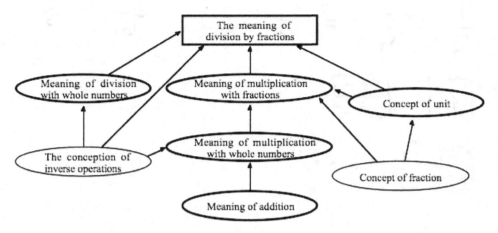

multiplication like 2/3 × 4 to a fraction by fraction multiplication like 2/3 × 3/4 is not made.

As suggested by Ma (1999) for fraction division, the meaning of fraction division is placed on the top layer of major fraction concepts and operations (see Figure 4). A deep conceptual understanding of fraction division should be built upon a deep conceptual understanding of those prior concepts and operations.

Our analyses of the fraction division activities on the tutorial website of Visual Fractions also revealed limited connection with the network of prior knowledge, such as the meanings of whole number division and fraction multiplication, shown in Figure 4. For example, the simulated samples for fraction division from this website, pictured in Figure 5, are all embedded in the structure of equal-groups measurement and interpreted as how many sets of divisors can fit into the dividend. They are not connected to users' prior knowledge on whole number division, nor do they relate to the structure of equal-groups partition, which involves the process of forming fair shares and has been treated as the first goal in the development of fraction concepts (Van de Walle, 2007).

CONCLUSION

Although challenges facing web-based instruction were observed, the potential of web-based instruction remains promising, based on the findings of positive experiences gained by preservice teachers. To realize this potential, we would like

Figure 5. Virtual simulation of fraction division

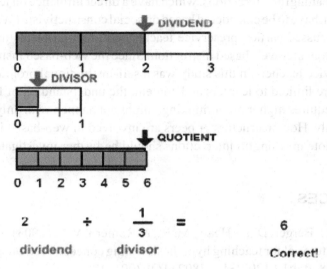

to propose the following solutions and recommendations to improve the current environment and functions of web-based instruction.

First, web-based instruction will be more meaningful and conceptual by adding more realistic examples. The two mentioned websites–National Library of Virtual Manipulatives (NLVM) and Visual Fractions–only focus on visual modeling rather than descriptive reasoning using real-world examples. Web-based amenities for promoting deep understanding such as video clips about real-world application in fractions should be added to the websites. Word problems, which can serve as an avenue for developing and assessing an individual's understanding in mathematics (Barlow & Drake, 2008; English, 1998; NCTM, 2000) should accompany the visual models.

Second, linkages between each level of knowledge need to be established on websites. Relevant concepts in the same knowledge network should be marked on websites and hyperlinked to their details. Research focusing on the developmental progression like the concept map proposed by Ma (1999) in Figure 4 can be applied to the development of a knowledge network.

Third, the web-based instruction can be richer and more diverse by including more resources into the development of teaching materials on websites. There is a significant gap between teaching materials found on websites and teaching materials published as books or articles. Generally speaking, teaching materials established on websites were not as well developed like those in books or articles with regard to fraction multiplication and division.

Finally, meaningful interactions, which have a direct influence on learners' intellectual growth, have to be considered based on social constructivism (Woo & Reeves, 2007). As discussed earlier, preservice teachers still had problems understanding fraction division after web-based instruction. Since the web-based instruction taken by the preservice teachers in this study was a self-instructional program where the interactions are limited to learners and content, the understanding of fraction division, which requires higher order thinking, might not happen with only this kind of interaction only. How instructors or peers are involved in web-based instruction in order to promote meaningful interactions should be further investigated.

REFERENCES

Aberson, C. L., Berger, D. E., Healy, M. R., & Romero, V. L. (2003). Evaluation of an interactive tutorial for teaching hypothesis testing concepts. *Teaching of Psychology*, *30*, 75–78. doi:10.1207/S15328023TOP3001_12

Barlow, A. T., & Drake, J. M. (2008). Division by a fraction: Assessing understanding through problem writing. *Teaching Children Mathematics*, *13*, 326–332.

Bliwise, N. G. (2005). Web-based tutorials for teaching introductory statistics. *Journal of Educational Computing Research*, *33*(3), 309–325. doi:10.2190/0D1J-1CE1-5UXY-3V34

Bliwise, N. G. (2005). Web-based tutorials for teaching introductory statistics. *Journal of Educational Computing Research*, *33*(3), 309–325. doi:10.2190/0D1J-1CE1-5UXY-3V34

Doering, A., Hughes, J., & Huffman, D. (2003). Preservice teachers: Are we thinking with technology? *Journal of Research on Technology in Education*, 35, 342-361.

English, L. D. (1998). Children's problem posing within formal context and informal contexts. *Journal for Research in Mathematics Education*, *29*, 83–106. doi:10.2307/749719

Fletcher-Flinn, C. M., & Gravatt, B. (1995). The efficacy of computer-assisted instruction (CAI): A meta-analysis. *Journal of Educational Computing Research*, *12*, 219–241. doi:10.2190/51D4-F6L3-JQHU-9M31

Isiksal, M., & Askar, P. (2005). The effect of spreadsheet and dynamic geometry software on the achievement and self-efficacy of 7th-grade students. *Educational Research*, *47*(3), 333–350. doi:10.1080/00131880500287815

Ma, L. (1999). *Knowing and teaching elementary mathematics: Teachers' understanding of fundamental mathematics in China and the United States*. Hillsdale, NJ: Erlbaum.

McNeil, B. J., & Nelson, K. R. (1991). Meta-analysis of interactive video instruction: A ten year review of achievement effects. *Journal of Computer-Based Instruction*, *18*, 1–6.

National Council of Teachers of Mathematics (NCTM). (2000). *Principles and standards for school Mathematics*. Reston, VA: Author.

National Mathematics Advisory Panel. (2008). *Foundations for success: The final report of the National Mathematics Advisory Panel*. Washington, DC: U.S. Department of Education.

Olkun, S., Altun, A., & Smith, G. (2005). Computers and 2D geometric learning of Turkish fourth and fifth graders. *British Journal of Educational Technology*, *36*(2), 317–326. doi:10.1111/j.1467-8535.2005.00460.x

Sinclair, M. (2004). Working with accurate representations: The case of preconstructed dynamic geometry sketches. *Journal of Computers in Mathematics and Science Teaching, 23*(2), 191-208.

Van de Walle, J. A. (2007). *Elementary and middle school mathematics: Teaching developmentally* (6th ed). Boston, MA: Allyn and Bacon.

Woo, Y., & Reeves, T. C. (2007). Meaningful interaction in web-based learning: A social constructivist interpretation. *The Internet and Higher Education, 10*, 15–25. doi:10.1016/j.iheduc.2006.10.005

Chapter 30
The Pathway to Nevada's Future:
A Case of Statewide Technology Integration and Professional Development

P.G. Schrader
University of Nevada, Las Vegas, USA

Terra Graves
Washoe County School District, USA

Neal Strudler
University of Nevada, Las Vegas, USA

Shawn L. Pennell
University of Nevada, Reno, USA

Loretta Asay
University of Nevada, Las Vegas, USA

Sara Stewart
Clark County School District, USA

EXECUTIVE SUMMARY

An online, statewide technology professional development project was implemented for middle school teachers in Nevada. This document reports the preliminary findings associated with the planning, development, and implementation of Module 1 of the Pathway to Nevada's Future project. Baseline data, participant characteristics, findings, and results from participation in Module 1 are reported. Data sources include online surveys, online discussions, and informal interviews of project personnel.

During the planning phase, the milestones outlined in the grant proposal were accomplished. In terms of project implementation, Module 1 was designed, developed, and implemented. A schedule for Module 2 was developed for the summer and implemented during June and July 2010.

DOI: 10.4018/978-1-61350-492-5.ch030

At the beginning of Module 1, base-line data were collected and examined to describe the general profile of Pathway participants. Overall, these data suggested that the population of participants was an appropriate cross section of Nevada teachers. Participants indicated that they held a high opinion of the role of technology in the classroom and reported being moderately skilled in technology use. There were many areas, however, in which they were not skilled and had room to benefit from the planned modules. Overall, the group was well suited to interact with the professional development materials, provide formative feedback for refining the modules, and apply their learning in classrooms across Nevada.

Module 1 primarily involved an overview of resources, tools, and strategies intended for a variety of settings. Activities ranged from conceptual readings, webinars, videos, and discussions, to hands-on assignments that exposed participants to a range of tools.

Results indicated that participants significantly increased in their knowledge, attitudes, and self-efficacy associated with technology and technology integration. However, analysis of progress, assignments, and online discussions indicated that the amount of material was overwhelming for the majority of participants. As a result, adjustments to the delivery of Module 1 were implemented during the professional development. These modifications were also implemented in subsequent Modules, allowing participants to explore applications of interest at a deeper level.

BACKGROUND INFORMATION

Digital technologies and their uses have pervaded nearly every segment of society. For example, informed citizens may find their news via television, online news outlets, papers, magazines, blogs, forums, and/or podcasts, just to name a few. People may find respite in virtual worlds like Second Life, World of Warcraft, or EverQuest. Others may simply consume media and movies on smartphones, portable MP3 players, or tablet computers. Regardless of the medium, students also find themselves in a world that is pervaded by technology, media, and knowledge. Technology has clearly provided new affordances for the presentation and storage of information.

These contemporary environments also allow users to participate in the creation and exchange of information in dynamic ways (Dede, 2008; Schrader, Lawless, & McCreery, 2009). On the World Wide Web (WWW), there has been a shift from a passive information retrieval system to a dynamic, interactive model in which users are active participants in authoring, editing, evaluating, and disseminating content (Dede, 2008; O'Reilly, 2005). Often termed Web 2.0, the modern Internet and WWW have changed the way people share their views (e.g., blogs), engage in communities of practice (e.g., social networks), and collaborate on ideas (e.g., wikis) (Dede, 2008; Jenkins, 2006; 2007; 2008). When compared to an industrial society, this difference is profound and requires an entirely different set of skills to be productive (Goldman, 2004).

Collectively, the presentation, consumption, and production of information across resources and modes have given rise to a wide array of educational difficulties. Although 17 million students in the United States regularly use the Internet in school (Pew Internet and American Life, 2001, 2005), we know very little about the skills students require to negotiate these information environments (Lawless & Schrader, 2008). As a result, little emphasis is placed on training students to become competent 21st century learners within formal school settings (Manning, Lawless, Gomez, McLeod, Braasch, & Goldman, 2008). This is not only true of the United States, but countries like Australia and the United Kingdom where there is a similar push toward understanding educational technology and technology integration for the 21st century (Kitson, Fletcher, & Kearney, 2007; New London Group, 1996). Unfortunately, what students are trained to do in school does not necessarily align with the expectations of what they need to do in their futures (Apple, 2007; Gee, 2006; Leu, 2000; Schrader et al., 2009).

As a result of these concerns, educators in Nevada developed a statewide program to facilitate the integration of technology in Nevada's schools as part of a national funding initiative. This chapter describes and characterizes the conceptualization and implementation of this project as it may pertain to other broad-scale technology integration projects. Findings associated with the planning and development phase of the Pathway project's first professional development module (of four) are reported. Several sources of data are included to provide a context for the case. Specifically, these include qualitative interviews with instructors/trainers, trainee artifacts, discussions, and quantitative data from various instruments. Further, baseline data were examined to describe the general profile of Pathway participants. Overall, these data suggest that the population of participants is an appropriate cross section of Nevada teachers. In general, participants hold a high opinion of the role of technology in the classroom and report being moderately skilled in technology use. There are many areas, however, in which they are not skilled and have room to benefit from the modules planned. Overall, the group appears well suited to interact with the professional development materials, provide formative feedback for refining the modules, and apply their learning in classrooms across Nevada.

Case Background

The State of Nevada is characterized by two urban areas, Las Vegas and Reno, and a vast landscape of relatively isolated smaller cities and towns, and has educational funding at a national low (Per Pupil Expenditures by State, 2004). Nevada is a large state in terms of land area, covering 109,826 square miles but has a population of 2,783,733, the majority of whom live in or near Las Vegas. Las Vegas lies within the Clark County School District (CCSD), which is the fifth largest district in the United States.

The student population in Nevada reflects diversity in many ways. For example, of the 429,362 students enrolled in Nevada schools, 39.4% are eligible for free or reduced lunch. More than 10% are enrolled in limited-English proficiency programs and approximately 11% of students have an Individualized Education Plan (IEP). Across the state, nearly 20% of students are enrolled in Title I schools. In terms of racial backgrounds, more than half of the student population is from traditional ethnic minorities of which Hispanic students comprise 36.4% of the school population. Black (11.0%), Asian/Pacific Islander (7.9%), American Indian/Alaskan Native (1.5%) and White (43.1%) students account for the rest.

Unfortunately, Nevada students fare poorly in terms of funding, resources, and testing when compared to other students in the United States (Institute of Education Sciences, 2010; National Education Association, 2010). For example, Nevada spent $7,292 per student in 2007 (NEA, 2010). While that figure increased to $8,029 in 2010, the National Education Association still ranked Nevada 48th in this category (IES, 2010; NEA, 2010). This may be due to fallout from the largest period of growth in Nevada's history. The population of Nevada increased 45.5% from 1997 to 2007. The influx of school age children, combined with geographic isolation and low levels of funding compared to other states, has stretched resources to the breaking point.

Overall, these unique characteristics place tremendous demands on the state's Department of Education. The tremendous breadth of needs among constituents in Nevada creates challenges in terms of teacher preparation and training. Nevada education and educators must serve the needs of urban students as well as isolated rural students, whose link to the world depends on technology. More importantly, all Nevada students deserve the benefits of technology for their academic achievement, collaboration, aspirations, and cultural awareness. Nevada students must be prepared to compete with the rest of American students as well as with an increasingly competitive global workforce.

Setting the Stage: Pathway to Nevada's Future Project

To address the major challenges in Nevada (i.e., geographic, ethnic, and economic diversity), individuals from the Nevada Department of Education and several school districts throughout the state anticipated that the use and integration of technology was an appropriate way to improve the preparation of students in Nevada. Similarly, technology provided the means to train teachers across the state. Specifically, the Pathway to Nevada's Future Project (http://cpdmoodle.ccsd.net/pathway/) is a statewide initiative intended to change teachers' technology integration practices as a result of the development and implementation of an online professional development program. Additionally, the project is intended to identify appropriate packages of effective classroom technology.

The Pathway Project grew out of the Nevada Educational Technology Plan and statewide concern about student engagement and achievement. Participating teachers and administrators are taking part in a two-year professional development program, funded through Federal ARRA. The project is focused on recognizing and addressing the needs of 21st century students through the framework of the revised Nevada Educational Technology Standards, which align to ISTE's National Educational Technology Standards for Students (NETS-S).

There are two primary objectives of the Pathway project: (1) change teacher behavior through online, collaborative professional development about technology integration; and (2) determine packages of effective classroom technology resources and professional development for planning and budgeting purposes. In pursuit of these objectives, the Pathway Project attempts to resolve Nevada's challenges associated with geographic, ethnic, and economic diversity by developing effective and efficient training for teachers that leverages distance education tools in maximizing instructional value through appropriate technologies. These objectives relate to an overall goal of increasing student achievement by providing engaging and motivating classroom experiences made possible by technology integration. To accomplish these goals, the Project has a professional development component for teachers and a tandem component for their supervising administrators.

To organize, manage, and monitor the Pathway Project, three specific groups were formed. An advisory committee, with an administrator representative from every District, meets regularly online for Project decisions about such things as equipment standards, budget, and logistics. Project staff includes professional development facilitators, geographically housed at opposite ends of the state and a technical support person. They work closely with faculty from the two large universities in Nevada in developing and providing the professional development. Finally, an evaluation group monitors and provides feedback to both the advisory committee and Project staff, as well as to fiscal agents. This Project organization requires that all of these groups work online; this is an unusual situation, which puts the Project organizers into much of the same situation as the participants.

THE CASE

All of the professional development is being conducted in an online Course Management System (CMS). In this case, the software suite Moodle was selected because it allowed for customized assignments using a Web 2.0 interface, enabled dynamic interaction, and is open source (i.e., no additional cost to buy software). Curriculum specialists, online technology experts, and higher education professors have worked together to develop and refine four modules, each equivalent to three graduate credit-hour courses.

This chapter outlines the development and implementation of Module 1. All modules will be archived for future professional development needs across the state. To facilitate the implementation of strategies learned, each participating teacher has access to a minimum set of technological tools, including student laptops and mobile handheld devices (iPod Touches). Data have been gathered on the use of these tools to inform future budgeting, planning, and professional development.

The Nevada Pathway Project reflects an extensive collaboration between school districts across the state to provide professional development for teachers and administrators that supports and enhances teaching and learning with technology. In considering the number of entities involved, the project has done well in implementing the scheduled activities outlined above. Several synchronous online meetings enhanced project planning and implementation with district representatives serving on the Project's advisory committee. Meetings were conducted and archived through Clark County School District's Centra system and consistent efforts have been made by project leaders to set a collaborative and inclusive climate for the advisory meetings.

One hundred eighty teachers and administrators, representing all 17 districts, were selected to participate in the two-year professional development program. Two teachers and one administrator were selected per school, largely at the middle school level. Participating teachers began interacting via the Moodle online software on November 20, 2009 and engaged in an orientation module comprised of three weeks of activities designed to orient users to the Moodle environment and start building a culture within the group. The kickoff webinar, featuring Cheryl Lemke, took place on December 1, 2009. Registration for university credit began soon thereafter and Module 1 began in January 2010, as planned, and was completed on May 11, 2010.

Pathway Online Professional Development Environment

The online Professional Development environment is delivered via Moodle (http://cpdmoodle.ccsd.net/) (Figure 1). Moodle logs user interaction, participation, and all of their contributions. As a result, this system was leveraged to collect information about the state of the online professional development at this point. These data indicate that the project involved 189 total participants, including school administrators, teachers, project coordinators, and project staff. Of these, 38 did not access the online professional development. However, 131 participating teachers were actively engaged in the online professional development at some point during Module 1. These logs indicated that only eight teacher participants were inactive for more than four weeks and 12 were inactive for more than three weeks.

Participating teachers were assigned to one of eight small groups—two for English language arts, two for mathematics, two for science, and two for social studies. In addition, larger groups were configured for each of the subject area groups (i.e., one for English language arts, one for mathematics, one for science, and one for social studies) and an "All" group includes all participants for broad discussion topics. A few teachers from non-core subjects (e.g., foreign language, performing arts, visual arts) were able to pick which content group to join.

Figure 1. The Pathway Project's Moodle environment

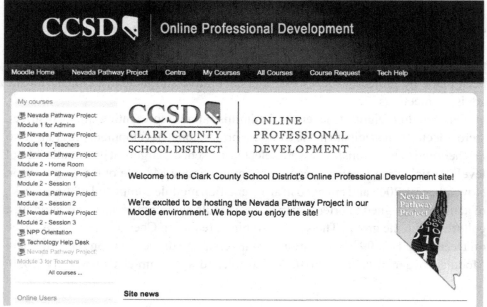

Module 1 Content

Learning modules included a wide range of activities and online resources, including both large and small group discussion forums. The content in Module 1, titled "Building Knowledge and Skills," was primarily an overview of resources, tools, and strategies that may be implemented in a wide range of settings (Figure 2). The theoretical orientation of the project was driven by a vision for how learning and teaching should change and a framework for what students should know and be able to do based on the Nevada Educational Technology Standards (based on the NETS-S) and the Partnership for 21st Century Skills (P21). In addition, the project employed the TPACK framework (Koehler & Mishra, 2008; Mishra and Koehler, 2006) for guiding learning activities for teacher development and curriculum implementation.

Beyond conceptual readings, webinars, videos, and discussions, hands-on assignments exposed participants to a range of tools. Within the assignment titled Engage in Web 2.0 Tools, resources explored included Google Docs, Social Bookmarking, Twitter, VoiceThread, Blogs, Podcasts, YouTube/TeacherTube, Photosharing, Skype, and Wordle. In addition, Vimeo (http://www.vimeo.com) was shared as a way to publish and exchange educational video.

Figure 2. Module 1: Building knowledge and skills

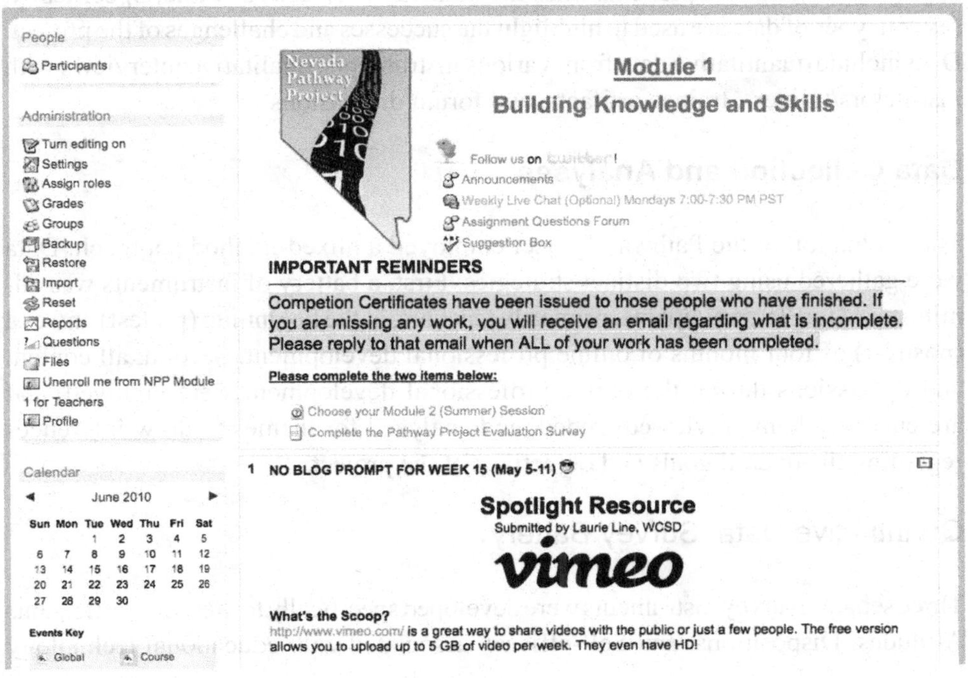

An ongoing curriculum mapping assignment helped bridge the gap between the resources explored and their application in the classroom. Mapped with the Nevada Educational Technology Standards and P21 framework, teachers built a database of lesson ideas that served as a resource for further lesson planning. Subsequently, participants created SMART Goals (in this case, Specific, Measurable, Attainable, Relevant, and Timely; see Doran, 1981), which will ultimately lead to the development of a Measurable Achievement Plan (MAP), a variation of action research to be developed in a future Module. In addition participants created elements to be included in an e-portfolio. They also continued to explore 21st Century learning resources and Web 2.0 tools that fit with their interests and goals. Activities that extended beyond the Pathway project were shared using a Diigo site (http://www.diigo.com/user/nevadapathway) and two databases housed within Moodle (i.e., App junction and a think tank glossary), which allowed participants to research, share, and collaborate in groups around a particular topic.

Lessons Learned: Evaluation of Objectives

The Pathway Project is highly complex, involving numerous entities, outcomes, and variables. As a result, the project evaluation is employing a mixed methods approach to triangulate the results and contextualize inferences. Although detailed analyses of the Pathway Project may be found elsewhere (see Strudler, Schrader, & Asay, under review), this chapter examines the Pathway Project as a whole. Specifically, several types of data are used to highlight the successes and challenges of the project. Data include quantitative data from various instruments, qualitative interviews with instructors/trainers, trainee artifacts, and forum discussions.

Data Collection and Analyses

The evaluation of the Pathway Project employed a mixed-method approach. Data were gathered using two distinct strategies. First, a battery of instruments was administered to 135 participants, primarily teachers, at the beginning (pretest) and end (posttest) of four months of online professional development. Second, all content and discussions during the online professional development were archived, and are currently being reviewed, coded, and analyzed for themes to draw inferences regarding the overall goals and objectives of the project.

Quantitative Data: Survey Battery

Three separate survey instruments were developed specifically to measure participants Attitudes, Dispositions, and Self-efficacy associated with educational technology and teaching with technology. Items from a fourth instrument, TPACK, were adapted from an existing set of items developed by Schmidt et al. (2009). Items on the Attitudes Toward Technology Tools survey pertained to questions about technology in general and its potential in education. Items on the Dispositions Toward Teaching with Technology survey pertained to teachers' perceptions of technology and its role as an educational tool. The items on the Self-Efficacy survey pertained to participants' confidence in performing a variety of tasks (e.g., building a web page, emailing attachments) that involve technology. Finally, the items on the TPACK survey involved participants' evaluation of their technological, pedagogical, and content knowledge.

Qualitative Data

All course materials and online discussions within the Moodle forums were exported as text files and are being coded using HyperRESEARCH Qualitative Analysis Tool. Using the constant comparative method (Strauss, 1987), data analysis began as data were first collected and will continue throughout the study. Data are being triangulated as our review of documents and field notes from the online materials have served to confirm the trustworthiness (Lincoln & Guba, 1985) of the data gathered.

Course discussions, artifacts, and field notes were read and reviewed. Guided by the evaluation questions, the data are being coded, beginning with a common set of codes established by the researchers. Codes have been revised as necessary to reflect the data that were analyzed.

Participants' Profile

Demographics

From base-line data, the teachers in the Pathway project appear to represent an appropriate cross section of participants. The participants ranged in age from 21 to older than 55 years, with the greatest frequency of participants reporting that they were between 35 and 39 years of age (21.3%). The majority of participants reported that they were white (75.7%) and female (72.8%). Other races/ethnicities were also reported, including: Black (2.9%), Hispanic (3.7%), Asian or Pacific Islander (2.9%), and American Indian or Alaskan Native (1.5%). A total of 18 participants did not report an ethnicity (13.2%). Participants were either middle school teachers (83.8%) representing all major content areas, or administrators (6.6%). Thirteen participants (9.6%) did not specify their role in schools.

Attitudes toward Technological Tools Survey

As expected, participants indicated that some tools might be more useful than others. In general, respondents were familiar with common tools (e.g., Word, PowerPoint, the WWW, etc.) and less familiar with specialized, subject-specific tools (e.g., modeling software, educational games, etc.). However, while participants varied in their appreciation of the common tools, those who were familiar with specialized tools valued them more highly. For example, although participants varied in their acceptance of concept mapping software as a useful tool, relatively few were unfamiliar with the category (11.9%). Alternatively, proportionally more participants (33.7%) were unaware of probeware and the associated data collection tools. However, those who reported some knowledge of probeware also indicated that it was a useful tool. This trend was evident in ratings associated with common Instant Messaging tools and Web 2.0 tools like blogs and wikis, as they compared to more specialized tools like interactive simulations and website creation software.

Dispositions toward Teaching with Technology Survey

In general, the participants have high opinions of the role of technology in the classroom. The average rating on a 5-point Likert-type scale, which ranged from 1 (strongly disagree) to 5 (strongly agree), was above four in every case with the exception of item seven: "Technology should be central to instruction," which was rated a 3.8 on average. From these data, we infer that all participants value the use of technology but would assert that content is principal in instruction. Items in the TPACK instrument (below) address how content, pedagogy, and technology may be intertwined.

Technology Self-Efficacy (Confidence) Survey

Similar to their awareness of tools as reported in the Attitudes section, participants reported high self-efficacy ratings associated with easy skills (e.g., email, grades, search, etc.) but low self-efficacy with respect to more complex skills (e.g., video chat, web page creation, etc.). This suggests that the population has a solid foundation to begin a professional development program.

Technology, Pedagogy, and Content Knowledge (TPACK) Survey

Common across the TPACK items was participants' high rating of their strengths associated with their content areas. In general, participants believe that they know their content areas, can engage in a way of thinking aligned with their content area, and provide meaningful instruction associated with that content area. At this point, the findings also support the notion that the integration of technology, pedagogy, and content is an area in which participants might improve. While they have reported skills in their content area, preliminary data analysis suggests opportunities for growth.

Overall Profile of Pathway Participants

From these data, we conclude that the teacher participants in the Pathway Project represent an appropriate cross section of trainees. Participants are experienced (at least three years) and confident in both their ability to apply basic tools and to teach in their content areas. At a minimum, this group reports that they have the requisite skills to engage with the Pathway professional development. Further, we assert that this group has the potential for improvement to allow for an appropriate evaluation of the Pathway modules and training materials as specified in the project objectives. Lastly, the majority of participants were recruited early. Preliminary analysis of participants' goals suggests that they are commensurate with the characteristics required of successful online professional development and learning. Ultimately, the group of individuals appears well suited to interact with the professional development materials in a meaningful way and provide important feedback for the future improvement and delivery of instruction.

Results

Based on findings reported by Strudler, Schrader, and Asay (under review), Principal Components Analysis of participant responses on the Attitudes Toward Technology Tools scale revealed four stable components (Interactive tools, production tools, delivery tools, and specialized tools). Analysis of the Dispositions Toward Teaching with Technology revealed two stable components (Student Centric Uses and Teacher Guided Uses). Analysis of the Self-Efficacy survey revealed two stable components (Daily Tasks and Pedagogical Tasks). Analysis of the TPACK survey revealed six components (Technological Knowledge, Pedagogical Knowledge, Technological Pedagogical Knowledge, TPACK, Content Knowledge, and Models of TPACK).

Strudler et al. also reported that there were significant gains in major areas associated with the Pathway professional development. Specifically, participants' attitudes toward production and specialized tools increased as a result of Pathway. Production tools include tools to create media, web pages, and other authoring applications. Specialized tools include those with specific uses, such as modeling software or simulations.

Strudler et al. also indicated that participants' ratings on the TPACK scales changed significantly. Specifically, participants' self-efficacy associated with pedagogical activities, technological and content knowledge, and models associated with TPACK all increased. Because the professional development was delivered online, TPACK provided the conceptual framework for the Pathway Project. Further, the content in Module 1 was based in the TPACK approach. Participating teachers were asked to consider this framework as a way to conceptualize their own technology integration.

Strudler et al. also described the analysis of qualitative data. Although the outcomes were not necessarily universal, the data support the effectiveness of the online professional development to support teacher change in attitudes, self-efficacy, and TPACK. As might be expected, the time involved in the professional development component of the project was cited as a key variable and obstacle for many of the participants. Specifically, participants questioned the time that was necessary to complete assignments. In many cases, they cited several hours beyond what the Pathway instructors had allocated for the work. This may be partially explained by the need to learn the Moodle environment in addition to module content.

Strudler et al. also indicated that school and subject culture exert a further influence on teachers' attitudes about the project goals for classroom implementation.

While results shared by Strudler et al. provided an indication that the Pathway Project has made positive impacts in terms of professional development, the post-Module 1 evaluation also included open-ended items that provided much more detailed data about perceived successes and challenges. Specifically, participants were asked to list "3 things you think are going well" and "3 things you would improve." Responses were examined for similarity and like responses were combined. The most frequently identified strength of the Project centered on high levels of learning. One respondent noted, "My eyes have definitely been opened to new opportunities and options." Another stated, "I have learned a lot about the technologies out there. I am excited to try more of them in my class." Many cited various Web 2.0 resources and other useful websites, increased knowledge of the iPod Touches, and use of the Moodle content management system.

Respondents also frequently lauded the increased access to technology that resulted from participation in the project, "using the awesome technology—iPods and laptop cart." Teachers also noted that the student use of technology was going well as was the motivation that both students and teachers were experiencing. Finally, many teachers cited the collaboration that they were experiencing with Pathway teachers as a major strength of the project. They noted that teachers are able to share successes and difficulties and get new ideas through their online collaboration. As one teacher explained, people "seem pressured in terms of the time that it takes and the vast amount of resources to explore. The peer support for this level of change appears quite helpful."

Although Module 1 exhibited many positive attributes, there were a few areas that needed to be addressed. The most frequently cited area for improvement related to the amount of work required. While the content and range of resources were identified as positive aspects of the Module, some respondents suggested that less emphasis should be placed on the quantity of resources explored. Specifically, some participants suggested that more time be allocated for working directly with the technologies and applications for implementation in the classroom. One teacher noted: "Assignments were almost too varied-it was hard to choose where to start and how to focus. I am hoping in future modules the scope will narrow just a bit." Another teacher added, "I appreciate being shown what's out there, but now I need more practice and guidance using it."

The next most frequently cited improvement focused on having greater clarity for some assignments in terms of expectations, directions, and grading criteria. One respondent requested "more elaboration or examples on what to do for some of the assignments." A couple of others specifically referred to "communication about expectations as far as grades go." In addition, a number of participants commented that the organization of the Moodle site could be clearer and more "user-friendly" for accessing course materials. One teacher noted, "After Moodle was revamped, it definitely got better, but having 2 or 3 places to look for things gets confusing." Another concurred, "The page set up is often confusing....Simplicity would be nice."

Other suggestions for project improvement included eliminating delays in getting equipment to some of the sites and addressing various issues in getting the technology up and running. In this project, such technology-related issues are the responsibility of the districts and their participating schools. In addition, several people noted their preference for some face-to-face meetings. As one teacher noted, it would be nice to have "local collaborative informal meetings to discuss what we have learned, what is working, and brainstorm what is not."

CONCLUSION

Modifications to Module 1

Based on participant feedback through emails, comments, and discussions, facilitators reported making several modifications during the implementation of Module 1. As evident from the open-responses, a key challenge to the Pathway Project involved time and the complexity of assignments. Pathway instructors indicated that they received numerous emails detailing the tremendous time involved in completing the assignments. This trend was confirmed by tracking surveys administered from Moodle, allowing facilitators to quickly determine how much time participants spent on each block. In some cases, the time spent was 10 or more hours in excess of the time anticipated. Based on this feedback, the facilitators opted to reduce the number of assignments and created weekly checks to avoid overloading project participants.

Another prominent change involved altering the Moodle layout. For example, assignments were changed to give them a visual "priority." Further, content was delivered in blocks and the most recent block was moved to the top of the page. Previous blocks were arranged in order from the most recent toward the top of the page to the oldest toward the bottom of the page. This contrasts to the standard organization of Moodle, which sequences activities in a linear progression down a single page. Although this change did not solve all of the clarity issues, a review of participant comments confirmed that these design changes were helpful in improving navigation and clarity for some.

Participants' comments in Moodle suggested that these changes were well received and helped contribute to what appears to be a very positive online environment. Although participants expressed a desire for additional time to experiment with the technology and tools involved in the project, the facilitators appear to have achieved a pragmatic balance between structured professional development activities and time for experimentation. The facilitators confirmed their efforts in this regard in interviews and have incorporated greater flexibility in some of the subsequent learning activities.

Current Challenges

With respect to increasing skill and knowledge, the professional development appears successful. One goal of the project is to identify cost-effective packages for technology integration. An appropriate package is defined as a list of software and tools as well as the professional development that is necessary to implement those tools. However, a challenge with the current professional development is the ability to package and replicate the experience. The first step in this project involves determining which aspects of the professional development are successful (i.e., discussions, group work, assignments, authentic 21st century projects, etc.) and then identifying ways to divide those into smaller parcels for distribution. The integrated nature of technology, participants, activities, and all other aspects of the Pathway Project make it difficult to parse the influence of specific aspects or assignments with respect to their influence on technology integration.

There is also a need to support project facilitators and personnel during future implementations of the Pathway Project. During Module 1, project facilitators were extremely involved and active on Moodle. In most cases, questions or comments were answered within a single day. Additionally, they encouraged participants to request individual help sessions via Skype or phone conferences. Facilitators also commented on the degree and nature of their guidance through somewhat challenging material. While facilitators acknowledged that the group became comfortable answering questions and helping one another toward the end of the project, the initial levels of guidance were significant. One may conclude that the packaging and deployment of Module 1 to thousands of teachers across the state will require similar degrees of human intervention. Without the ability to support facilitators, it is unlikely that the professional development will achieve similar learning gains. While this level of support is planned in Nevada, not all professional development efforts enjoy similar resources.

The tremendous amount of facilitator involvement was also an indicator of the time participants spent working on assignments, collaborating with peers, and participating in the project. Although many participants expressed concern over the amount of time involved and facilitators adjusted the requirements, technology integration is highly complex and requires considerable thought and practice. This balance is a challenge for any online professional development.

Another significant challenge for the project was attrition. During Module 1, a few participants did not participate in Moodle, others ceased participation in the project altogether, and two teachers lost their teaching positions due to budget reductions. For example, in the largest Project district, Clark County School District (CCSD) is the fifth largest school district in the United States. Within CCSD, teachers have a great deal of flexibility in terms of teaching location. Several participants moved to schools that were not part of Pathway Project. Other districts were short on personnel to recruit teachers. The variety of hurdles resulted in two other challenges: late enrollment and low levels of engagement and motivation.

Initially, teachers volunteered to participate in Pathway. As some of these individuals left the project, participants who were actively recruited replaced them. In some cases, their principals urged these teachers to participate. Facilitators described this latter group as "reluctant participants." They were often difficult to motivate and appeared disengaged in the activities. However, this may have resulted from a later start time and a difficulty integrating into the group and project.

The Pathway participants could be considered early adopters of technology. Early adopters are typically motivated to overcome challenges and take risks. However, research also suggests that later adopters will likely be less willing to explore vast amounts of resources and may require more clearly identified packages or "solutions" (McKenzie, 1999). Because later adopters may comprise the majority of participants in future iterations of the project, this creates a challenge for the professional development.

Lastly, the Pathway Project is a finitely funded initiative. Naturally, this funding provides technical support, infrastructure, and support for facilitators. Without this support, future implementations of the professional development would clearly be difficult and will have to be re-shaped according to available resources. Stipends, which may be used for materials or other items, were given to participants who completed Module 1. It would appear that many people worked harder than they might have and persevered through a wide range of learning activities. This resulted in meaningful learning gains for a majority, but a clear overload and frustration for others. The overall approach appears to have a good balance between "carrot" and "stick." This has implications in terms of motivation and also for the ability to replicate the project. Overall, facilitators' expectations and intended rigor are not necessarily in line with practical implementations of Pathway beyond the current case, without adequate funding for stipends and equipment.

The advisory committee and staff conceptualize the Pathway Project as a sandbox for experimenting and gathering information. Data on relationships between content area and online professional development, the components needed for students to participate in statewide, collaborative projects, and the human resources needed to support online professional development are all being gathered to inform future online environments.

Themes from Pathway

The Nevada Pathway Project is an ambitious statewide initiative with excellent potential to create viable models for professional development that impact student learning with technology. In considering the number of entities involved and the scope of the project, Pathway staff and participants have done well in implementing the initial activities as scheduled. Module 1 has been delivered and modified based on helpful feedback. Findings from this Module indicate that it was successful in terms of project objectives. Specifically, Module 1 has already impacted participant learning in key ways (e.g., knowledge, TPACK, self-efficacy, and attitudes). Further, project logistics that arose were addressed. Equipment has been purchased and distributed and management issues are being resolved. Consistent efforts were made by project leaders and staff to establish a collaborative and supportive climate in both the administration of the project as well as in the online learning activities. Overall, participating teachers actively participated in the professional development, experienced meaningful gains, and are in a position to benefit from subsequent modules and project-related initiatives.

Another important outcome that resulted from Module 1 is the development of a statewide online community of practice to support innovative teaching. This includes participants from remote rural areas who would not readily receive this type of professional development in their local districts. While several participants noted that they would like to include some face-to-face meetings, the project appears to be working for a majority of the participants. Classroom implementation will be a greater focus during Year 2 of the project, but the professional development component appears to have much promise for supporting large-scale change once the major challenges have been addressed.

Overall, these data indicate that the project is having an impact on teachers' technology integration. It is important to remember that these results reflect the first of four Modules, which span two academic years. Although these data reflect a single module of the project, they are encouraging. Specifically, outcomes analyzed thus far show significant changes in teacher attitudes, self-efficacy, and TPACK. Most importantly, these areas are of particular interest because they imply a solid foundation for change in classroom practice.

An unexpected outcome has been increased collaboration among instructional technology personnel across the state. In some districts, one person is responsible for grants, instructional technology, and technology support. In others, there are more staff members and these tasks are divided. A variety of webinars and online discussions, on topics not specifically tied to the Pathway Project, have spontaneously emerged as a direct result of the collaboration needed in the Pathway Project. There has been a dramatic increase in the sharing of resources and ideas among districts.

Dede et al. (2009) stated that a review of the literature in the field of online professional development reveals that much work is anecdotal and lacks a rigorous research methodology. The authors concluded that until more systematic research is conducted in this area, educators will be hard pressed to know the best design features to include and guidelines for where to direct their support. Such research is critical for understanding teacher change and the effective implementation of technology-enhanced learning environments. Case studies such as this provide data to contribute to the systematic research that is needed.

Support Material

Overall, there are many areas in which the first of four Modules was successful in increasing knowledge, attitudes, and self-efficacy associated with technology. However, the project facilitators learned many key lessons about their expectations and level of interaction with students. These lessons will inform future Modules. Regardless of the specific outcomes, it is clear that professional development is a complicated endeavor. Professional development involves many theoretical approaches and perspectives and when it is combined with technology that serves as both the content and context, additional challenges arise. The following materials are intended to continue the discussion and extend these ideas beyond the confines of this particular case.

REFERENCES

Apple, M. W. (2007). Ideological success, educational failure? On the politics of No Child Left Behind. *Journal of Teacher Education, 58,* 108–116. doi:10.1177/0022487106297844

Dede, C. (2008). New horizons: A seismic shift in epistemology. *EDUCAUSE Review, 43*(3), 80–81.

Doran, G. T. (1981). There's a S.M.A.R.T. way to write management's goals and objectives. *Management Review, 70*(11).

Gee, J. P. (2006). Foreword. In Shaffer, D. W. (Ed.), *How computer games help children learn* (pp. ix–xii). New York, NY: Palgrave/Macmillan.

Goldman, S. R. (2004). Cognitive aspects of constructing meaning through and across multiple texts. In Shuart-Ferris, N., & Bloome, D. M. (Eds.), *Uses of intertextuality in classroom and educational research* (pp. 313–347). Greenwich, CT: Information Age Publishing.

Institute of Education Sciences. (2010). *NAEP data explorer*. Washington, DC: IES National Center for Education Statistics. Retrieved July 15th, 2010, from http://nces.ed.gov/nationsreportcard/naepdata/

Jenkins, H. (2006). *Convergence culture: Where old and new media collide*. New York, NY: New York University Press.

Jenkins, H. (2007). From YouTube to YouNiversity. *The Chronicle of Higher Education Review, 53*(24), 9.

Jenkins, H. (2008). Public intellectuals in the new-media landscape. *The Chronicle of Higher Education, 54*(30), 18–20.

Kitson, L., Fletcher, M., & Kearney, J. (2007). Continuity and change in literacy practices: A move towards multiliteracies. *Journal of Classroom Instruction, 41*(2), 29–41.

Lawless, K. A., & Schrader, P. G. (2008). Where do we go now? Understanding research on navigation in complex digital environments. In Coiro, J., Knobel, M., Lankshear, C., & Leu, D. J. (Eds.), *Handbook of new literacies* (pp. 267–296). Hillsdale, NJ: Lawrence Erlbaum Associates.

Lincoln, Y. S., & Guba, E. G. (1985). *Naturalistic Inquiry*. Beverly Hills, CA: Sage Publications, Inc.

Manning, F. H., Lawless, K. A., Gomez, K. G., McLeod, M., Braasch, J., & Goldman, S. R. (2008). *Sources of information in the classroom: Characterizing instruction through a model of multiple source comprehension for inquiry learning.* Paper presented at the annual meeting of the Association of Psychological Science, Chicago, IL.

McKenzie, J. (1999). *Reaching the reluctant teacher*. Retrieved August 21, 2005, from http://www.fno.org/sum99/reluctant.html

National Education Association. (2010). *Rankings & estimates: Rankings of the states 2009 and estimates of school statistics 2010*. Atlanta, GA: National Education Association. Retrieved August 1, 2010 from http://www.nea.org/assets/docs/010rankings.pdf

New London Group. (1996). A pedagogy of multiliteracies: Designing social futures. *Harvard Educational Review, 66*(1), 60–92.

O'Reilly, T. (2005). *What is Web 2.0?: Design patterns and business models for the next generation of software*. Sebastopol, CA: O'Reilly Network. Retrieved June 13, 2008, from http://www.oreillynet.com/pub/a/oreilly/tim/news/2005/09/30/what-is-web-20.html

Pew Internet & American Life Project. (2001). *The Internet and education: Findings of the Pew Internet & American Life Project*. Retrieved March 12, 2007, from http://www.pewInternet.org/reports

Pew Internet & American Life Project. (2005). *The Internet at school*. Retrieved March 12, 2007, from http://www.pewinternet.org/PPF/r/163/report_display.asp

Schrader, P. G., Lawless, K. A., & McCreery, M. (2009). Intertextuality in massively multiplayer online games. In Ferdig, R. E. (Ed.), *Handbook of research on effective electronic gaming in education* (*Vol. III*, pp. 791–807). Hershey, PA: Information Science Reference.

Strauss, A. (1987). *Qualitative analysis for social scientists*. New York, NY: Cambridge University Press. doi:10.1017/CBO9780511557842

Strudler, N., Schrader, P. G., & Asay, L. (under review). *An evaluation of statewide online professional development for integration of laptops and mobile devices in the middle school curriculum*. Paper submitted to the Annual Meeting of AERA, April 8th-April 12th, New Orleans, LA.

Chapter 31
Using Technology to Support Algebra Teaching and Assessment:
A Teacher Development Case Study

Sandra L. Richardson
Lamar University, USA

Shirley L. Barnes
Alabama State University, USA

David S. Torain II
Hampton University, USA

EXECUTIVE SUMMARY

The current reform agenda in mathematics education promotes the view that mathematics should be taught and assessed in a variety of meaningful and authentic ways, including incorporating technology in the mathematics classroom. However, the incorporation and sustained use of technology into mathematics classrooms presents technological, content, and pedagogical challenges to teachers and students. As the necessity and availability of technology in mathematics classrooms increases, so must supporting technology usage in teachers' content delivery and assessment practices and their professional development (Roblyer & Edwards, 2000; Newby, Stepich, Lehman, & Russell, 2000).

DOI: 10.4018/978-1-61350-492-5.ch031

This empirical case study reports on the advancement of 8th grade Algebra I teachers' mathematical assessment practices of technology-based activities and classroom artifacts during a two year professional development program. As a part of the professional development program, participating teachers documented their use of examining and assessing algebraic work on a handheld Computer Algebra System (CAS).

BACKGROUND INFORMATION

This two-year professional development initiative offered professional development to twenty 8th grade mathematics teachers from six urban schools in a tri-county region of Texas. The professional development sessions guided teachers in using technology to explore elements of teaching, learning, and assessment in Algebra I. Goals of the professional development program included: (1) enhancing participating teachers' formulation and communication of algebraic content, pedagogical, technological, and assessment knowledge; and (2) using technological tools to develop, support, and assess teacher and student algebraic thinking.

Prospective teachers interested in program participation were required to apply for the program via an online program application. Approximately 70% of the applicants were accepted as program participants. Three of the participating teachers had three or fewer years of teaching experience, eight had been teaching for at least 10 years, and the remaining teachers had teaching experience ranging from three to 10 years. With the exception of one participant, all teachers were teaching at least one 8th grade Algebra I course with an average of 21 students per class. All participating teachers possessed general middle school teaching certifications. No participating teacher held a secondary mathematics certification.

All participants were paid a small stipend for program participation and were provided with materials and supplies to supplement their mathematics teaching. At the completion of the two-year project, each participant received 240 professional development hours including 60 hours of summer professional development per year and 60 hours of academic year professional development. Summer sessions focused on conceptual knowledge while the academic year agenda targeted pedagogical techniques for developing and implementing effective Algebra I classroom activities and instruction for students in urban schools, particularly those from underrepresented groups.

Setting the Stage

All professional development sessions incorporated technology usage as a tool for cooperative work, reflection on teaching experiences, and exploration of a variety of solution strategies. In particular, a Computer Algebra System (CAS) was extensively used as a tool for numerical routines and symbolic algebra, spreadsheet capabilities for dealing with data, and analysis and evaluation of algebraic solutions. Project data comprised predominantly of teacher-created lesson plans that incorporated CAS usage, CAS created files, teacher reflections and evaluations, participant journal entries, and observations of participant interactions and discussions.

The professional development sessions were primarily organized and conducted by the first author, a mathematics educator charged with the responsibility of preparing pre-service mathematics teachers and delivering continuing education to in-service mathematics teachers.

THE CASE

Research has confirmed that student difficulties with certain types of algebra problems are results of instructional factors (Knuth, 2005). Activities and discussions from the program's professional development sessions focused on using technology as an instructional tool to represent algebraic ideas in verbal, symbolic, and graphic forms–known as transfer representations (Cunningham, 2005).

This case study presents the case of Ashley and Dominique (given pseudonyms), two in-service teachers whose instructional understanding about representing and assessing algebraic ideas using technology evolved during a series of professional development sessions. Instances of Ashley and Dominique's evolution are noted through an example of a mathematical task where teachers explored the meaning of solutions to an equation using tabular, algebraic, and graphical representations.

Task: An example that elicited the most discussion read as follows: Solve $4x-15 = 5(x-3)-x$ (Equation 1) for x. Although all participating teachers were able to successfully solve Equation 1 in algebraic form by attempting to isolate the variable x, Ashley and Dominique had difficulty interpreting the equation's solution $0 = 0$ and hence difficulty assessing the accuracy of explanations of the solution.

In an effort to address how to understand and assess students' interpretation of the solution of $0 = 0$, Ashley and Dominique explored possible solution representations other than the traditional algebraic manipulation of isolating the variable x. After extensive mathematical discussion and reasoning, Dominique suggested to first examine solving the equation using a graphical approach. Using a Computer Algebra System (CAS), Ashley and Dominique used the technology tool to graph

Figure 1. CAS screenshot of graph for equation 1

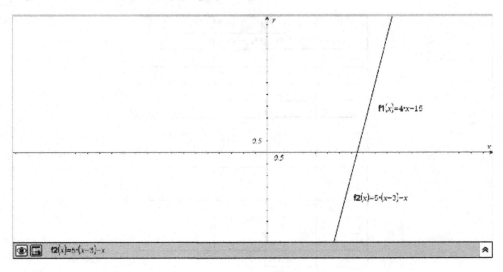

both sides of Equation 1(see Figure 1) and then compare the outputted table of values for Equation 1 (see Figure 2).

Through manipulation and comparison of both the graphical and tabular representations shown on the CAS, Ashley and Dominique were able to justify that the meaning of the Equation 1 solution $0 = 0$ is that Equation 1 is true for all real values of x.

Current Challenges Facing the Organization

The appeal for Ashley and Dominique to use technology as an approach in explaining the meaning of the solution $0 = 0$ lead to investigation of the questions: (i) How should teachers explain, assess, and compare different algebraic solution strategies to the same problem (i.e. compare a strategy that generates a solution using algebraic manipulation and a strategy that uses a graphical device to generate a solution)? and (ii) What do exploration of different algebraic strategies reveal about what both teachers and students know or understand?

Algebra I is a multi-representational subject focused on applications and symbolic reasoning. Because of this new face of algebra, there are many obstacles to using technology to adequately match new ways of learning to algebraic understanding and assessment. While many teachers note that the use of technological mathematical tools has great potential for student learning and development of a teacher's pedagogical potential, only teachers who receive effective professional development

Figure 2. CAS screenshot of table of values for equation 1

x	f1(x):= ▼ 4*x−15	f2(x):= ▼ 5*(x−3)−x	
-5.	-35.	-35.	
-4.	-31.	-31.	
-3.	-27.	-27.	
-2.	-23.	-23.	
-1.	-19.	-19.	
0.	-15.	-15.	
1.	-11.	-11.	
2.	-7.	-7.	
3.	-3.	-3.	
4.	1.	1.	
5.	5.	5.	
6.	9.	9.	
7.	13.	13.	
8.	17.	17.	
9.	21.	21.	
10.	25.	25.	
-23.			

on integrating features of the tool into their instruction and assessment practices benefit from the potential of such tools.

CONCLUSION

Both Ashley and Dominique advanced to utilizing a technological representation to serve as a catalyst for their thinking and to amplify their conceptual understanding. As a result of the technology usage, both teachers became more involved in asking and answering "what if", "how to teach", and "how to assess" questions that challenged their pedagogical and content knowledge.

Analysis of the changing discourse over the course of the professional development sessions indicated that the participating teachers' discussion of appropriate content and assessment usages of CAS and other technological tools became deeper and more mathematically coherent, as well more focused on unpacking their students' understanding relative to the underlying mathematical concepts. As seen in the case of Ashley and Dominique, teachers can use technology, such as CAS, to pose questions and justify answers that stimulate reasoning and explanation, document student thinking and reasoning, and gauge the effectiveness of instruction. In doing so, teachers increase their level of content knowledge, identify specific activities that guided their planning and teaching algebra, increase their knowledge and appropriate use of technology in the teaching and learning of algebra, and experiment with instructional and assessment strategies.

REFERENCES

Cunningham, R. (2005). Algebra teachers' utilization of problems requiring transfer between algebraic, numeric, and graphic representations. *School Science and Mathematics, 105*(2), 73–82. doi:10.1111/j.1949-8594.2005.tb18039.x

Knuth, E. (2005). Student understanding of the Cartesian coordinate connection: An exploratory study. *Journal for Research in Mathematics Education, 31*(4), 500–508. doi:10.2307/749655

Newby, T. J., Stepich, D. A., Lehman, J. D., & Russell, J. D. (2000). *Instructional technology for teaching and learning: Designing instruction, integrating computers and using media*. Columbus, OH: Prentice Hall.

Roblyer, M., & Edwards, J. (2000). *Integrating educational technology into teaching*. Upper Saddle River, NJ: Prentice-Hall.

Chapter 32

ABCs and PCs:
Effective Professional Development in Early Childhood Education

Cory Cooper Hansen
Arizona State University, USA

EXECUTIVE SUMMARY

Effective professional development holds the power to transform teaching practices that invigorate teachers and increase student engagement. Arizona Classrooms of Tomorrow Today (AZCOTT) was one such experience. Eighteen elementary teachers completed a yearlong, rigorous, sixty-hour workshop experience that focused on integrating technology in content area instruction. Participants integrated technology effectively, began to develop leadership skills, and experienced changes in attitude, beliefs, knowledge, and skills as technology influenced existing curricula.

BACKGROUND INFORMATION

Two successful models emerged in a review of the literature that build on the possibilities of transformation: Intel Teach to the Future and the Apple Classroom of Tomorrow (ACOT) project. The goal of the Intel program is to help teachers already familiar with technology to integrate those skills more effectively in the curriculum to enhance student learning (Kanaya, Light, & Culp, 2005). The ACOT project is a ten-year study of the impact of an infusion of technological resources and sustained

DOI: 10.4018/978-1-61350-492-5.ch032

professional development on teaching and learning (Sandholtz, Ringstaff & Dwyer, 1997). ACOT is student centered, driven by an essential question, encompasses the use of technology by teachers and students, and culminates in a student-created project. Key elements of effective programs structure both: format, duration, collective participation, inclusiveness, incentives, active learning opportunities, content focus, and coherence (SRI International, 2002). AZCOTT grew from those past successes and elements of the work of Wetzel, Zambo and Padgett (2001).

Setting the Stage

Poole (1995) helps us understand that transition from traditional teaching to teaching with technology involves a shift in teaching paradigms. It involves a cultural shift in the way we think about teaching that can be developed through effective professional development. Traditional models of professional development proliferate in the research literature, but many are what Watson (2001) consider retooling; integrating technology into the existing curriculum by providing specific skills and competencies. Watson espouses that a different model of professional development is required; re-forming. A re-forming model carries teachers through different stages during professional development with re-forming intentions. McKenzie (2001) agrees, noting that traditional programs lack a "generative" method during which behavior and daily practice change because of the training experience. Central to both ideas is rethinking traditional professional development into a model that takes teachers beyond skill acquisition to possibilities of transformation of teaching practice (Triggs & John, 2004). The purpose of this case study is to engage technology-leaders in planning professional development experiences for inservice teachers with promises to transform teaching practice.

A team of professionals collaborated to design a workshop experience based on input from content experts (English and Mathematics professors), technology users (inservice teachers currently in the field renowned for their technology rich classrooms), technology experts (professionals whose careers focused on technology), and teaching experts (professors from the local teacher preparation program).

THE CASE

Miss DeAndra. has been teaching second grade for 25 years and has seen approaches to teaching touted as innovative and effective come and go over–and sometimes come back again–during that time. The students she teaches in a poverty-stricken neighborhood have limited English speaking skills and let's not even go to where they are as writers! Regardless, Miss DeAndra is highly respected in the community and many parents request their children be assigned to her class because they have heard she is a fun teacher and children learn a lot of English with her. She loves to host student teachers from the local university and continues her gift of mentoring by lesson planning with "newbies" who join the teaching staff. The principal pretty much leaves her alone because the parents seem happy, the children are learning, and no complaints is a good thing.

Two male teachers recently transferred in from a different neighborhood school and seem to be shaking things up with their use of technology. Their purchase of a Smartboard funded through a local grant opportunity consumes the talk in the teachers' lounge and Miss DeAndra. finds herself a little confused and feels more than a little jilted that her place at the top of the second grade totem pole is in danger. Things get more complicated when the two guy teachers rush in after class one afternoon excited about the possibility of being part of a year-long technology-based, professional development experience if they can get a grade level team to apply. At the core of Miss DeAndra's professional image is a small worry that perhaps she too should jump on this computer-driven bandwagon, but she needs to be convinced. After all, there is already too much to be taught in the second grade curriculum and these children need to develop as speakers of English in order to have a chance of academic success. She has been highly effective in the past, so why rock the boat?

Current Challenges

Many American children have grown up with technology and accept it as just another tool to get information. For many of our teachers, this is not the case. Cuban, Kirkpatrick, and Peck (2001) found that, despite the billions of dollars invested in educational technology, little or no computer use in teaching is still common. Wheatley (2004) attributes that statement to some exemplary teachers who grew up without technology and were not educated in teacher preparation programs that included integration of modern learning technologies. Russell, Bebell, O'Dwyer and O'Connor (2003) found that even if teachers were familiar with technology, they used it more for preparation and communication than for delivering instruction or assigning learning activities that required the use of technology.

CONCLUSION

The participants in this actual study completed daily exit tickets commenting on the effectiveness of the workshop, instructional content, and speculation on how content would play out in the classroom. Discussion results formulated the next workshop and provided qualitative data. Responses were collated electronically and coded for recurring topics of interest and interpretations of meaning. The last exit ticket invited participants to reflect upon their AZCOTT experience and how it had affected their classroom community. These responses were particularly rich and the following categories emerged in data analysis:

Positive Reactions to Teaching with Technology

Fifteen participants were unanimous in positive reactions to teaching with technology. Teachers noted differences in ways they felt about themselves as teachers and their students as learners.

Changing View of Self as Teacher

One participant summed up how most of the teachers had changed over the course of the AZCOTT year: "I now feel better equipped and better qualified to teach in the 21st century." Many stated that technology had changed the way that they taught: technology was at the core of their teaching, an integral part of lesson planning, and it was instrumental in changing their view about their students.

Changing View of Students as Learners

Integrating technology into their classrooms changed how teachers viewed their students. Technology as a "great motivator" was repeated often and the participants collectively noticed an increase in levels of engagement, independence, ability to work with others, and confidence in their students.

One participant captured the essence of AZCOTT when she wrote, "This was one of the most growth filled, exciting educational experiences I have had. Thank you so much for this opportunity." When asked to reflect upon unexpected outcomes of the AZCOTT experience, one participant wrote, I didn't expect my whole teaching philosophy to be shaped and restructured with a technology foundation."

AZCOTT positively impacted the teaching lives of eighteen participants and the countless numbers of children and education students in the future who will benefit from their commitment to teaching effectively with technology. The careful structure of AZCOTT may lead to systemic reform and is reaching toward that goal.

Here are the unexpected results:

- Establishment of technology-rich classrooms for preservice interns and student-teachers
- Leadership skills in the local educational community through participant presentations in district staff development

- Willingness to continue professional growth through co-presentations with university faculty at state and national educational technology conferences

Technology influences the experiential base of students and changes instruction faster than research can document (Hansen, in review). Increased academic achievement is at the heart of pedagogical change, and participation in scientifically based professional development is a means for teachers to meet highly qualified requirements which, in turn, increases the academic achievement of students in core subjects (Vandevoort, Amrein-Beardsley, & Berliner, 2004).

REFERENCES

Cuban, L., Kirkpatrick, H., & Peck, C. (2001). High access and low use of technologies in high school classrooms: Explaining an apparent paradox. *American Educational Research Journal, 38*(4), 813–834. doi:10.3102/00028312038004813

Hansen, C.C. (in review). *Changing attitudes, beliefs, knowledge, and skills: Effective technology-based professional development.*

SRI International. (2002, May). *Technology-related professional development in the context of educational reform: A literature review.* Prepared for the U.S. Department of Education under GSA Contract #GS-35F-5537H.

Kanaya, T., Light, D., & Culp, K. M. (2005). Factors influencing outcomes from a technology-focused professional development program. *Journal of Research on Technology in Education, 37*(2), 313–329.

McKenzie, J. (2001). *How teachers learn technology best.* Retrieved March 31, 2010, from http://www.fno.org/mar01/howlearn.html

Poole, B. (1995). *Education for an information age.* Madison, WI: WCB Brown Benchmark.

Russell, M., Bebell, D., O'Dwyer, L., & O'Connor, K. (2003). Examining teacher technology use: Implications for preservice and inservice teacher preparation. *Journal of Teacher Education, 54*(4), 297–310. doi:10.1177/0022487103255985

Sandholtz, J. H., Ringstaff, C., & Dwyer, D. C. (1997). *Teaching with technology: Creating student-centered classrooms.* New York, NY: Teachers College Press, Columbia University.

Triggs, P., & John, P. (2004). From transaction to transformation: Information and communication technology, professional development, and the formation of communities of practice. *Journal of Computer Assisted Learning, 20*(6), 426–439. doi:10.1111/j.1365-2729.2004.00101.x

Vandevoort, L. G., Amrein-Beardsley, A., & Berliner, D. C. (2004, September 8). National board certified teachers and their students' achievement. *Education Policy Analysis Archives, 12*(46). Retrieved March 31, 2010, from http://epaa.asu.epaa/v12n46

Watson, G. (2001). Models of information technology teacher professional development that engage with teachers' hearts and minds. *Journal of Information Technology for Teacher Education, 10*(1 & 2), 179–190. doi:10.1080/14759390100200110

Wetzel, K., Zambo, R., & Padgett, H. (2001). A picture of change in technology-rich K-8 classrooms. *Journal of Computing in Teacher Education, 18*(1), 5–11.

Wheatly, K. F. (2004). Increasing computer use in early childhood teacher education: The case of a "computer muddler". *Information Technology in Childhood Education*, 135-56.

Chapter 33

Designing District-Wide Technology-Rich Professional Development

Drew Polly
University of North Carolina at Charlotte, USA

Clif Mims
University of Memphis, USA

Brenda McCombs
Kannapolis City Schools, USA

EXECUTIVE SUMMARY

This case will focus on the following situation: As the technology coordinator for a school district you receive a state grant to provide technology resources and professional development for every teacher in the intermediate (Grades 5-6), middle (Grades 7-8) and high school (Grades 9-12) classrooms in your district. Your superintendent and school board have asked you to:

- *Design differentiated professional development to meet all teachers' needs*
- *Include some outside consultants but quickly build teacher capacity so future professional development can be facilitated by district employees*

DOI: 10.4018/978-1-61350-492-5.ch033

- *Provide educational materials for teachers and parents about internet safety and legal issues*
- *Determine that the use of technology has positively impacted student learning outcomes*
- *This case study describes the story of how one school district responded to this challenge.*

BACKGROUND INFORMATION

This case takes place in a high-need school district in North Carolina. Approximately 80% of the students qualify for free and reduced lunch. The school district is supportive of technology integration, and the Superintendent, school board and all administrators believe that more technology needs to be incorporated into instruction. However, there is a lot of uncertainty among everyone about what effective technology integration looks like.

Through part of a large grant from the state's Department of Public Instruction, every teacher in each of the three schools–intermediate (Grades 5-6), middle (Grades 7-8) and high school (Grades 9-12)–received a teacher laptop, flash drive, projector, and interactive whiteboard in each classroom. There was also money for schools to purchase additional technologies such as document cameras, video cameras, or printers. Each teacher also received at least 5 days of technology integration professional development. However, the design and the content of the professional development was left to the determination of the technology coordinator.

THE CASE

While the general outline of the professional development was written into the grant, once it was funded the technology coordinator needed to determine how to provide effective professional learning experiences for over two hundred teachers in all three schools. Using a framework of learner-centered professional development (National Partnership for Excellence and Accountability in Teaching, 2000; Polly & Hannafin, in press), the professional development was targeted to:

- address problematic areas regarding student learning outcomes
- provide explicit connections between technology use and concepts that teachers taught
- give teachers choices about where teachers would focus their attention
- facilitate collaboration among grade levels and subject areas

- include follow-up support during the school year based on teachers' needs and
- administrators' analysis of technology use

These goals were carried out in a few different ways that will be discussed later in this chapter.

Building Teacher-Leader Capacity

As a result of the need to build teacher-leader capacity and serve a large number of teachers, a team of teacher-leaders–called the Vanguard team–was formed. The Vanguard team consisted of early adopters and technology-using teachers in the district who were already using internet-based activities, interactive whiteboards, or teachers who had expressed a passionate interest for integrating technology into their instruction. These Vanguard team members participated in one week of professional development that was designed to mirror the same type of experience that they would co-facilitate with their colleagues during the remainder of the summer.

The Vanguard week included sessions that were facilitated by district leaders, teacher-leaders and higher education partners. Vanguard members learned about higher-order thinking skills and Revised Bloom's Taxonomy, designing effective technology-rich lessons, Web. 2.0 tools, and educational games. Further, Vanguard team members also spent a day preparing professional development sessions that they facilitated to their colleagues later that summer.

Technology Concerns

The major technology concerns focused on supporting the district-wide infrastructure that was essential in establishing a technology-rich district. The grant provided money to purchase laptops, projectors and interactive whiteboards for every 5th-12th grade teacher. The ample amount of technology could be purchased because the district opted to purchase Mimio technologies rather than other interactive whiteboard options. Mimio was between 1/3 and 1/2 of the cost of other whiteboard technologies. Further, using other funds, the district was able to upgrade the wireless connectivity speeds in the intermediate, middle and secondary schools.

One of the primary concerns was preparing teachers to effectively and appropriately use the internet as a tool to facilitate their teaching and their students' learning. Many teachers at the three schools had experience using the Internet to locate educational resources, but they were limited in designing activities where their students access the internet to locate, synthesize, compile or create representations of content about which they are learning.

Technology Components: Addressing Technology Concerns

This concern was addressed by spending time with Vanguard and other teachers learning about the power of leveraging the Internet to expand students' exposure to concepts. Teachers learned about virtual field trips, WebQuests, telecollaboration using wikis and Google Documents, internet-based communication, organizational tools such as Diigo and Delicious, and various web-based productivity tools that allow students to create scrapbooks, posters, ebooks, websites or podcasts online. A few of these are detailed further in this section.

Collaborative Sharing: Wikis

Groups of teachers used a wiki site (www.pbworks.com) to establish internet-based spaces for teachers to store, share, and organize educational resources. The high school and middle school teachers were grouped by department and subject area, while the intermediate school teachers were grouped by both grade level and subject area. Resources included links to videos and other resources, activity sheets, pacing guides, and assessments. Since the wiki was private, teachers felt comfortable posting ideas and resources without anxiety about the quality of the resources.

Wikis were chosen for a few main reasons. First, teachers could contribute and access the wiki from any internet-connected computer. Prior to wikis, teachers stored all of their resources on secure drives on their school's server, which required them to be in the school building to access those resources. Second, wikis allowed multiple people to view and access the resources. Rather than a word processing document or spreadsheet that had to be e-mailed to various teachers, the wiki allowed numerous teachers to benefit from the resource at the same time. Third, wikis were an easy technology to learn how to use. Rather than other website development packages, wikis allowed students to link to resources with a few simple clicks of their mouse.

Increased Access to Information: Internet-Based Activities

During the professional development, teachers spent time exploring and learning about internet-based activities including virtual field trips and WebQuests. During the Virtual Field Trip session, teachers were situated in a setting where they had to locate specific virtual trips that aligned to their curriculum, design follow-up activities, and then write a letter to their Principal defending the use of the Internet in their classroom. During the workshop, teachers became more involved in this task than the professional developers expected. Teachers found numerous virtual field trips and posted them to the wiki and their online bookmarking account for later use.

Another internet-based task that teachers participated in was WebQuests. WebQuests are online activities in which learners investigate a complex task or problem, find information related to the task, and then create a product based on the information that they have found. Teachers completed a few different WebQuest tasks during workshops. First, as learners, teachers completed a WebQuest about WebQuests, where their task was to evaluate and determine the quality of WebQuests that had been created by other teachers. Second, they explored WebQuest resources housed by San Diego State University–where WebQuests were first created. Third, teachers had time to adapt or create their own WebQuest that aligned to their state standards. Both the WebQuest and Virtual Field Trip tasks allowed teachers to experience the process of using the Internet to increase their access to information, and identify or create resources that they could use in their own classroom. In future workshops, these topics were blended in a workshop that focused on many telecollaborative experiences.

Formative Assessment: Clickers

As part of a major focus of the state Department of Education, teachers also worked with hand-held devices called Clickers that could be used to assess students during a lesson. Two teachers in the district who were experts at using these technologies facilitated the workshop. Teachers were given the opportunity to use Clickers as if they were students and then had time to create quizzes using the software. Teachers were asked to bring instructional materials to the workshop. so many of them were able to spend time creating assessments they could use with their students during the following school year.

During the year after the professional development, these digital assessments on the Clickers began to permeate classrooms. In some cases, teachers used Clickers to replace paper-based assessments. Moreover, teachers used these clickers in the midst of a lesson and modified their instruction based on data that they were collecting on students' progress. As part of the professional development, teachers needed support connecting the Revised Bloom's Taxonomy levels with writing high-level questions in the Clickers system.

Management and Organizational Concerns

As with any professional development effort, there were concerns from district leaders and professional development facilitators regarding logistics and organizational issues. The concerns and how they were addressed are detailed below.

Bridging Technology and Curriculum

Project leaders held to the notion that the goal of teachers' professional development was to build knowledge and skills that would substantially impact teachers' practices and their students' learning. During the workshops, teachers had a half day to hone their expertise on one or two technologies that they had learned about earlier in the week. That time allowed them to go create technology-rich resources that they could use in their classroom.

On the last day of the five-day workshop, teachers met with grade levels or departments (subject areas) to plan how they would integrate technology into their curriculum. The planning day allowed participants to work on a variety of tasks based on teachers' needs and interests. Tasks included pacing out the curriculum, infusing higher-order thinking skills into lessons, creating technology-rich resources, collaborating with other subject area teachers to integrate two or more curriculum goals with technology tools, creating assessments, and further examining how to use technology to support their teaching and their students' learning.

Focusing on Student Learning

While fostering student learning was a focal point from the beginning of the project, in the first year of the professional development most of the teachers' attention was on learning various technologies and connecting them to curriculum so that these technologies would enhance their own teaching and their students' learning experience. As the first summer of workshops concluded, it became clear that future efforts should be more explicit and pointed towards addressing student learning barriers as identified in data from statewide tests, unit tests, and more formative assessments. While this conversation and approach could have been employed from the beginning of the project, both district leaders and professional developers decided to hone their attention on the technologies and the process of integrating technology into their classroom. From there, attention was given to supporting teachers, preventing the feeling of being overwhelmed, and being persistent as teachers attempted to use these technologies with their students.

During the follow-up professional development throughout the year, individual schools took different approaches to addressing the student learning-barrier concern. Despite their different methods, all schools spent time analyzing multiple data sources, unpacking state standards, and then modifying or creating curriculum to address both the state standards and deficiencies in student learning as identified in the data.

Establishing a System of Sustainability

District leaders wanted to build capacity for teacher-leadership through the professional development project. As a result, the Vanguard team, which was explained earlier, served as the foundation for building teacher-leaders in the district. These Vanguard team members were charged with developing the necessary knowledge and skills to effectively teach with technology, facilitate workshops, and lead teachers at their school regarding technology integration.

As a result of the Vanguard team and the professional development format, each of the three schools had a cadre of teacher–leaders that served during the year as a group that other teachers could seek out for additional assistance and ideas. These individuals, since that time, continue to be catalysts in modeling technology integration, developing students' higher-order thinking skills, and supporting their colleagues.

CONCLUSION

As a result of our experiences, we offer recommendations which we feel were mission critical to the success of the project. Many of these build upon early themes that we have shared.

First, technology integration experts frequently write about the need to connect technology to curriculum. In this project we were able to develop teachers' technology skills while simultaneously providing them with opportunities to analyze how technology could effectively influence their teaching and their students' learning. As a result, teachers left the professional development with increased knowledge, skills, and also resources they could immediately use in their classroom.

Further, this project's success was heavily dependent on giving teachers' ownership of their own professional learning. During the week-long workshop, teachers were able to choose some of the sessions that they attended, which technologies they were going to deepen their understanding of, and how they planned on integrating technology into their classroom. All teachers were able to focus their learning based on their own interests and perceived needs.

Current Challenges

Designing district-wide professional development for teachers of Grade 5-12 students was a powerful experience that has substantially impacted teaching and learning in the school district. However, there are a number of specific challenges to consider based on our experience.

One challenge was the maintenance of technologies. Similar to other technology initiatives, technologies break and need to be repaired. Each school has their own technology specialist to handle troubleshooting. During the school year these technology specialists provided just in time help repairing technologies. However, that was not the specialists' only role. All three technology specialists also had instructional expertise at using technology, so each of them supported teachers' integration of technology into their curriculum by working with teachers during planning or with small groups or whole classes of students on various projects. These projects included creating student-produced videos using iMovie, setting up student blogs, and other projects that allowed students to use technology to deepen their understanding of concepts while also creating technology-rich artifacts.

Finding time to provide continuous follow-up has also been a challenge for the three schools. Through continued funding and administrator buy-in, the culture has been established that all teachers will engage in ample amounts of professional development, including summer workshops. However, with other district and state-wide initiatives it was challenging trying to find time for teachers to participate in follow-up professional development during the school year. This included classroom support. While technology specialists were available to provide some support, many teachers who sought in-class support could not receive assistance due to demands placed on technology specialists. In many cases, the Vanguard teachers provided support during their planning periods or the times before or after the school day.

Another challenge was including elementary schools in this initiative. In order for this initiative to be district-wide, there was a need to get the five elementary schools (Kindergarten through 4th grade) caught up with both technology and the instructional practices associated with using technology. With subsequent funding, one of the elementary schools was able to participate in professional development 2 years after the beginning of this project. Still, four elementary schools had access to technology and some professional learning experiences to develop teachers' knowledge and skills.

Compilation of References

Aberson, C. L., Berger, D. E., Healy, M. R., & Romero, V. L. (2003). Evaluation of an interactive tutorial for teaching hypothesis testing concepts. *Teaching of Psychology, 30*, 75–78. doi:10.1207/S15328023TOP3001_12

Alton, L. (2003). *Quality teaching for diverse students in schooling: Best evidence synthesis.* Wellington, New Zealand: Ministry of Education Policy Division.

Amory, A., & Seagram, R. (2003). Educational game models: Conceptualization and evaluation. *The Journal of Higher Education, 17*(2), 206–217.

Anderson, J., & Rainie, L. (2008). *The future of the Internet III.* Washington, DC: Pew Internet & American Life Project.

Anderson, L. W., & Krathwohl, D. R. (2000). *A taxonomy for learning, teaching, and assessing: A revision of Bloom's taxonomy of educational objectives.* Boston, MA: Allyn and Bacon.

Angeli, C. (2004). The effects of case-based learning on early childhood preservice teachers' beliefs about the pedagogical use of ICT. *Journal of Educational Media, 29*, 139–151. doi:10.1080/1358165042000253302

Apple, M. W. (2007). Ideological success, educational failure? On the politics of No Child Left Behind. *Journal of Teacher Education, 58*, 108–116. doi:10.1177/0022487106297844

Barlow, A. T., & Drake, J. M. (2008). Division by a fraction: Assessing understanding through problem writing. *Teaching Children Mathematics, 13*, 326–332.

Basham, J. D., Lowrey, K. A., & Jones, M. L. (2006). Making use of the net: Internet based videoconferencing and online conferencing tools in teacher preparation. In Crawford, D. A. Willis, R. Carlsen, I. Gibson, K. McFerrin, J. Price, & R. Weber (Eds.), *AACE handbook* (pp. 1440-1444). Retrieved September 25, 2009, from ED/IT Lib.

Beaudin, L., & Hadden, C. (2005). Technology and pedagogy: Building techno pedagogical skills in preservice teachers. *Innovate 2*(2). Retrieved November 9, 2009, from http://www.innovateonline.info/index.php?view=article&id=36

Compilation of References

Becker, H., & Ravitz, J. (1999). The influence of computer and Internet use on teachers' pedagogical practices and perceptions. *Journal of Research on Computing in Education, 31*(4), 356–385.

Becker, H. J., Ravitz, J. L., & Wong, Y. (1999). *Teaching, learning and computing: 1998 national survey (Report #3)*. University of California and University of Minnesota: Center for Research on Information Technology and Organizations.

Becker, H. J. (2001). *How are teachers using computers in instruction?* Paper presented at the 2001 Meetings of the American Educational Research Association.

Befiore, P., Auld, R., & Lee, D. (2005). The disconnect of poor-urban education: Equal access and a pedagogy of risk taking. *Psychology in the Schools, 42*(8), 855–863. doi:10.1002/pits.20116

Berson, M. J., Lee, J. K., & Stuckart, D. W. (2001). Promise and practice of computer technologies in the social studies: A critical analysis. In Stanley, W. (Ed.), *Critical issues in social studies research for the 21st century* (pp. 209–229). Greenwich, CT: Information Age Publishing.

Bliwise, N. G. (2005). Web-based tutorials for teaching introductory statistics. *Journal of Educational Computing Research, 33*(3), 309–325. doi:10.2190/0D1J-1CE1-5UXY-3V34

Bliwise, N. G. (2005). Web-based tutorials for teaching introductory statistics. *Journal of Educational Computing Research, 33*(3), 309–325. doi:10.2190/0D1J-1CE1-5UXY-3V34

Bokyeong, K., Hyungsung, P., & Youngkyun, B. (2009). Not just fun, but serious strategies: Using meta-cognitive strategies in game-based learning. *Computers & Education, 52*(4), 800–810. doi:10.1016/j.compedu.2008.12.004

Breuleux, A. (2001). Imagining the present, interpreting the possible, cultivating the future: Technology and the renewal of teaching and learning. *Education Canada, 41*(3), 1–9.

Brown, D., & Warschauer, M. (2006). From the university to the elementary classroom: Students' experiences in learning to integrate technology in instruction. *Journal of Technology and Teacher Education, 14*(3), 599–621.

Brown, J., Collins, A., & Duguid, P. (1989). Situated cognition and the culture of learning. *Educational Researcher, 18*, 32–42.

Brown, A., & Green, T. D. (2007, March 2007). *Podcasting and video podcasting: How it works and how it's used for instruction*. Paper presented at the Society for Information Technology and Teacher Education (SITE) Conference 2007, San Antonio, TX.

Bryman, A. (2001). *Social research methods*. New York, NY: Oxford University Press.

Bull, G., Thompson, A., Searson, M., Garofalo, J., Park, J., Young, C., & Lee, J. (2008). Connecting informal and formal learning: Experiences in the age of participatory media. *Contemporary Issues in Technology & Teacher Education, 8*(2). Retrieved from http://www.citejournal.org/vol8/iss2/editorial/article1.cfm.

Center for Educational Policy. (2008). *Instructional time in elementary schools: A closer look at changes for specific subjects*. Retrieved February 19, 2008, from http://www.cep-dc.org

Clausen, J. (2007). Beginning teachers' technology use: First-year teacher development and the institutional context's affect on new teachers' instructional technology use with students. *Journal of Research on Technology in Education, 39*(3), 245–261.

Colby, S., & Colby, R. (2008). A pedagogy of play: Integrating computer games into the writing classroom. *Computers & Education, 25*(3), 300–312.

Cox, M., Abbott, C., Webb, M., Blakeley, B., Beauchamp, T., & Rhodes, V. (2003). *ICT and attainment: A review of the research literature. ICT in Schools Research and Evaluation Series – No.17*. British Educational Communications and Technology Agency.

Cuban, L. (2001). *Oversold and underused computers in the classroom*. London, UK: Harvard University Press.

Cuban, L., Kirkpatrick, H., & Peck, C. (2001). High access and low use of technologies in high school classrooms: Explaining an apparent paradox. *American Educational Research Journal, 38*(4), 813–834. doi:10.3102/00028312038004813

Cunningham, R. (2005). Algebra teachers' utilization of problems requiring transfer between algebraic, numeric, and graphic representations. *School Science and Mathematics, 105*(2), 73–82. doi:10.1111/j.1949-8594.2005.tb18039.x

Darling-Hammond, L. (2000). Teacher quality and student achievement: A review of State policy evidence. *Education Policy Analysis Archives, 8*(1).

Davies, A. (2007). *Making classroom assessment work*. Courtenay, Canada: Connections Publishing, Inc.

Davis, B., Sumara, D., & Luce-Kapler, R. (2000). *Engaging minds: Learning and teaching in a complex world*. Mahwah, NJ: Lawrence Erlbaum.

Dede, C. (2008). New horizons: A seismic shift in epistemology. *EDUCAUSE Review, 43*(3), 80–81.

Dewey, J. (1997). *How we think*. Mineola, NY: Dover.

Dexter, S., & Riedel, E. (2003). Why improving preservice teacher educational technology preparation must go beyond the college's walls. *Journal of Teacher Education, 54*, 334–346. doi:10.1177/0022487103255319

Dixon, A. (2000). Free blankets or depth charges: choices in education for citizenship. *Forum, 42*(3), 94–99.

Doering, A., Hughes, J., & Huffman, D. (2003). Preservice teachers: Are we thinking with technology? *Journal of Research on Technology in Education, 35*(3), 342–361.

Doran, G. T. (1981). There's a S.M.A.R.T. way to write management's goals and objectives. *Management Review, 70*(11).

Compilation of References

Downes, T. (1999). Playing with computing technologies in the home. *Education and Information Technologies*, *4*(1), 65–79. doi:10.1023/A:1009607432286

Drent, M., & Meelissen, M. (2008). Which factors obstruct or stimulate teacher educators to use ICT innovatively? *Computers & Education*, *51*, 187–199. doi:10.1016/j.compedu.2007.05.001

DuFour, R., DuFour, R., & Eaker, R. (2008). *Revisiting professional learning communities at work: New insights for improving schools*. Bloomington, IN: Solution Tree.

English, L. D. (1998). Children's problem posing within formal context and informal contexts. *Journal for Research in Mathematics Education*, *29*, 83–106. doi:10.2307/749719

Facer, K. (2003). *Computer games and learning: Why do we think it's worth talking about computer games and learning in the same breath?* A discussion paper for FutureLab.

Fahlberg, T., Fahlberg-Stojanovska, L., & MacNeil, G. (2006). Whiteboard math movies. *Teaching Mathematics Applications*, *26*(1), 17–22. doi:10.1093/teamat/hrl012

Fahlberg-Stojanovska, L., Fahlberg, T., & King, C. (2008). Mathcasts: Show-and-tell math concepts. *Learning and Leading with Technology*, *36*(1), 30–31.

Fang, Z. (1996). A review of research on teacher beliefs and practices. *Educational Research*, *38*(1), 47–65. doi:10.1080/0013188960380104

Fletcher-Flinn, C. M., & Gravatt, B. (1995). The efficacy of computer-assisted instruction (CAI): A meta-analysis. *Journal of Educational Computing Research*, *12*, 219–241. doi:10.2190/51D4-F6L3-JQHU-9M31

Fosnot, C. T. (1996). Constructivism: A psychological theory of learning. In *Constructivism: theory, perspectives and practice*. New York: Teachers College Press.

Friedman, T. (2006). *The world is flat: A brief history of the twenty-first century* [Updated and expanded]. New York, NY: Farrar, Straus and Giroux.

Gee, J. P. (2006). Foreword. In Shaffer, D. W. (Ed.), *How computer games help children learn* (pp. ix–xii). New York, NY: Palgrave/Macmillan.

Goldman, S. R. (2004). Cognitive aspects of constructing meaning through and across multiple texts. In Shuart-Ferris, N., & Bloome, D. M. (Eds.), *Uses of intertextuality in classroom and educational research* (pp. 313–347). Greenwich, CT: Information Age Publishing.

Gregory, K., Cameron, C., & Davies, A. (1997). *Knowing what counts: Setting and using criterion*. Courtenay, Canada: Connections Publishing, Inc.

Gros, B. (2007). Digital Games in Education: The Design of Games-Based Learning Environments. *Journal of Research on Technology in Education*, *40*(1), 23–38.

Grunwald., & Associates, L. L. C. (2010). *Educators, technology and 21st century skills: Dispelling five myths*. Retrieved November 23, 2010, from http://grunwald.com/pdfs/Educators-Technology-21stCentury-Skills.pdf

Gusky, T. R. (2007). Using assessment to improve teaching and learning. In Reeves, D. (Ed.), *Ahead of the curve*. Bloomington, IN: Solution Tree.

Haney, J. J., & McArthur, J. (2002). Four case studies of prospective science teachers' beliefs concerning constructivitst teaching practices. *Science Education, 86*(6), 783–802. doi:10.1002/sce.10038

Hansen, C.C. (in review). *Changing attitudes, beliefs, knowledge, and skills: Effective technology-based professional development*.

Harris, S. (1999). Secondary school students' use of computers at home. *British Journal of Educational Technology, 30*(4), 331–339. doi:10.1111/1467-8535.00123

Hayes, D. (2007). ICT and learning: Lessons from Australian classrooms. *Computers & Education, 49*, 385–395. doi:10.1016/j.compedu.2005.09.003

Heid, M. K. (2005). Technology in mathematics education: Tapping into visions of the future. In Masalski, W. J., & Elliott, P. C. (Eds.), *Technology-supported mathematics learning environments, the sixty-seventh yearbook of the National Council of Teachers of Mathematics*. Reston, VA: National Council of Teachers of Mathematics.

Higgins, S. (2003). *Does ICT improve learning and teaching in schools?* United Kingdom: British Educational Research Association.

Hug, B., Krajcik, J., & Marx, R. (2005). Using innovative learning technologies to promote learning and engagement in an urban science classroom. *Urban Education, 40*(4), 446–472. doi:10.1177/0042085905276409

Information Highway Advisory Council. (1997). *Preparing Canada for a digital world*. Ottawa, Canada: Industry Canada: Final Report of the Information Highway Advisory Council.

Institute of Education Sciences. (2010). *NAEP data explorer*. Washington, DC: IES National Center for Education Statistics. Retrieved July 15th, 2010, from http://nces.ed.gov/nationsreportcard/naepdata/

International Society for Technology in Education. (2008). *Technology and student achievement: The indelible link*. Retrieved August 3, 2010, from http://www.iste.org/Content/NavigationMenu/Advocacy/Policy/59.08-PolicyBrief-F-web.pdf

IPCC. (2008). *Summary for policymakers*. Geneva, Switzerland: IPCC.. *Climatic Change*, 2007.

Isiksal, M., & Askar, P. (2005). The effect of spreadsheet and dynamic geometry software on the achievement and self-efficacy of 7th-grade students. *Educational Research, 47*(3), 333–350. doi:10.1080/00131880500287815

Ito, M., Horst, H., & Bittanti, M. boyd, d., Herr-Stephenson, B., Lange, P., … Robinson, L. (2008). *Living and learning with new media: Summary of findings from the Digital Youth Project*. Chicago, IL: The John D. and Catherine T. MacArthur Foundation.

Compilation of References

Jacobsen, M., Clifford, P., & Friesen, S. (2002). Preparing teachers for technology integration: Creating a culture of inquiry in the context of use. *Contemporary Issues in Technology & Teacher Education, 2*(3), 363–388.

Jenkins, H. (2006). *Convergence culture: Where old and new media collide.* New York, NY: New York University Press.

Jenkins, H. (2007). From YouTube to YouNiversity. *The Chronicle of Higher Education Review, 53*(24), 9.

Jenkins, H. (2008). Public intellectuals in the new-media landscape. *The Chronicle of Higher Education, 54*(30), 18–20.

Johnson, D., & Johnson, R. (1993). Cooperative learning and feedback in technology-based instruction. In Dempsey, J., & Sales, G. (Eds.), *Interactive instruction and feedback* (pp. 133–159). Englewood Cliffs, NJ: Educational Technology Publications.

Jonassen, D. H. (1995). Supporting communities of learners with technology: A vision for integrating technology with learning in schools. *Educational Technology, 35*(4), 60–63.

Kafai, Y. B. (2001). *The educational potential of electronic games: From games–to–teach to games–to–learn.* Chicago, IL: Playing by the Rules Cultural Policy Center, University of Chicago.

Kanaya, T., Light, D., & Culp, K. M. (2005). Factors influencing outcomes from a technology-focused professional development program. *Journal of Research on Technology in Education, 37*(2), 313–329.

Katz, L. (1998). What can we learn from Reggio Emilia? In Edwards, C., Gandini, L., & Forman, G. (Eds.), *The hundred languages of children: The Reggio Emilia Approach- advanced reflections* (2nd ed.). Norword, NJ: Ablex.

Kendall, M. (2000). Citizenship is lifelong learning: The challenge of information and communications technology. In D. Benzie & D. Passey (Eds.), *Proceedings of Conference on Educational Uses of ICT.* Beijing, China: Publishing House of Electronics Industry.

Kirriemuir, J., & McFarlane, A. (2004). *Literature review in games and learning: A report for NESTA.* United Kingdom: FutureLab.

Kitson, L., Fletcher, M., & Kearney, J. (2007). Continuity and change in literacy practices: A move towards multiliteracies. *Journal of Classroom Instruction, 41*(2), 29–41.

Kleiner, B., Thomas, N., & Lewis, L. (2007). *Educational technology in teacher education programs for initial licensure* (NCES 2008-040). Retrieved April 13, 2010, from http://nces.ed.gov/

Knuth, E. (2005). Student understanding of the Cartesian coordinate connection: An exploratory study. *Journal for Research in Mathematics Education, 31*(4), 500–508. doi:10.2307/749655

Kozma, R. (2003). ICT and educational change. In Kozmo, R. (Ed.), *Technology, innovation, and educational change: A global perspective. A report of the second information technology in education study: Module 2* (pp. 6–18). International Association for the Evaluation of Educational Achievement.

Kozman, R. B. (2005). *ICT, education reform and economic growth*. White Paper for INTEL.

Lai, K. W., Pratt, K., & Trewern, A. (2001). *Learning with technology: Evaluation of the Otago secondary schools technology project*. Dunedin, FL: The Community Trust of Otago.

Lankes, R. D. (2008). Trusting the Internet: New approaches to credibility tools. In Metzger, M. J., & Flanagin, A. J. (Eds.), *Digital media, youth, and credibility* (pp. 101–122). Cambridge, MA: The John D. and Catherine T. MacArthur Foundation Series on Digital Media and Learning.

Lawless, K. A., & Schrader, P. G. (2008). Where do we go now? Understanding research on navigation in complex digital environments. In Coiro, J., Knobel, M., Lankshear, C., & Leu, D. J. (Eds.), *Handbook of new literacies* (pp. 267–296). Hillsdale, NJ: Lawrence Erlbaum Associates.

Lehman, J. D., & Richardson, J. (2007). *Linking teacher preparation programs with k-12 schools via videoconferencing: Benefits and limitations*. Retrieved from http://p3t3.education.purdue.edu/AERA2007_Videoconf_Paper.pdf

Lei, J., & Zhao, Y. (2007). Technology uses and student achievement: A longitudinal study. *Computers & Education, 49*, 284–296. doi:10.1016/j.compedu.2005.06.013

Lenhart, A., Ling, R., Campbell, S., & Purcell, K. (2010). *Teens and mobile phones*. Washington, DC: Pew Internet & American Life Project.

Levine, P. (2008). A public voice for youth: The audience problem in digital media and civic education. In Bennett, W. L. (Ed.), *Civic life online: Learning how digital media can engage youth* (pp. 119–138). Cambridge, MA: The MIT Press.

Lim, C. (2008). Global citizenship education, school curriculum and games: Learning Mathematics, English and Science as a global citizen. *Computers & Education, 51*(3), 1073–1093. doi:10.1016/j.compedu.2007.10.005

Lincoln, Y. S., & Guba, E. G. (1985). *Naturalistic Inquiry*. Beverly Hills, CA: Sage Publications, Inc.

Ma, L. (1999). *Knowing and teaching elementary mathematics: Teachers' understanding of fundamental mathematics in China and the United States*. Hillsdale, NJ: Erlbaum.

Magliaro, J., & Ezeife, A. (2007). Preservice teachers' preparedness to integrate computer technology into the curriculum. *Canadian Journal of Learning and Technology, 33*(3), 95.

Mann, D., Shakeshaft, C., Becker, J., & Kottkamp, R. (1998). *West Virginia story: Achievement gains from a statewide comprehensive instructional technology program*. Santa Monica, CA: Milken Exchange on Educational Technology.

Compilation of References

Manner, J. C. (2007, March 2007). *Widening the audience: Using podcasting to share student work*. Paper presented at the Society for Information Technology and Teacher Education International Conference (SITE) 2007, San Antonio, TX.

Manning, F. H., Lawless, K. A., Gomez, K. G., McLeod, M., Braasch, J., & Goldman, S. R. (2008). *Sources of information in the classroom: Characterizing instruction through a model of multiple source comprehension for inquiry learning*. Paper presented at the annual meeting of the Association of Psychological Science, Chicago, IL.

McCrory, R. (2008). Science, technology, and teaching: The topic-specific challenges of TPCK in science. In Technology, A. C. I. a. (Ed.), *Handbook of technological pedagogical content knowledge (TPCK) for educators* (pp. 193–206). New York, NY: Routledge.

McFarlane, A., Sparrowhawk, A., & Heald, Y. (2002). *Report on the educational use of games: An exploration by TEEM of the contribution which games can make to the education process*. Cambridgeshire, UK: TEEM, St Ives.

McKenzie, J. (1999). *Reaching the reluctant teacher*. Retrieved August 21, 2005, from http://www.fno.org/sum99/reluctant.html

McKenzie, J. (2001). *How teachers learn technology best*. Retrieved March 31, 2010, from http://www.fno.org/mar01/howlearn.html

McLeod, J., & Vasinda, S. (2008). Electronic portfolios: Perspectives of students, teachers and parents. *Education and Information Technologies, 14*, 29–38. doi:10.1007/s10639-008-9077-5

McLeod, J., Lin, L., & Vasinda, S. (in press). Children's power for learning in the age of technology. In Blake, S., Winsor, D., & Allen, L. (Eds.), *Technology and young children: Bridging the communication-generation gap*. Hershey, PA: IGI Global. doi:10.4018/978-1-61350-059-0.ch003

McLeod, J., & Vasinda, S. (2009a). Web 2.0 affordances for literacys: Using technology as pedagogically strong scaffolds for learning. In Kidd, T. T., & Chen, I. (Eds.), *Wired for learning*. Charlotte, NC: Information Age Publishing.

McNeil, B. J., & Nelson, K. R. (1991). Meta-analysis of interactive video instruction: A ten year review of achievement effects. *Journal of Computer-Based Instruction, 18*, 1–6.

Milton, P. (2003). *Trends in the integration of ICT and learning in K-12 systems*. Report for the Canadian Education Association.

Mishra, P., & Koehler, M. J. (2006). Technological pedagogical content knowledge: A framework for teacher knowledge. *Teachers College Record, 108*(6), 1017–1054. doi:10.1111/j.1467-9620.2006.00684.x

Mumtaz, S. (2000). Factors affecting teachers' use of information and communication technology: A review of the literature. *Journal of Information Technology for Teacher Education, 9*(3), 319–341. doi:10.1080/14759390000200096

Mumtaz, S. (2001). Children's enjoyment and perception of computer use in the home and the school. *Computers & Education, 36*(4), 347–362. doi:10.1016/S0360-1315(01)00023-9

National Council of Teachers of Mathematics. (n.d.). *Appendix: Table of standards - Process standards.* Retrieved August 1, 2010, from http://standards.nctm.org/document/appendix/process.htm

National Council of Teachers of Mathematics (NCTM). (2000). *Principles and standards for school Mathematics.* Reston, VA: Author.

National Education Association. (2010). *Rankings & estimates: Rankings of the states 2009 and estimates of school statistics 2010.* Atlanta, GA: National Education Association. Retrieved August 1, 2010 from http://www.nea.org/assets/docs/010rankings.pdf

National Mathematics Advisory Panel. (2008). *Foundations for success: The final report of the National Mathematics Advisory Panel.* Washington, DC: U.S. Department of Education.

National Research Council. (1996). *National science education standards.* Washington, DC: National Academy Press.

New London Group. (1996). A pedagogy of multiliteracies: Designing social futures. *Harvard Educational Review, 66*(1), 60–92.

Newby, T. J., Stepich, D. A., Lehman, J. D., & Russell, J. D. (2000). *Instructional technology for teaching and learning: Designing instruction, integrating computers and using media.* Columbus, OH: Prentice Hall.

Niederhauser, D. S., & Stoddart, T. (2001). Teachers' instructional perspectives and use of educational software. *Teaching and Teacher Education, 17*, 15–31. doi:10.1016/S0742-051X(00)00036-6

Niess, M. L. (2005). Preparing teachers to teach science and mathematics with technology: Developing a technology pedagogical content knowledge. *Teaching and Teacher Education, 21*, 509–523. doi:10.1016/j.tate.2005.03.006

Niess, M. L. (2010, May). *Using classroom artifacts to judge teacher knowledge of reform-based instructional practices that integrate technology in mathematics and science classrooms.* Paper presented at the 2010 Annual Meeting of the American Educational Research Association. Denver, CO.

Nworie, J., & Haughton, N. (2008). The unintended consequences of the application of technology in teaching and learning environments. *TechTrends, 52*(5), 52–58. doi:10.1007/s11528-008-0197-y

Nye, B., Konstantopoulos, S., & Hedges, L. (2004). How large are teacher effects? *Educational Evaluation and Policy Analysis, 26*, 237–257. doi:10.3102/01623737026003237

O'Reilly, T. (2005). *What is Web 2.0?: Design patterns and business models for the next generation of software.* Sebastopol, CA: O'Reilly Network. Retrieved June 13, 2008, from http://www.oreillynet.com/pub/a/oreilly/tim/news/2005/09/30/what-is-web-20.html

Compilation of References

Oblinger, D. (2004). The next generation of educational engagement. *Journal of Interactive Media, 8*, 1–18.

Olkun, S., Altun, A., & Smith, G. (2005). Computers and 2D geometric learning of Turkish fourth and fifth graders. *British Journal of Educational Technology, 36*(2), 317–326. doi:10.1111/j.1467-8535.2005.00460.x

Paas, L., & Creech, H. (2008). *How information and communications technologies can support Education for sustainable development: Current uses and trends.* International Institute for Sustainable Development.

Papastergiou, M. (2009). Digital game-based learning in high school computer science education: Impact on educational effectiveness and student motivation. *Computers & Education, 52*(1), 1–12. doi:10.1016/j.compedu.2008.06.004

Paraskeva, F., Mysirlaki, S., & Papagianni, A. (2010). Multiplayer online games as educational tools: Facing new challenges in learning. *Computers & Education, 54*(2), 498–505. doi:10.1016/j.compedu.2009.09.001

Patrick, S. (2008). ICT in educational policy in the North American region. In *International handbook of Information Technology in primary and secondary education* (pp. 1109–1117). US: Springer International Handbooks of Education. doi:10.1007/978-0-387-73315-9_70

Pelgrum, W. J. (2001). Obstacles to the integration of ICT in education: Results from a worldwide educational assessment. *Computers & Education, 37*(2), 163–178. doi:10.1016/S0360-1315(01)00045-8

Pelgrum, W. J., & Plomp, T. (2005). *The turtle stands on an emerging educational paradigm.* Netherlands: Springer.

Pelgrum, W. J., & Law, N. (2008). Introduction to SITES 2006. In *Pedagogy and ICT use in schools around the world: Findings from the IEA Sites 2006 study,* (pp. 1-11). CERC Studies in Comparative Education. Netherlands: Springer.

Pew Internet & American Life Project. (2001). *The Internet and education: Findings of the Pew Internet & American Life Project.* Retrieved March 12, 2007, from http://www.pewInternet. org/reports

Pew Internet & American Life Project. (2005). *The Internet at school.* Retrieved March 12, 2007, from http://www.pewinternet.org/PPF/r/163/report_display.asp

Plankis, B. J., & Weatherly, R. (2008, March 2008). *Engaging students and empowering researchers: Embedding assessment, evaluation and history into podcasting.* Paper presented at the Society for Information Technology and Teacher Education International Conference (SITE) 2008, Las Vegas, NV.

Pollock, J. E. (2007). *Improving student learning one teacher at a time.* Alexandria, VA: Association for Supervision and Curriculum Development.

Polly, D. (2008). Modeling the influence of calculator use and teacher effects on first grade students' mathematics achievement. *Journal of Technology in Mathematics and Science Teaching, 27*(3), 245–263.

Polly, D. (2011). Examining teachers' enactment of TPACK in their mathematics teaching. *The International Journal for Technology in Mathematics Education, 30*(1).

Polly, D., & Hannafin, M. J. (in press). Examining how learner-centered professional development influences teachers' espoused and enacted practices. *Journal of Educational Research, 104*(2).

Polya, G. (2004). *How to solve it: A new aspect of mathematical method*. Princeton, NJ: Princeton University Press.

Poole, B. (1995). *Education for an information age*. Madison, WI: WCB Brown Benchmark.

Prensky, M. (2001). Digital natives, digital immigrants. *NCB University Press, 9*(5), 1–15.

Ramirez, R. (2001). A model for rural and remote information and communication technologies: A Canadian exploration. *Telecommunications Policy, 25*(5), 315–330. doi:10.1016/S0308-5961(01)00007-6

Rheingold, H. (2008). Using participatory media and public voice to encourage civic engagement. In Bennett, W. L. (Ed.), *Civic life online: Learning how digital media can engage youth* (pp. 97–118). Cambridge, MA: The MIT Press.

Robertson, J., & Howells, C. (2008). Computer game design: Opportunities for successful learning. *Computers & Education, 50*(2), 559–578. doi:10.1016/j.compedu.2007.09.020

Roblyer, M. D. (2006). *Integrating educational technology into teaching* (4th ed.). NJ: Pearson Education.

Rowley, J., Dysard, G., & Arnold, J. (2005). Developing a new technology infusion program for preparing tomorrow's teachers. *Journal of Technology and Teacher Education, 13*(1), 105–123.

Russell, M., Bebell, D., O'Dwyer, L., & O'Connor, K. (2003). Examining teacher technology use: Implications for preservice and inservice teacher preparation. *Journal of Teacher Education, 54*(4), 297–310. doi:10.1177/0022487103255985

Sandholtz, J. H., Ringstaff, C., & Dwyer, D. C. (1997). *Teaching with technology: Creating student-centered classrooms*. New York, NY: Teachers College Press, Columbia University.

Sang, G., Valcke, M., van Braak, J., & Tondeur, T. (2010). Student teachers' thinking processes and ICT integration: Predictors of prospective teaching behaviors with educational technology. *Computers & Education, 54*(1), 103–112. doi:10.1016/j.compedu.2009.07.010

Schrader, P. G., Lawless, K. A., & McCreery, M. (2009). Intertextuality in massively multiplayer online games. In Ferdig, R. E. (Ed.), *Handbook of research on effective electronic gaming in education* (*Vol. III*, pp. 791–807). Hershey, PA: Information Science Reference.

Compilation of References

Selwyn, N. (2007). Technology, schools and CE: A fic too far? In *Young citizens in the digital age - political engagement, young people and new media* (pp. 129–142). London, UK: Routledge Taylor and Francis Group.

Selwyn, N. (2008). An investigation of differences in undergraduates' academic use of the internet. *Active Learning in Higher Education, 9*(1), 11–22. doi:10.1177/1469787407086744

Shapka, J. D., & Ferrari, M. (2003). Computer-related attitudes and actions of teacher candidates. *Computers in Human Behavior, 19*(3), 319–334. doi:10.1016/S0747-5632(02)00059-6

Shuler, C. (2007). *D is for digital: An analysis of the children's interactive media environment with a focus on mass marketed products that promote learning.* Retrieved June 14, 2010, from http://www.joanganzcooneycenter.org/pdf/DisforDigital.pdf

Shulman, L. (1987). Knowledge and teaching: Foundations of a new reform. *Harvard Educational Review, 57*(1), 1–22.

Shulman, L. S. (1986). Those who understand: Knowledge growth in teaching. *Educational Researcher, 15*(2), 4–14.

Smith, S. D., Salaway, G., & Caruso, J. B. (2009). *The ECAR study of undergraduate students and information technology, 2009.* Boulder, CO: EDUCAUSE Center for Applied Research.

Souviney, R. J. (1994). *Learning to teach mathematics.* Columbus, OH: Merrill Publishing Company.

Souviney, R. J. (2005). *Solving math problems kids care about.* Tucson, AZ: Good Year Books.

Squire, K. (2005). Changing the game: What happens when video games enter the classroom? *Innovate, 1*(6), 82–89.

SRI International. (2002, May). *Technology-related professional development in the context of educational reform: A literature review.* Prepared for the U.S. Department of Education under GSA Contract #GS-35F-5537H.

Stiggins, R. (2005). *Student-involved assessment FOR learning* (4th ed.). Upper Saddle River, NJ: Pearson.

Strauss, A. (1987). *Qualitative analysis for social scientists.* New York, NY: Cambridge University Press. doi:10.1017/CBO9780511557842

Strong, M. (1995). *Connecting with the world: Priorities for Canadian internationalism in the 21st century. International Development Research and Policy Task Force. International Development Research Centre (IDRC); International Institute for Sustainable Development (IISD); North-South Institute.* NSI.

Strudler, N., Schrader, P. G., & Asay, L. (under review). *An evaluation of statewide online professional development for integration of laptops and mobile devices in the middle school curriculum.* Paper submitted to the Annual Meeting of AERA, April 8th-April 12th, New Orleans, LA.

Tezci, E. (2009). Teachers' effect on ICT use in education: The Turkey sample. *Procedia - Social and Behavioral Sciences, 1*(1), 1285-1294.

The University of the State of New York. (1996). *Learning standards for social studies*. Albany, NY: New York State Department of Education.

The University of the State of New York. (1999). *Social studies resource guide with core curriculum*. Albany, NY: New York State Department of Education.

Thomas, D., & Brown, J. (2009). Why virtual worlds can matter. *International Journal of Learning and Media, 1*(1), 37–49. doi:10.1162/ijlm.2009.0008

Tondeur, J. (2008). ICT integration in the classroom: Challenging the potential of a school policy. *Computers & Education, 51*(1), 212–223. doi:10.1016/j.compedu.2007.05.003

Tondeur, J., van Braak, J., & Valcke, M. (2006). Curricula and the use of ICT in education: Two worlds apart? *British Journal of Educational Technology, 38*(6), 1–14.

Triggs, P., & John, P. (2004). From transaction to transformation: Information and communication technology, professional development, and the formation of communities of practice. *Journal of Computer Assisted Learning, 20*(6), 426–439. doi:10.1111/j.1365-2729.2004.00101.x

U.S. Department of Education. (2003). *Federal funding for educational technology and how it is used in the classroom: A summary of findings from the integrated studies of educational technology*. Retrieved December 10, 2009, from http://www.ed.gov/rschstat/eval/tech/iset/summary2003.pdf

U.S. Department of Education. (1993). *Using technology to support education reform*. Washington, DC: U.S. Department of Education, Office of Research.

van Braak, J., Tondeur, J., & Valcke, M. (2004). Explaining different types of computer use among primary school teachers. *European Journal of Psychology of Education, 19*(4), 407–422. doi:10.1007/BF03173218

Van de Walle, J. A. (2007). *Elementary and middle school mathematics: Teaching developmentally*. Boston, MA: Allyn and Bacon.

Van Lehn, K., Graesser, A. C., Jackson, G. T., Jordan, P., Olney, A., & Rose, C. P. (2007). When are tutorial dialogues more effective than reading? *Cognitive Science, 30*, 3–62. doi:10.1080/03640210709336984

Vandevoort, L. G., Amrein-Beardsley, A., & Berliner, D. C. (2004, September 8). National board certified teachers and their students' achievement. *Education Policy Analysis Archives, 12*(46). Retrieved March 31, 2010, from http://epaa.asu.epaa/v12n46

vanDijck, J. (2009). Users like you? Theorizing agency in user-generated content. *Media Culture & Society, 31*(1), 41–58. doi:10.1177/0163443708098245

VanFossen, P. J. (2005). Reading and math take so much of the time.. .: An overview of social studies instruction in elementary classrooms in Indiana. *Theory and Research in Social Education, 33*(3), 376–403.

Compilation of References

Vasinda, S., & McLeod, J. (2011). Extending readers theater: A powerful and purposeful match with podcasting. *The Reading Teacher, 64*(7). doi:10.1598/RT.64.7.2

Vasinda, S., McLeod, J., & Morrison, J. (2007). 1+1=3: Combining language experience approach with Web 2.0 tools. *LEA SIG (of the International Reading Association). Newsletter, 38*(1), 6–10.

Vasinda, S. (2004). *Reinventing Reggio through negotiated learning: Finding a place for voice and choice in an American standards-based elementary classroom*. Unpublished doctoral dissertation. Texas A&M University-Commerce.

Vogler, K. E., Lintner, T., Lipscomb, G. B., Knopf, H., Heafner, T. L., & Rock, T. C. (2007). Getting off the back burner: Impact of testing elementary social studies as part of a state-mandated accountability program. *Journal of Social Studies Research, 31*(2), 20–34.

Vygotsky, L. (1986). *Thought and language*. Cambridge, MA: MIT Press.

Ward, L., & Parr, J. (2010). Revisiting and reframing use: Implications for the integration of ICT. *Computers & Education, 54*(1), 113–122. doi:10.1016/j.compedu.2009.07.011

Watson, G. (2001). Models of information technology teacher professional development that engage with teachers' hearts and minds. *Journal of Information Technology for Teacher Education, 10*(1 & 2), 179–190. doi:10.1080/14759390100200110

Wenglinsky, H. (1998). *Does it compute? The relationship between educational technology and student achievement in mathematics*. Educational Testing Service Policy Information Center. Retrieved September 10, 2002, from www.mff.org/pubs/ME161.pdf

Wetzel, K., Zambo, R., & Padgett, H. (2001). A picture of change in technology-rich K-8 classrooms. *Journal of Computing in Teacher Education, 18*(1), 5–11.

Wheatly, K. F. (2004). Increasing computer use in early childhood teacher education: The case of a "computer muddler". *Information Technology in Childhood Education*, 135-56.

White, G. (2005). *Beyond the horseless carriage: Harnessing the potential of ICT in education and training*. Australia: Education.au Limited.

Williamson, A. (2003). Shifting the centre: The Internet as a tool for community activism. In *Proceedings of the 5th International Information Technology in Regional Areas (ITiRA) Conference*, (pp. 149-155). Rockhampton, Australia: Central Queensland University.

Woo, Y., & Reeves, T. C. (2007). Meaningful interaction in web-based learning: A social constructivist interpretation. *The Internet and Higher Education, 10*, 15–25. doi:10.1016/j.iheduc.2006.10.005

Yin, R. (2003). Applied Social Research Methods Series: *Vol. 34. Applications of case study research* (2nd ed.).

About the Contributors

Irene L. Chen received her Doctor of Education in Instructional Technology. Dr. Chen has a diverse professional background. She previously served as an instructional technology specialist, and computer programmer/analyst. Her current research interests are: instructional technology, assessment and evaluation, multicultural education, urban education, business education, and curriculum and instruction. She has delivered K-12 in-service professional development activities for both faculty and staff. She is the co-author of *Technology Applications for K-12 Teachers* and a co-editor of *Wired for Learning: An Educator's Guide to Web 2.0.*

Dallas McPheeters is an award winning Educational Technologist passionate about helping others feel at home with technology. His peer-reviewed and published research focuses on the mashup generation of uncertainty facing an unknowable future and how to engage such minds as they prepare for tomorrow. Most recently, McPheeters received a Service Recognition Award from the President for his contribution to the field of education within multi-user virtual environments. Results from McPheeters' research have been presented both nationally and internationally to educators and professionals interested in adapting emerging technologies to the next generation of learners and workers, whether face-to-face or in the Cloud. McPheeters' work demonstrates how the elimination of space-time and identity barriers opens new avenues for learning previously unavailable in traditional venues. More about Mr. McPheeters can be discovered online at http://dallasmcpheeters.com.

* * *

Sina Andegherghis was born in Eritrea and moved to the United States at the age of four. She is currently pursuing a Master's Degree in Instruction and Curriculum with a concentration in English Second Language.

Loretta Asay serves as the Coordinator, Instructional Technology and Innovative Projects, in Clark County School District, Las Vegas, NV. Her role is to increase the integration of technology into classroom activities. She was a science teacher and a school technologist, then worked as a trainer for school technologist. She served as the Coordinator for Science and became the Instructional Technology coordinator in 2007. Mrs. Asay is finishing a doctorate in educational psychology at the University of Nevada, Las Vegas.

Shirley Barnes is an Assistant Professor of Foundations and Psychology at Alabama State University in Montgomery, AL. She received her Ph.D. in Educational Psychology from Auburn University, M.Ed. in Counseling and Student Development Services from Tuskegee University, and B.A. in Sociology from Auburn University. Dr. Barnes teaches graduate courses in foundations of education assessment, statistics, measurement, and evaluation. Her experience includes years of experience of online teaching. Dr. Barnes' research interest includes teacher self-efficacy in content areas, assessment, and multicultural issues in education. She holds several national certifications, including being a National Certified Psychologist, Board Certified Clinical Psychotherapist, and National Certified Counselor. She has served as a National Testing and Assessment Administrator with Psychological Corporation and Educational Testing Services (ETS), including supervising and administering admissions national tests and tests for national licensure/certification. She has received numerous scholarly awards and honors and is an active scholar in the field.

Chelsea Bruner is striving to become more proficient with electronics to keep up with her students and the future.

Susan Gibson is a Professor in the Department of Elementary Education in the Faculty of Education at the University of Alberta, Edmonton Alberta, Canada. She teaches social studies education in the undergraduate teacher education program. Her areas of research expertise include the preparation of social studies teachers, infusing technology into teaching and learning, and preparing preservice and practicing teachers for teaching in a digital age.

Amanda Gordon recently completed her second year of teaching as an eighth grade reading teacher. While in college, I played basketball for four years and met life-long friends and gained experiences that she carries with her daily. She feels blessed to have a job that challenges her daily!

Terra Graves has been an educator in Nevada for 18 years. She is currently the State Online Professional Development Coordinator for the Nevada Pathway Project. In this ARRA funded position, she collaboratively created and facilitated four online professional development modules for the 120 statewide teacher participants. She is also a teacher in the Washoe County School District Office of Staff Development in Reno, Nevada. As a former classroom teacher, Terra has supported teachers for the past eight years in the areas of classroom management, instructional strategies and 21st Century skills/technology integration. Terra is the author of The Organized Teacher, A Guide for Beginning Teachers, editor of various resources such as NETS-S and P21 Framework Correlation, Web 2.0 Tools and Resources for Teaching 21st Century Skills, and Using Games and Simulations in the Classroom.

S. Selcen Guzey is a Research Associate at the STEM Education Center at the University of Minnesota. Dr. Guzey's research interests are focused on technology integration into secondary science teaching, learner-centered science instruction, and motivation theory. Her specific areas of research consider the effects of intrinsic motivation on teachers' technology-enhanced classroom practices.

Cory Cooper Hansen, Ph.D., is an Associate Professor in the Mary Lou Fulton Teachers College at Arizona State University. She is the Early Childhood Program Director and teaches courses in language and literacy at the undergraduate and graduate levels. Dr. Hansen's Bachelor's Degree is from the University of Calgary in Alberta, Canada and her graduate degrees are from Arizona State University. Her research agenda includes best practice in instruction at all levels which includes effective integration of technology to meet the needs of 21st century students. As principle investigator, she has led two years of an Arizona Classrooms of Tomorrow Today grant funded through the Arizona Board of Regents Improving Teacher Quality Program. Most recently, she is collaborating with doctoral students engaged in action research to positively impact learning environments for young children.

Alison Horstman is now in her tenth year of teaching first grade. Once she achieves her Master's degree, she hopes to teach undergraduate education courses.

Rarshunda Hudson is a teacher in an urban elementary school.

Nick Lawrence is a teacher at East Bronx Academy for the Future, a public school in the Bronx, New York. He teaches U.S. history and German to students ranging from eighth to tenth grade. His research interests include finding ways that learning platforms can promote collaborative skills and improve academic achievement in the K-12 classroom as well as how digital participatory media can support civic engagement.

Cheng-Yao Lin is an Associate Professor of Mathematics Education at Southern Illinois University Carbondale. He is interested in the integration of technology into mathematics education, the preparation of pre-service teachers and cross-cultural research on pre-service teachers' knowledge of fractions. He has published in many peer-reviewed journals for research in mathematics education. Dr. Lin has served in many official positions in professional organizations - Program Chairperson of the 21st -28th Annual Conferences on Teaching Mathematics [ICTM/ Southern Section], SIUC, Carbondale. IL; Membership Committee of the School Science and Mathematics Association (2006-2009); session chair for Research in Mathematics Education on the program of the 2011 AERA Meeting in New Orleans; Discussant on the program of the 2010 AERA Meeting in Denver; session chair of Research in Mathematics Education on the program of the 2008 AERA Meeting in New York City.

Jane-Jane Lo is an Associate Professor in the Department of Mathematics at Western Michigan University. Dr. Lo has a long-term research interest in studying the process of mathematical learning and concept development. This focus has been pursued in three complementary areas: the development of ratio and proportion concepts, classroom discourse, and international comparative. Since arriving at Western Michigan University in 2001, Dr. Lo has combined this particular research interest with her primary teaching assignments: mathematics courses for prospective elementary and middle school teachers. In addition to working with prospective teachers, Dr. Lo serves as the Project Co-Director of the Kalamazoo Area Algebra Project (KA2P) that provides professional development opportunities for local middle and high school mathematics teachers to strengthen their knowledge for teaching algebra.

Fenqjen Luo is an Assistant Professor of Mathematics Education in the Montana State University's Department of Education. Principally, she teaches elementary mathematics methods. She received her Ph. D. in 2000 in Mathematics Education from the University of Texas at Austin. Prior to joining the Montana State University, she worked as an Assistant Professor of Mathematics Education at the University of West Georgia and an Assistant Professor of Mathematics and Computer Science at the Chung Yu Institute of Technology in Taiwan. She is a co-author of elementary school mathematics textbook series published by Kang Hsuan Educational Publishing Group between 2002 and 2008 in Taiwan. Her research interests include the application of Web-based instruction in teacher education, the impact of on-line learning on students' mathematical performance and attitudes, international comparisons among mathematical teachers, and cognitive processing of mathematical knowledge.

Alicia Martinez, with roots in Mexico, is currently an elementary school teacher with a focus on bilingual education.

Evelyn Martinez is a public school teacher specialized in bilingual education.

Brenda McCombs is the Director of Instructional Technology of a school district.

Christian McGlory is a first grade teacher. She has been teaching first grade for the past 8 years. She is certified to teach pre-k-4th grade and also holds an ESL certification for EC-12th grade. She loves to watch students grow into great readers, mathematicians, scientists, artists, and computer whizzes.

Julie McLeod currently teaches technology integration courses at the University of North Texas where she earned her doctoral degree in Learning Technologies. She also teaches mathematics for Allen ISD where she and her students use many technologies during their learning. Julie's research interests include exploring children's curiosity, power and motivation as they use technology to learn. She has also published book chapters and journal articles that discuss powerful ways to integrate technology by purposefully matching a proven learning strategy with the affordances of the technology to create a learning experience that maintains the integrity of the proven strategy while creating something not possible without the technology.

Clif Mims (http://clifmims.com/blog/) is an Associate Professor in the Department of Instructional Design and Technology at the University of Memphis and the Director of the Martin Institute for Teaching and Learning in Memphis, TN. His interests involve supporting teachers' integration of technology through professional development and other professional learning experiences.

Jessie Munks is a certified K-12 music educator in the state of Texas and is currently serving as a fifth year elementary school music teacher and a fourth year department head. She earned a Bachelor of Arts degree in Music (Voice emphasis). She is currently pursuing a Master of Science degree in Educational Management and aspires to be a public school principal. Ms. Munks devotes her spare time to singing and writing short stories.

Joe O'Brien is an Associate Professor in the Department of Curriculum & Teaching at the University of Kansas. He teaches courses in middle and secondary social studies instructional practices, research and theory and has received numerous teaching awards. His research interests include the relation between digital participatory media and civic engagement and the use primary sources to promote students' ability to think historically.

Venus Olla is interested in the use of Internet-based virtual environments as a new pedagogical approach in the teaching of citizenship.

Shawn Pennell is a faculty of the Raggio Research Center at the University of Nevada, Reno. She holds a MA Ed in Curriculum, Teaching, and Learning with an emphasis in Educational Technology from UNR. As a licensed Nevada teacher, she has taught social studies both in the classroom as well as online. Shawn has co-authored two articles and made contributions to a Chinese textbook in teaching Chinese as a Second Language. She is a reflective practitioner to excess, and enjoys travel, her husband's good humor, and engaging in 21st century endeavors of teaching and learning at all times. Shawn is married and has one son from the belly and two daughters from the heart.

Drew Polly (drewpolly@gmail.com) is an Assistant Professor in the Department of Reading and Elementary Education at UNC Charlotte. His research agenda focuses on examining how to best support the integration of technology-rich learner-centered tasks in elementary school classrooms.

Kate Popejoy (kate.popejoy@uncc.edu) is an Assistant Professor in the Department of Reading and Elementary Education at UNC Charlotte. Her research agenda focuses on supporting scientific inquiry in elementary school classrooms.

Martina Ramos-Rey is a 4th grade writing teacher. She has been teaching for 10 years and recently graduated with her Master's in Teaching with a focus in Curriculum and Instruction. Like many teachers, Martina looks for new ways to incorporate technology into her elementary classroom. Her students come from diverse backgrounds that have limited use of computers and other technologies. Therefore, Martina feels it's important for her to learn about and incorporate new technology as much as she can in her classroom. Her hope is that by exposing her students to what she's learned in the technology classes her graduate program offered, she will somehow bridge the technology gap that challenges her students.

Diana Ramirez is interested in looking at current libraries and how they are changing to address the technology that is now available and that will change the overall purpose and use of the library. She has taught over 30 years both as an early childhood teacher and now as a librarian for an urban high school.

Sandra Richardson holds a joint appointment as an Associate Professor at Lamar University in the Department of Mathematics and Department of Professional Pedagogy. She received both her M.S. and Ph.D. in Mathematics Education from

Purdue University and her B.S. in Mathematics from Dillard University. While at Lamar University, she has taught a range of undergraduate and graduate courses. Her research and scholarly interests include developing effective tools for mathematics curricula, advancing technological pedagogical content knowledge of mathematics teachers, studying minority and underrepresented students' mathematical thinking at all levels of school mathematics, and mathematics teacher education. Dr. Richardson has received over $1 million dollars in grants to fund her research and scholarly pursuits. She has received numerous honors and awards, including the University Excellence in Teaching and Research Merit Award and the Texas State Teachers Association Student Programs Advisor of the Year Award.

Blanca Rodriguez is certified to teach early childhood through fourth grade as well as special needs. She currently teaches first grade. One of her three children is autistic, so she enjoys spending time with discussion groups and sharing ideas with other parents of children on the autism spectrum.

Gillian Roehrig is Co-Director of the STEM Education Center and an Associate Professor of science education in the department of Curriculum and Instruction at the University of Minnesota. Dr. Roehrig's teaching and research is focused on the preparation and retention of beginning secondary science teachers and the implementation of inquiry-based instruction and technology integration in secondary science classrooms. Her research agenda is focused on the constraints experienced by teachers as they implement inquiry-based instruction and/or integrate technology in their classrooms and how these constraints can be mitigated through participation in professional development.

P.G. Schrader is an Associate Professor of Educational Technology at the University of Nevada, Las Vegas. Dr. Schrader's recent work involves understanding learning in complex nonlinear digital environments like Massively Multiplayer Online Games and Hypertext. In these contexts, he has examined aspects of expertise, literacy, and the dynamic exchange of information. His work has appeared in a number of journals, books, and national and international conferences.

Leanne Spinale, a teacher candidate, is married with a 9 year old daughter and resides in the state of Texas.

Sara Stewart has been an educator in Clark County School District for the past 12 years. Throughout this time, she has taught middle school life science and high school biology. Her Master's degree is in Curriculum and Instruction, with emphasis on technology integration. This helped prepare her for her most current positions, educational computing strategist, and presently, a project facilitator in Instructional Technology (IT). As an IT project facilitator, her main focus has been instructional designer and facilitator for the Nevada Pathway Project. This project is a collaborative learning community comprised of 124 middle school teachers throughout the state of Nevada. The professional development focuses on 21st Century learning, iPods, and effective technology integration. She also provides professional development for effective technology integration for technology specialists, administrators, and teachers throughout the district.

Neal Strudler, a former seventh grade teacher and Assistant Principal, is a Professor of Educational Technology in the College of Education at the University of Nevada, Las Vegas. His research focuses on technology integration in both teacher education and K-12 schools. Along with P.G. Schrader, Dr. Strudler served as an evaluator for the Nevada Pathway Project. He has also served as a member of the Board of Directors of the International Society for Technology in Education (ISTE), as president of ISTE's Teacher Education Special Interest Group (SIGTE) and as President of AERA's SIG- TACTL (Technology as an Agent of Change in Teaching and Learning). Most recently he was the Research Paper Chair for ISTE 2011. Dr. Strudler is a recipient of ISTE's "Making It Happen Award."

David S. Torain II is an Associate Professor of Mathematics and the Chair of the Department of Mathematics at Hampton University. He received a Ph.D. in System Science/Mathematics from Clark Atlanta University and was awarded a M.S. in Applied Mathematics and B.S. in Mathematics from North Carolina State University. Dr. Torain's research area is in Mathematical Modeling and Partial Differential Equations. He has presented his research at numerous national, state, and local conferences. As the Chair of Department of Mathematics at Hampton University, Dr. Torain has engaged students in active learning through the implementation of a series of technological supplements, including WebAssign and MyMathLab, in various undergraduate mathematics courses. He has received numerous professional awards for his teaching and scholarship.

Ngoc Tran has taught Kindergarten for four years at a Title 1 school. Teaching has been her passion, and the Internet is her hobby.

Sheri Vasinda is a classroom teacher and Adjunct Professor for Texas A&M University-Commerce. During her thirty year career she has taught Kindergarten, first, third, fourth, and third-fourth multiage. She has also been a reading resource teacher, dyslexia therapist, and educational researcher. Her research interests include purposeful and powerful technology integration, teaching into the intentions of the learner while meeting state and national standards, teacher research, involving students in their own assessment, and equipping learners to uncover their own power.

Anabel Vallejo has been a teacher for four years. She is the first in her family to pursue a Master's degree.

Deepak Verma is currently a middle school Math teacher. He has been teaching profession for 7 years. His teaching philosophy is that all students can learn and enjoy learning if they are provided with a good encouraging support and environment and a great teacher. He is a strong believer in keeping a work family balance in his life.

Tamika Washington is a recent college graduate. She completed the Generalist Early Childhood through 6th grade teacher's certification course through an alternative certification program. Currently, she is a substitute teacher. She is also perusing her Master's Degree in Speech Pathology.

Index